Truly Rich

Truly Rich

Practical Wisdom and a
Proper Perspective for an Enriched Life

C. ZACH IVEY

Library of Congress Control Number:		2006907640
ISBN 10:	Hardcover	1-4257-3131-7
	Softcover	1-4257-3130-9
ISBN 13:	Hardcover	978-1-4257-3131-1
	Softcover	978-1-4257-3130-4

To order additional copies of this book, contact:
Xlibris Corporation
1-888-795-4274
www.Xlibris.com
Orders@Xlibris.com
34016

Contents

Introduction 9

Chapter 1   Porsches And Prozac 13
Chapter 2   Adam, Eve, And The Mega-mall........................ 19
Chapter 3   Designer Theology.. 26
Chapter 4   Mammon, Man, And Our Maker...................... 33
Chapter 5   Planning For The Trip Called Life.................... 50
Chapter 6   The Imaginary Finish Line 63
Chapter 7   Blocking And Tackling 77
Chapter 8   The Flight Attendant Hand Jive 90
Chapter 9   The Psychologically Impaired Investor............ 102
Chapter 10 The Raw Materials In The Construction Of Wealth 114
Chapter 11 Investing Serious Money 131
Chapter 12 The President's Cabinet 138
Chapter 13 More Pearls To Ponder.................................. 152
Chapter 14 Homework 160

Bibliography.. 163

*Wealth is not measured by the things you have
but by the things you have for which you
would not take money.*

To God, for His love, grace, and mercy to me and my family and for giving me the desire to share this message;

To my beautiful wife, Sarah, for being the Godly woman and mother she is and for her constant support and encouragement in all that I do;

To my children, Anderson and Julia, for being all that I could ever hope for – may you learn these lessons early in life;

To my parents, Carl and Paula Ivey, for all of their love and support and for the entrepreneurial spirit that they have given me which has allowed me to pursue my career;

To my friends, colleagues, and mentors who have given me so much joy and taught me so many meaningful lessons; and

To my clients, for their trust and allowing me to be a part of their lives.

INTRODUCTION

A few years ago, after having read numerous books and having had exposure to mentors, preachers, friends, and clients, I began to get a nagging feeling about the message I hope to share with you in this book. As a financial planner by profession, I have had the unique opportunity to be involved in the lives of a number of families and have seen and experienced firsthand many of the issues of life, both good and bad. As a Christian, I have also had the wonderful privilege to read and study God's word and be taught by wonderful teachers. I would be remiss if I also didn't point out that I have been extremely blessed to have wonderful parents and friends with whom I have shared personal experiences and faced a number of life lessons that I will discuss in this book. This book flows out of those experiences, encounters, and truths that I have learned; my prayer is that they will prove as insightful and beneficial for you as they have for me.

The tugging feeling that I kept feeling dealt with reconciling my profession of financial planning with deeper spiritual truths that I firmly hold. As a financial planner and being in a professional community, it should be of no surprise that most of the clientele we serve would be categorized as "successful." Most individuals have good jobs and enjoy a level of material success that I certainly recognize as not the norm. In light of this, and drawing not only from my own experience but also from my colleagues in my profession, it is glaringly apparent to all involved that while there is great tangible value in what we do, there is also the interesting truth that the size of someone's net worth does not translate into a truly rich life.

Most all financial planners and advisors I know could easily bring to mind those individuals who have a full and happy life while at the same time think of those clients who were miserable yet had every visible advantage the world can provide. From time to time I would think about this phenomenon, but it started to get to a point where I couldn't just give it a cursory thought anymore. I had to investigate it deeper. While it may seem intellectually obvious to most that money doesn't buy happiness, there is something emotionally that causes most to try and achieve it through some sort of strategic allocation of dollars, whether it's buying the right house or picking the right stock. We all seem to also acknowledge that money is a means to an end, but to what end? With a little more thinking, most would recognize that money comes at a cost in the form of time, effort, and sacrifices and that we should be counting these costs instead of bullheadedly fixed on some preconceived dollar figure. It is these types of issues I will be exploring more and hopefully pointing you toward the optimal balance in life that God wants for you and your family.

What I have found and truly believe is that what most people are *really* striving for is to be *truly rich* – an ideal that encompasses so much more than money. I also believe that while a small percentage of people have a sort of internal compass or innate ability, certainly by God's grace, to do the right things and think the right thoughts, most of us need to be educated and/or reminded continually in order to stay on the path to this greater goal of true richness. I believe that without a changed heart, an intellectual foundation, and practical framework within which we can view life and make decisions, even the most well-meaning Christian can be hindered financially and in other ways from living to the full potential God intended.

My purpose of this book is multifold. I hope to convince you that material excess is not the mark of a truly rich life. I recognize that no right-minded person would admit to holding the view that it was; but unfortunately most Americans, even Christians, have fixated on the wrong things. Secondly, I hope to share with you God's purposes for money. Money is a unique tool used to accomplish a number of things, not all of which are obvious at first glance. Finally, as a financial planner I can't help but also give you some practical applications and knowledge to help educate you to make wise decisions in your pursuit of a truly rich life.

The most difficult part of writing this book for me has not been finding what I want to put in it, but rather, what do I leave out. I hope that my efforts will spur you to seek more information, advice, and guidance on these topics and others. I love my profession of financial planning and will talk in some detail about its benefits, but the purpose of this book is to address a much larger and deeper issue of defining what being truly rich is and how to strive for it more effectively for God's glory. I will quickly admit to you that I don't do many of these topics justice by the amount of print I give them, and virtually all of my subjects can and do fill volumes of books. I do, however, hope to have captured many of the "high points" and some ideas which are not widely discussed. I also will admit that this book places an overemphasis on things financial in nature. This should not mislead you into thinking that I believe that sound financial management is the primary means to achieve a truly rich life; I rightly give a relationship with Christ that credit. My reason for overemphasis of financial issues is simple and twofold: First, as a financial planner, that is what I deal with regularly and where I feel I have specific expertise and insight. Second, the ways in which we do view and use money do have a profound effect on our lives. I hope that this book may serve as a stepping stone to greater learning for this worthy pursuit.

I can tell you with a great degree of confidence that I have already gotten more out of this book than most readers will obtain. I have gained a sharper focus of what is important and strengthened my commitments to God and His plans for me. For those of you who know me personally or professionally, you might recognize that I can't claim to have life "all figured out"; and I will confess my utter humbleness in presenting such a lofty topic. However, I hope you and even those who don't know me will concentrate less on how I, or anyone else for that matter, line up with these principles and look introspectively to see how these truths have application in *your* life. My hope and prayer is that this book will give you a new or strengthened perspective on what being truly rich means and motivate you to press on toward a life which is *truly rich.*

CHAPTER 1

Porsches and Prozac

To the world around us, America is considered to be one of the richest nations in the world; to our credit, we do represent the lion's share of the world's monetary wealth. However, I plan to build the case that many Americans are not *truly* rich, regardless of financial comparativeness. I hope to start to build the foundation of what I believe being truly rich is and maybe, surprisingly, what it is not. My purpose in sharing this topic with you is not to add a feather to your academic hat or to make you say, "Wow, those people need to get it together!" My hope is that you will take an introspective look to see if any of these characteristics describe you and your life. I will admit humbly that I find evidence of some of them in mine, but I also realize that only by the acknowledgment of the situation can I then begin to institute change and live a richer life.

It is really hard to find a great place to start, so let me just jump into the thick of it. Starting with spending, it is probably no surprise to learn that most people, Americans especially, enjoy spending money. However, would it surprise you to know that on average, Americans spend six hours a week shopping? Even more disturbing is the fact that the same "average American" only spends forty minutes playing with their kids.[1] In fact, research shows that we spend more on the most trivial things than most people in other countries spend on everything. For instance, in 2001 Americans spent $25 billion on personal watercraft – more than the entire GDP of North Korea. A United Nations Environmental Program did a study which showed that Americans spend more for trash bags than 90 percent of the world's 210 countries spend for everything combined.[2] This study was shocking to me; but after my initial shock wore off, my first response was to point out why the numbers are that way. Other countries are much smaller which accounts for some of it and, of course, it includes all of those countries that are in total poverty, so that explains why the numbers are so dramatic. Now thinking about it for a minute, should that make me feel any better?

My assumptions are true: other countries may be smaller, and one-fifth of the world's populations, some one billion people, live in abject poverty.[3] How can that make any of us feel any better? People die of hunger every day, and we complain that our clothes are out of season. Another statistic that has been getting a lot of press lately, and one that we are all very aware of because it affects our vanity, is the problem of obesity. In America today, obesity is a greater health threat than starvation. To me, that is sobering; and while some may speculate on the causes of obesity, we certainly know of one: eating too much. So while others are dying of hunger for lack of food, our problem has to do with gluttony!

Not only is the abundance and overindulgence of food began to hurt our health, we now have so much stuff that we can't fit it all in our houses. This, even though our average house size is 2, 250 square feet compared to the average 1950's home of 1,100 square feet that seemed quite comfortable at the time. There are now over thirty thousand self-storage facilities in the United States, and that business has expanded fortyfold since the 1960s from virtually nothing to over a $12 billion-a-year industry.[4] For many of those with substantial wealth, they acquire second homes, vacation homes, condos, or all of the above to enjoy and store their abundance of stuff. In the year 2005, according to the National Association of Realtors, 39.9 percent of all home purchases in America were second homes. Given the sheer volume of that number, it can easily be seen that this abundance is not limited to the elite upper class.

Another interesting fact is that in America, we have almost as many cars as we have licensed drivers. Compare that to fifty years ago and you will notice the growing trend of material wealth of the average American. I will insert here before I continue: *I do not condemn the possession of wealth; in fact I help people to attain it. Rather I am pointing to a symptom of a problem growing in our society.* Let me continue.

There is no doubt in my mind that we are a nation that has had God's hand of providence abundantly supplying our needs, but have we taken it too far? Our spending does not go without effect; and as a result, debt is rampant in our country. The average American has around $9,000 in credit card debt, with an average interest rate of 18 percent.[5] We simply spend tomorrow's cash today. It is this type of behavior which puts us on what Thomas Stanley, author of *The Millionaire Next Door*, refers to the "perpetual earn-and-consume treadmill." Unfortunately this treadmill doesn't seem to shut off or slow down for most people, and the end result is nothing short of extreme exhaustion or worse. This earn-to-consume cycle is one of the factors that I believe explains what has caused time to have seemingly sped up. I can remember summers as a kid that felt like they lasted forever, but now they go by in the blink of an eye; days, weeks, and months are only distinguishable by certain holidays or memorable weather.

Recent studies show that 95 percent of our workers say they wish they could spend more time with their families and 69 percent say they'd like to slow down and live a more relaxed life. [6] Despite these numbers, most continue on as usual, and not because they necessarily want to but because they have started a viscous cycle that is hard to break. Americans don't just plot along in their consumer behavior; many peoples' thirst for immediate gratification has turned into a full-on obsession. Our nation is now characterized as one that shouts at a microwave oven to hurry up, revs the engine at stoplights, pulls its hair out while waiting on high-speed Internet, and will literally push people down at the local Wal-Mart to get "the toy" during Christmas. Did these things characterize the lives of our parents or grandparents? As I have heard in many recent articles, many Americans are so busy today making a living that there seems to be no time to make a life. Spending and consuming are what we do; it is who we are, and it is even a self-proclaimed hobby of many Americans. We shouldn't think for one second that this behavior isn't self-destructive as well as hurting the generations to come; it already is.

Today, 93 percent of teenage American girls rate shopping as their favorite activity.[7] The average teenager now spends $5,252 annually, and one in three teenagers carries a credit card, according to Teen Research Unlimited in Northbrook, Illinois.[8] This behavior we are practicing and teaching our kids, surprisingly, does not yield the intended result of happiness but instead, is often characterized by a later lifestyle ruled by stress and financial ruin. We should stop to consider that the lifestyle and standard of living we are showing our children may be putting a ton of pressure on them to be able to replicate when they get older. As Americans, we all inherently recognize that part of the American dream is that each succeeding generation should be more successful than the one preceding it. With this in mind, it should be no surprise when our children become "successful" workaholics with debt and marriage problems; the standard of living for many may be too high. If Daddy is a doctor and his wife and daughter's favorite activity is shopping, it should not be surprising to guess that this pattern being developed might cause a point of contention in the future if his daughter's husband doesn't have the same robust income to support this recreational spending. Or will our children seek out spouses based on material assets as opposed to internal assets, and what impact will that have down the road? I think you can see my point.

Let's take another example of the indoctrination of our children into American materialism: the celebration of Christmas. Without being a killjoy, I think that many would agree that much of the focus of this holiday is truly not the birth of our Savior but more a holiday of materialistic chaos. Parents often buy so much for Christmas that they pay for it for the next three months of the year. Stop and think about most people's favorite question to ask kids during this time of year: what do you want for Christmas? Christmas has been commercialized to the point that Christ is almost nonexistent. As a Christian, we know that Christmas is not about giving presents; it is about God giving us a savior, a fact that has taken a backseat to the "gotta have gadget of the season."

I believe many Americans' increasingly affluent lifestyles may be robbing their kids of a lot of what being a kid is all about. We wouldn't dare give a two-year-old a beer and tell them to learn to like it, but we do take away the box and force them to play with the fancy toy. After a short while, we have addicted them to the same things that we like; and before you know it, we have brand-conscious teenagers filling our shopping malls. I certainly recognize I am ignoring other factors, but parenting and modeling behavior is certainly part of the issue.

Yet another side effect of this spend-to-consume behavior is the lack of preparedness that most families have. Most people are just one financial hiccup (ex. a short-term disability or unemployment or even an unexpected bill) away from a financial disaster. Harvard University economist Juliet Schor writes, "Sixty percent of families have so little in the way of financial reserves that they can only sustain their lifestyles for about a month if they lose their jobs. The next richest can only hold out for three and a half months." [9] Unfortunately, many have not escaped those financial hiccups, and bankruptcy has been their only way out. Personal bankruptcy filings have almost doubled since 1994 to a record 1.66 million in the fiscal year ending September 2003.[10] For those who may fair better than the previous statistics, most are still grossly unprepared for inevitable events such as retirement or college cost. The corresponding stress from financial difficulties and trying not to fall off the earn-to-consume treadmill that has now sped up to an unmanageable speed has a tremendous effect on the individual and the family.

Many people site worries about financial issues, and those worries often compound into more severe issues. Consider that today the rate of clinical depression is ten times what it was before 1945.[11] Now I am sure that psychologists might argue with me over the cause of the increase in depression (citing diagnosis primarily); but I can imagine that financial strains, if not at the root, significantly contributed to many of the cases. The family, along with the individual, is suffering as shown by the fact that the divorce rate is double what it was in 1950s; and money is the precipitating factor in 90 percent of all divorces. Many recent numbers indicate around 50 percent of all marriages end in divorce, and the rate for first marriages is around 35 percent. While there are a number of issues relating to the divorce rate which are notable, I would just like to point to the strains caused by financial issues. Certainly being financially sound wouldn't save all or even a majority of these divorces; but to be sure, it would relieve a lot of tension and could have untold effects on a number of areas including each person's work life and "spare" time. I do wish to add an interesting tidbit, for what it is worth: the divorce rate for couples who "pray together regularly" is around one out of 150.

Another example of our materialistic pursuit is evidenced by the overwhelming popularity of the dual-income family. While I certainly recognize there are a plethora of circumstances surrounding this issue and don't want to come across as judgmental, the sheer percentages of Americans which have chosen this path signals a change in the values of some. For those of you who either have to work, feel a calling in your work, or have a flexible arrangement which allows for time as a parent . . . that is great. My point is not to judge your heart's desires, but to get you to judge your heart's desire to make sure you aren't one of these I am referring to who are falling victim to the fallacy of the advantages of the dual-income family. The people I do wish to address are those whose main desire is to maintain a certain standard of living, focusing primarily on the material things. There is often a feeling of "we can't afford to live on one income." For many, the reality is they are choosing a certain level of material affluence versus a reduction in that lifestyle to be able to support the traditional arrangement. The result for many is not a better standard of living at all. Sure there may be more money, even after child care, taxes, work clothes, work lunches, and commuting expenses; but to be sure, there is a trade-off. Life is busier, and there are new emotional strains that often manifest themselves into all kinds of issues. It is very hard to put a price tag on what a healthy marriage and family life are worth. Unfortunately, there are many who still believe the lies of the advantages of the dual-income family; and for the most part, they aren't any happier for it.

All of this being said, I don't think this characterizes a country, a people, a family, or a person who is truly rich. In fact, I would characterize it more as the authors did in the book titled *Affluenza*. They describe America as a nation in epidemic infected with a disease called affluenza : "Affluenza is described as a painful, contagious, socially transmitted condition of overload, debt, anxiety, and waste resulting from the dogged pursuit of more."[12] While these characteristics may not characterize you, by the very nature of statistics, they do characterize somebody. To take that thought even further, if they don't include you, then someone else's situation is even worse than previously described. Fortunately most people I know and come in contact with are far from this label of being infected with "affluenza"; and to be quite honest, my purpose is not to judge whether or not this label fits you. What I do think is beneficial is to examine if you think it describes any part of your life or thoughts; and if so, isn't it robbing you of happiness and peace?

I find it almost ironic that America which is in this condition of hyper-consumerism was settled by the Puritans who fled England to get away from the oppression of England and its church which had been tainted with material obsession. The Puritans came to America to practice simple living and to honor and worship God. Today, Americans seem to relegate God far from the limelight and continue to pursue their lifestyles of the rich and famous.

Ponder this: isn't it interesting that despite America's gross national product (GNP) being twice what it was in the 1950s, we really don't feel that much richer?[13] To be more specific, the average American's purchasing power has tripled since WWII; and during this same time period, large amounts of extremely low-income immigrants have entered the country driving those averages down. All of this and the percentage of Americans who describe themselves as "happy" haven't budged in fifty years.[14] In fact, the University of Chicago's National Opinion Research Center has found that from 1957 to 1996, the percentage of those saying they were "very happy" has declined slightly from 35 percent to 30 percent.[15] One of the most fascinating bits of research to me, and really the study which most exemplifies my beliefs, was a survey given to those listed in Forbes Magazine's list of the four hundred wealthiest Americans.

These megamillionaires and billionaires were asked to rate their life's satisfaction from "extremely dissatisfied" (1) to "extremely satisfied" (7). The common perception and worldview that most hold would suggest that of course these people, among all else, would be the most satisfied with their lives. Not surprisingly to me, the respondents' average rating was 5.7, only slightly above the average rating.[16] Even more insightful was that they took this same life-satisfaction survey to the East African country of Kenya to the Masai tribesmen. While they lived in dirt huts, herded cattle for a living, and had no money or modern conveniences, they also rated themselves as a 5.7 on the life-satisfaction scale.[17] This scale must be broken! Surely these researchers failed math and can't add and divide! Or could this be revealing a richness that isn't entirely dependent on big bank accounts and flashy cars?

If this is the case, and Americans don't feel richer, but instead, are more debt laden, more rushed in their lives, more anxious about the future, and less content with what they have, then how and why has this happened? No one would willingly choose such a destructive path – would they? In this next chapter, I will discuss why we are like this and what has happened.

CHAPTER 2

Adam, Eve, and the Mega-mall

I think with the little amount of evidence that I have shown, we can agree that many Americans, possibly including ourselves, are hindered by the chains of materialism and it is preventing us from enjoying life to its fullest. The question becomes, how has American society slipped into such a rut, and more specifically, how have we individually gotten immersed into this mind-set and lifestyle?

While I could point the finger of blame at almost everyone and their brother, from the marketing executives at the luxury car manufacturers to those darn Joneses down the street, I find it most helpful to start at the root cause and work my way forward. In doing so, the couple I will first accuse is not the Joneses that we are all so familiar with but that other infamous couple, Adam and Eve. You see, theologically the case can be made that the first sin was this and that; but the manifestation of Adam and Eve's sin was in the act of wanting more – greed. God gave them the entire Garden of Eden except one tree, yet they wanted more. Because of their transgression, sin entered the world; now for all of the corruption and ungodly behavior that we (all mankind) exhibit, we can thank our ancestral heritage.

Now I am sure there are those who would say, "Zach, that is a little silly to blame my desire for material things on 'the fall of man'; and secondly, there is nothing wrong with wanting things." While there is nothing wrong or sinful about wanting things, I will address this point in detail in a later chapter; it is the *obsession* with things that I *am* addressing. What did take place at the fall *is* the reason for what I have described. God made man originally to be in perfect communion with him. God has set eternity in the heart of every man and woman; and only a right relationship with Him can fill that desire, that emptiness that we all feel apart from Him. At the fall, that perfect relationship was destroyed; and from that day forward, people have been in constant pursuit to try and meet nonmaterial needs such as spiritual fulfillment and true happiness with material excess and other forms of idolatry. Every man simply has a God-shaped hole that cannot be filled any other way. This materialistic approach leads only to disappointment and destruction, and unfortunately, it has been replicated since the very beginning.

In an article "Money and Happiness," author Steve Moeller points out that biologists have proved that all higher species, from frogs to humans, are biologically programmed to seek pleasure, "Everything we do, we do because we consciously or unconsciously believe that it will make us happy."[18] Taking this further, it is no leap to recognize that we pursue money and things because we *think* it will make us happy. Science may talk in terms of a biological programming; I believe the Bible refers to this exact thing – a sin nature. Because of this sin nature, we inevitably have sinful behavior and attitudes; and some of which are even hard to shake for those of us who have been saved by God's grace and given a new heart and a new nature.

I could spend the rest of this book on the effect of sin and lack of reconciliation and relationship with God as the reason for so many destructive paths, but let me continue by looking at some more surface causes that have contributed to the problem and led us in this direction.

Without question, another cause of our slide to materialism deals with a major societal demographic shift that has occurred. Even as recent as one hundred years ago, our country was primarily agrarian. A large majority of the population lived in rural communities and stayed close to the rest of the family. Things were simple, work was hard, families were close, time seemed to move at a slower pace, and overall, many of the inner feelings of contentment and security were met. There was a general feeling that if things got tough, you always had the kids, or Mom and Dad, to pitch in and help and things would be okay. I can remember Zig Ziglar, a popular motivational speaker and child of the Depression, saying that his dream of financial security as a young man was to grow up and buy a house on the outskirts of town on about an acre of land. He said he needed an acre of land just in case he got on hard times so he could have a garden and supply his family with food and have a little left over to sell to the neighbors. This, in his mind, was making it – financial security. Many in this time period have similar feelings and talk of a sense of community, collectiveness, and care for one another, a thought that is foreign to many of us today.

As time passed throughout our nation's history, technology improved and the economy became industrialized. This change in technology *had* the ability to lessen work hours, but it didn't. It is funny to think that people speculated many years ago that technology would shorten the workday to as little as four hours a day. People fled to the cities where the jobs were, leaving behind extended family and the close relationships of small town USA. People left the trades they once practiced, and many of the craftsmen became assembly-line workers. Many contend that because of this systemization, and the specialization of tasks, work became more monotonous and less fulfilling – the so-called death of the craftsman.

Now let's jump ahead to today. We are arguably the most industrialized nation in the world. Much of the population lives in urban cities, and few live in the same town as close relatives. Add on top of that, that out of the U.S. population of 294 million people, around forty million people move every year; and the average American moves every seven years.[19] Sociologist Will Miller speculates in his book *Refrigerator Rights* that it is because of this phenomenon there is a loss of connectivity and deep personal relationships which is one of the main causes of stress and discontentment in Americans. I agree and also believe this fuels our need to consume material things, filling the void that is left.

Before I go on, I ask you to follow my thinking. Am I right? Could I be right? Is the introduction of sin in this world the reason for our financial issues? Does societal changes cause or add to the problem? Perhaps a better question to ask is why is it that so many turn to *material* things as the remedy to feelings of inadequacy or feelings of emptiness?

I contend that we are far more influenced in what we believe and crave by the world around us than most would dare mention. Let's start with what the world around us contains: stuff and lots of it. In fact, there are more products on this earth than number of living species.[20] So possibly just by default, out of the sheer quantity of "stuff" out there, we choose to consume. If that isn't a big enough influence, there are those marketing people that make stuff so darn appealing. I received my undergraduate degree in marketing, and part of my education was based on this whole concept of making products and services appealing to consumers. One great example of marketing at its best is none other than the American icon of the shopping mall. The "magic", so to speak, of mall marketing involves store layout, lighting, fixtures, models, signs, and sheer volume of merchandise. The result of the science of mall marketing is that when all of these things are combined, our consumer appetite is aroused, our buying button is pushed, and we cannot help but buy something. Research confirms this fact and shows that only about a quarter of people go to malls with a product in mind, so much of the purchasing that keeps these mega-malls thriving is none other than impulse buying.[21]

Of course I'm also going to bring up the Joneses, that infamous couple we all want to keep up with. Isn't this an interesting and undeniable phenomenon? Give a child a scoop of ice cream and they are happy as a lark. Give their brother two scoops while they have one and a tantrum is sure to happen – so childish. Consider adults: own a car which functions perfectly well and you are content. Your neighbor buys a new fancy sports car and you loathe your old beater every time you look at it in the driveway. Author William Bernstein, in his book *The Birth of Plenty*, refers to this as the neighborhood effect.[22] It isn't absolute wealth which makes us happy, but rather relative wealth. The question is not "is my house nice?" but "is it bigger than others I know?" Unfortunately, television and other media compound this problem by extending our neighborhood. We no longer compare ourselves to the Joneses on our street but to the Joneses in Beverly Hills, which is somewhat of a new phenomenon. In times past, the average man had little idea or made little thought of what the king was eating or how he was living; but today the average man is constantly bombarded with how the "rich and the famous," not mentioning the other affluent, are living. It is this constant reminder of where you fall on the social/economic ladder that causes a reduced level of happiness.

I think you will also find it interesting to look at a medium which is extremely effective at advancing consumerism and our materialistic worldview: television. Let's start by examining the shows that are on TV today. In order to keep this book somewhat timeless, I will refrain from naming specific names of shows and mention some of the common themes. Example number 1 is the game show/reality show where the contestant competes to win a *huge* cash prize. Some of these shows do have some entertainment quality, but stop to think if you would watch the show if the prize was something insignificant; probably not. You see, part of the emotional draw that makes the show entertaining is the excitement of winning something big, not the actual event or game. I would argue that Americans would watch thumb wrestling on TV if the grand prize was one million bucks. We like it because we live vicariously through the participant; we begin to ask ourselves, "What would I do with that amount of money?" It inconspicuously plants the seeds of discontentment. If you think that I'm stretching here, then please explain to me why many of these types of shows are popular; it surely isn't because we like watching some house mom from Omaha answer unimportant trivia questions.

Let's continue by looking at the genre of the "makeover" show (home makeover or personal). These types of shows seem to be especially popular today and are often masked in the air of charity or goodwill; after all, these people *need* help. I don't want to seem jaded, and I do recognize that in some of these shows people who do need help get it; that's wonderful. Please keep in mind, however, that the way these shows can be afforded is through the suppliers and advertisers who will ultimately benefit from the viewers who are now magically discontent with what they have. Often the subjects of the makeover are shown to be ostracized or pitied for how they lived before; but now, with a makeover thanks to Company X and Company Y, their life is wonderful and they have obtained true happiness. Now that I am beautiful or now since I have this great new house, my whole outlook on life is different. The connection is craftily tied between materialism and happiness. If getting that nice kitchen made that family so happy, it surely will make me happy too! We love it and feel altruistic by watching. I am not saying that nice things don't add pleasure; we would all enjoy a stay at a Ritz-Carlton over a Motel 6, but the degree and endurance of the happiness is in question.

My last example of TV shows that socialize us is none other than the time-honored sitcom. You may be thinking, "These don't try to sell us anything; how would they affect the way I think?" There are a number of ways I do think they influence us, but I will focus on the issue of materialism. I ask you to notice one thing in most all sitcoms: the characters' standards of living, e.g., houses, clothes, eating habits, cars, etc. If you don't think these standards of living are inflated, just compare them to the average American. Better yet, just compare the standard of living in relation to the jobs the characters supposedly have, if they even have one. It is not at all uncommon for these characters to have very normal (average income) types of jobs or maybe no real job at all. Interestingly, however, these same characters have huge well-furnished homes, travel regularly, eat out every day, constantly shop, yet somehow are never working. No wonder we like watching these people; they get to sit around and hang out with their friends, spend money like it grows on trees and never have to balance a checkbook. It is virtually opposite of reality TV. While I too may find these shows amusing at times, don't think for one second that your thoughts and values aren't shaped by what you watch.

Do these TV shows pose an influential risk? Admittedly, maybe not in moderation; however, most Americans haven't quite got a handle on moderation. The average child and adult male watch three to four hours of TV a day or roughly twenty-eight to twenty-nine hours a week, and adult women watch around thirty-four hours a week.[23] [24] Just think, by high school graduation most kids have watched about twenty-five thousand hours of television. If you break that down, that is the equivalent of watching TV twelve hours a day for six years straight. I pose the question to all, what other influence consumes this amount of time? Can one go unaffected by a constant bombardment of messages without being affected? My contention is no.

What is true in terms of content for TV is at least the same, if not even more exaggerated, in movies. Within the course of a two-hour movie, we see our heroes go from rags to riches. We see major successes in the time it takes us to mow the grass and they fit right into our grandiose self-image and instant-gratification lifestyle; and man, do we love the movies! Many movies not only confirm but promote the materialism that so often categorizes Americans, and they also facilitate the infatuation we have with Hollywood actors and actresses and their real-life extravagance. You don't have to look any farther than your doctor's office waiting room table or grocery store checkout line to see numerous magazines devoted to Americans' infatuation with celebrities. Americans imitate as best we can the "lifestyles of the rich and famous" despite the fact that most of us know that many of these beautiful people's lives are wrecks and that fame and fortune they have has not produced in them admirable qualities or the happiness we desire. We try to mimic their lifestyles despite also knowing that we don't have incomes to keep up with Hollywood Boulevard. I would speculate that many of these Hollywood types actually spend less as a percentage of income on their bling than those of us who try to imitate them.

Yet another one of the reasons why TV helps perpetuate this need for greed has little to do with the actual shows, but more to do with what is shown in between the shows: commercials. Never forget how networks afford to pay these actors so much money: advertising. Why do large companies spend millions of dollars a year on advertising? Because it works – it is as simple as that. While much of advertising's effectiveness is difficult to measure and quantify, if you are a marketer, one of the main keys you do know is that repetition is the key to effectiveness, so repetition is what we get. One hour of commercial TV is consumed by around seventeen minutes of commercials; it should be no wonder we want more stuff. I will add here, because

I am not going to address print media in detail, just flip through any magazine and notice how much space is devoted to advertising. You may buy a magazine to read some articles, but good luck finding them!

Surely you can start to agree with me. Much of TV contains messages that promote discontentment and lifestyles that are contrary to financial logic. Combine that with the constant bombardment of advertising telling us we need something new. Advertisers today are very clever people; they know that people make buying decisions emotionally rather than rationally. Why else would beer makers show how sexy and attractive you will be if you drink their beer or how a luxury car will calm all of your worries in life and get you cool friends? Just think about those statements for a minute. Beer is beer. Cars are transportation. However, most people due to the emotional aspects delivered in advertising have a deep-rooted feeling that those products will fill another need in their life. I know it sounds crazy; but trust me, it's big business.

Another phenomenon that is relevant with media is what I would call the displacement factor. The more time we spend watching TV and movies, the less interaction we have with the "real" world. I am not saying that the TV is evil and my family has not resorted to tossing ours out the window, but what I am saying is don't be oblivious to the fact that it is a major influence on our culture and our happiness. Much of what is shown promotes discontentment. I also bring it to your attention because the TV serves as today's baby-sitter. Don't be surprised in years to come as the youth of America continues down the path of trying to find happiness through material wealth and the religion of consumerism.

Although most know from personal experience, I feel I must inform you of the fact that materialism is addictive in nature. Materialism is addictive for the same reason that most other things are addictive; they only provide a short period of satisfaction. That new fancy car quickly turns into last year's model; that fashionable dress is all of a sudden a fashion mistake. The "shopper's high" is often immediately followed by "buyer's remorse." This phenomenon should shoot up huge red flares and warn us that something isn't right. Psychologists describe this state of reoccurring dissatisfaction as a "hedonic treadmill" which is created when we quickly adapt to our current level of wealth and need more or something new to make us happy. Psychology would say we are wired to continually be in a state of want, which I would agree, but with one exception which I will expound on soon. This phenomenon should be a continual reminder of the fact that things will not make us happy, at least not for very long.

While I have pointed to many causes for why many Americans are in the financial and emotional predicament that I have laid out, a main contributor I firmly believe is a lack of financial education. Although I have already painted a gloomy picture, I truly believe that education can help change attitudes and actions. If I didn't think so, to be honest I wouldn't have written this book.

Research by Jump$tart Coalition for Personal Financial Literacy, a not-for-profit advocacy group in Washington, shows that many high school graduates can't balance a checkbook. "Most simply have no insight into the basic survival principles involved with earnings, spending, saving, and investing," the coalition's Web site reports.[25] I ask you to think back to grade school, high school, and even college. Where in all of our halls of academia is financial literacy taught? To answer the question for you, it traditionally hasn't been. Only very recently have programs been developed to teach the basics of financial management to students; but for the most part, they are not required curriculum. I dare say that most parents don't teach their kids about money because they themselves aren't at a level of literacy where they feel comfortable talking about it. It is this basic education that will help to defend against all of the other influences out there. Education can allow a person to not emotionally but rather rationally make a decision based on the best financial outcome. I truly believe that everyone at least deserves that chance to be responsible in their decisions. If people still decide to use credit cards like they have no limits, then that is their personal choice; but at least they can't plead ignorant when the creditors start calling. I believe that a financial education *is* a *huge* step in not only making the right financial decisions but being able to live a less stressful, happy, and truly rich life.

To get this much-needed financial education, there are many sources. Books like this one are a great start. Friends and family who have their financial lives in order are another great resource. Many civic organizations and churches also may offer services and/or classes regarding finances. Finally, as I will discuss in a later chapter, a trusted advisor can be an invaluable resource of education and accountability to you and your family.

Finally, I must come back again to the most important reason for our inability to snap out of our materialistic malaise: our lack of a relationship with God and an ignorance or disregard for God's word, the Bible. If we do indeed agree, as most professing Christians do, that the Bible is the authoritative, inspired, and infallible word of God, then how can we remain ignorant of what it says? If you are not a Christian, I urge you to read the Bible for yourself and seek out someone who can explain the good news of Jesus Christ because as I will explain, everything else, money, careers, etc., is somewhat meaningless without that relationship. To say it in the most loving way that I can think of, there is no meaning or lasting fulfillment in life apart from God; you can try like many have to find it, but God is the one who created you, and apart from Him, all else is meaningless.

Throughout the rest of this book I will lay the groundwork for how to strive for a *truly rich* life. This is a life not characterized by material wealth but by a life that honors God in not only spirit but in practice. I believe that this life is the result of both a biblical perspective on money and life as well as a practical understanding of the aspects of financial management. Being truly rich deals with both the attitude and application of biblical principles in all aspects of life, and we will deal primarily with the financial aspects. I fully recognize that a truly rich life is not just about our dealings with money and things, but *it is* a big part. I encourage you to read and challenge yourself and others on these ideas I present; after all, doesn't everyone want to be truly rich?

CHAPTER 3

Designer Theology

To try and prescribe a formula for happiness, success, and a truly rich life apart from the acknowledgment, participation, and focus on God just seems plain silly. In fact, trying to shape your life with the focus being only *your own* happiness is not only narcissistic but seemingly ignores or discounts the reality that an awesome God exists. However, despite its futility, many do try to plot and scheme their way to success and happiness, and many do achieve at least some external measure of it. I believe, however, the vast amount of evidence would show that a relationship with God is at the center of those who would be characterized as truly rich. For those who have not put God as their focus and view money as an end instead of a means, to be frank, they often have lives which more closely resemble a soap opera. There are volumes of other books written with "proven" and "guaranteed" methods for giving you all that you want in life and ways to create your "ideal life." My only response to those who buy into those books is good luck, if you plan on doing it without God. I think many can attest to the emptiness that many of those strategies produce; and many who try those strategies end up jumping from one to another like others do diets, trying to find the one that works for them. While goal setting, planning, and positive thinking are all wonderful, we should not get ahead of ourselves in crediting them with too much power and should instead recognize a sovereign God who is in control of everything.

There *is* one book out there that does have the formula for true happiness and fulfillment: the Bible. While there may be some disagreement on that statement, I find that most professing Christians will agree with me, at least outwardly, and say that by far the Bible is the most influential book in the world and that it has the ability to change one's life; after all, that is what we are supposed to say, right? Unfortunately I would have to agree with my pastor, when he said that if you confiscated people's Bibles today, there would be little change. In fact, a quick examination of many people's Bible would show that besides their name in the front, their Bible is in returnable condition.

It should be of no surprise to say that many Christians have a lack of priority in reading and studying the Bible which logically leads to an inability in rightly applying biblical principles. I will contend, even if you grew up in the Bible belt, that much of what we "believe" is based on cultural influences or what someone has taught us concerning the Bible rather than actual biblical truth. Said a little differently, many Christians have quickly adopted a view or belief without taking the time to read what the Bible *actually* says concerning different issues. I believe that only through studying God's word can we arrive at a proper perspective on money or life and be able to properly respond. In this chapter, I will address some commonly held beliefs and popular false teachings that are being spread today by many in the visible church. While I certainly wouldn't consider myself as any kind of authority on these issues, I will point out some conclusions I have made. I will say this, if I am right in my interpretation of these Scriptures, then the authority in question is no longer mine but our Lord's, for they are His word. I fully recognize that I have already made some bold statements and I hope that they are not taken arrogantly because my prayer for *everyone* is that they will have a truly rich life. I cannot, however, dilute what I know to be true; and I sincerely pray that if you disagree with me at this point, you will continue reading.

It might be helpful to first point out why the Bible is helpful and applicable to us today and why we can glean wisdom for life and even financial wisdom in particular from it. As I have mentioned before, let us start with the fact that the Bible is the inerrant, authoritative, sufficient, and inspired word of God. With just agreeing on these previous qualities (which may be a stretch for some), then the Bible *must be* of utmost importance. It must contain truths and wisdom that God wanted us to know and apply. I would agree with the Westminster Confession of Faith in that it states that the Bible should be our *only* "rule for faith and life."[26] The Scripture confirms these previous statements as Paul explains to Timothy that "all Scripture is breathed out by God and profitable for teaching, for reproof, for correction, and for training in righteousness, that the man of God may be competent, equipped for every good work." (2 Tim. 3:16) We have God's word, His specific revelation to us about Himself and in it truths that can enrich our lives; let us not seemingly ignore it in so many areas of our lives.

I also believe that there is often a real disconnect between what many say they value and what they truly do. To put it another way, I think many people have a programmed response when it comes to answering questions about their values; after all, we don't want to think of ourselves, much less anyone else, that we are narcissistic or materialistic. Take the following example. When asked how one would prioritize their duties, most Christians would respond by prioritizing their life as God first, then family, then work, and then play. Many of those who would correctly respond are also the people who are overworked executives with low golf handicaps who can't understand why their kids are a pain in the neck. You see, many of us intellectually ascend to one set of beliefs but emotionally are pulled into a lifestyle that advertises something much different. Instead of being tossed around by the forces of this world, we are called to be controlled by the Holy Spirit and directed by God's word. I can make these arguments, not just by what I have observed from others but because of the personal struggles I have had with these issues as well. Jonathan Edwards, America's most renowned theologian, spurs on his readers to be charitable and addresses this very issue I am talking about:

> We are professors of Christianity, we pretend to be the followers of Jesus and to make the gospel our rule. We have the Bible in our houses. Let us not behave ourselves in this particular, as if we had never seen the Bible, as if we are ignorant of Christianity, and knew not what kind of religion it is. What will it signify to pretend to be Christians and at the same time to live in the neglect of those rules of Christianity which are mainly insisted on in it? [27]

It may sound as if I am beating up on all Christians, which I am certainly not. I am simply stating issues that many others have stated and issues you have probably dealt with, if not personally, then at least firsthand. It should come as no surprise that these issues exist. If others are anything like me, even as a Christian for many years, I had not read or been told much of what the Bible said, especially concerning things such as our finances. To further prove my point, allow me to point out just one small issue that is very familiar for most Christians: the tithe. While I will discuss giving in general very shortly, let's look at the following study done by the Barna Group. In total, one out of every twenty households (5 percent) in America gave a tenth of their pre-tax income to non profit organizations. Of those who did give a tenth, a large majority of them actually gave in excess of that percentage. When the survey examined the behavior of born-again adults – those who have made a significant personal commitment to Jesus Christ and who believe they will experience eternal life because of their confession of sins and acceptance of Jesus Christ as their savior – the outcome showed just *7 percent had given a tenth of their incomes* to their church. Sadly, more than twice as many "born-again" adults gave no money to a church in 2003 (18 percent).[28] There could be numerous statements made about this research, but the one I wish to make at this point is simply this: why are Christians giving so little?

I believe our tightfisted giving is due to our lack of a biblical perspective on money which stems from a number of issues, not the least of which is our lack of teaching and study of the Bible. Christ knew of the importance in teaching about money, and I hope to share that with you. As the late U.S. Senate chaplain Richard Halverson once said, "Jesus Christ said more about money than about any other single thing because when it comes to a man's real nature, money is of first importance." In fact, the Lord gave thirty-eight parables in the Gospels; and out of those thirty-eight, sixteen are in regard to how we handle our money. Christ arguably said more about money and possessions than about heaven and hell combined. In the Bible, there are over five hundred references to prayer, less than five hundred references to faith, but there are over two thousand references to money and possessions, with 288 of them found in the four Gospels. It is obviously a major issue and for good reason.

Before I begin in sharing with you God's wisdom as presented in the Scripture, I feel the need to address some of the rampant false teachings that are out there today regarding the area of finances. I am not in the least surprised that these false teachings exist for the Scripture tells us that "for the time is coming when people will not endure sound teaching, but having itching ears they will accumulate for themselves teachers to suit their own passions, and will turn away from listening to the truth and wander off to myths." (2 Tim. 4:3-4) After all, who doesn't want to hear about all the goodies that being a Christian will produce, which is precisely why our pul   re full with many of those we have today? Today many Christians exercise "designer theology," essentially believe what you want to concerning God as long as it makes *you* feel good. Many have adopted this philosophy; and as a result, we have preachers, teachers, and TV personalities telling us varied messages about what is truth.

The Scripture tells us to test everything against Scripture and not to accept it if it doesn't line up. We are to be like the Bereans in the book of Acts: to study the Scriptures and test what is taught to see if it is true. False teachers will not tell you that they are false and many are self-deceived or have "good intentions" so we must be shrewd. Don't assume just because someone preaches in Christ's name that they are of God, for the Scripture clearly warns of this in Matthew. "Many will say to Me, 'Lord, Lord, did we not prophesy [meaning taught or preached publicly] in your name?" to which Christ will respond, "I never knew you; depart from Me, you workers of lawlessness!" 24 (Matt. 7:23-24). This Scripture should be a grave reminder to us to always test what is being preached. Take what you have heard or read, go back and read it for yourself in the context it resides. What have credible scholars said of this same Scripture? How does it fit within the totality of Scripture (agrees with or contradicts)? How does it point us to Christ? Until then, do not accept it as truth, lest you be lead astray. I challenge you to do the same with all I present, for the ultimate responsibility is yours.

I think it is also important to point out that much of the false teaching that is out there is not completely contrary to orthodox teaching but rather a slight twist on it. Many times there may not even be a twist of the meaning of a Scripture but will simply be an omission of what the rest of the Bible says about that same subject. An overemphasis on a truth, not giving balance or proper weight to the promises of God, can lead you down a wrong path as well. As it is said, a clock without a battery is still right twice a day; so just because a message contains some truth (even from the Bible), be careful before accepting the full teaching.

Unfortunately, as the Scripture warned us about, there are many preachers, pastors, and evangelists today that fall somewhere in the camp of false teaching when it comes to the topic of money. The teaching I am referring to often goes by titles such as the "health and wealth gospel" or the "prosperity gospel" or may be characterized by statements such as "name it and claim it." These types of teachers are epitomized in the American icon of the TV evangelist (not including all of course). Quentin Schultze, in his book *Televangelism and American Culture*, writes, "Televangelist offer their own personalized expressions of the gospel as adapted from and directed to the American Culture. To put it more strongly, the faith of some televangelist is more American than Christian, more popular than historic, more personal than collective, and more experiential than biblical. As a result, the faith they preach is highly affluent, selfish, and individualistic." [29] Jim Bakker interestingly wrote a book while in prison entitled *I Was Wrong*. He put an ad in *Charisma* magazine promoting the book which read, "I taught people that God wanted above all for you to be rich and have money. That's a lie. That is not the truth . . . I was proof-texting all the time, and just looking up Scripture to prove my beliefs . . . I was wrong. How could I have taught people how to get rich? The Church is in trouble right now because we have taken Scripture out of context and have built our own doctrine . . . We have another Gospel and another Jesus and another spirit being preached . . . and the Church is going to end up in hell."

I have struggled with whether I should name names when discussing these false teachers, and I have come to the conclusion that it would be better not to because doing so may cause you to just take my word for it and make a snap judgment. Instead, I will leave these individuals anonymous and charge you with the responsibility to take *all* messages to the measuring stick of Scripture.

While you may have not sat under these types of flagrant teachings, and your soul may not be in danger, I would challenge you to search yourself for thoughts and beliefs you hold. I can remember having thoughts such as "If I do this or that, I can please God and he will prosper me" or "God wants me to be materially successful, I just know it!" I don't know if you have had similar thoughts but I can remember finding those Scriptures that I liked which confirmed my heart's desires and I then worked that into my own brand of theology which suited me. Looking back at those thoughts I once had, I find the crux of what much of this bad theology rests. It draws a connection between righteousness and prosperity and prosperity and righteousness; and it is all motivated by greed, a dangerous proposition. This brand of theology also is primarily focused on the here and now and not the eternal perspective, which we should be our focus. As Zig Ziglar once said, "research shows that I will be dead longer than I'm alive and for that reason I should have long range goals." This prosperity theology also is damaging in that it commonly puts limits, rules, and formulas as to how God chooses to work in individuals' lives. If there is one statement I feel very confident in saying, it is that you can't fit God into some neat little box.

The church at Laodicea in the book of Revelations boasted in their material prosperity saying, "I am rich and have become wealthy, and have need of nothing," to which is replied, "And you do not know that you are wretched and miserable and blind and naked." (Rev. 3:17) The Lord warns them that their earthly riches are of no spiritual benefit. We so quickly make this connection that if we are "good" we will be blessed materially and that "good" people are materially blessed. This seems like a great formula and one that we might manipulate for our own benefit, but we are also very inconsistent in our belief. If this is the formula for success and happiness, then how can we explain those who are dishonest or ungodly and prosper? Joe Magliato in his book *The Wall Street Gospel* states, "I can show you 50 atheists who will swear at God and wave their rebellious fist at heaven's laws and still have big diamond rings on their fingers and drive flashy cars, but who are neither blessed of God nor going to His heaven. Neither prosperity nor wealth is an indication of spirituality."[30] On the other hand, further destroying that formula of godliness equals prosperity is simply the life of both Jesus and the Apostles, as well as other godly people who have not been materially blessed. "The foxes have holes, and the birds of the air have nests; but the Son of Man has nowhere to lay His head" (Matt. 8:20).

Christ our king, fully man and fully God, humbled Himself to take the form of man, humbled Himself in material poorness, and humbled Himself to the point of death on a cross. The Apostle Paul, another tremendous example of godliness as presented in Scripture, experienced similar circumstances, "I have learned to be content in whatever circumstances I am. I know how to get along with humble means, and I also know how to live in prosperity; in any and every circumstance I have learned the secret of being filled and going hungry, both having abundance and suffering. I can do all things through Him who strengthens me." (Phil. 4:11-13) We see these vivid examples that I believe cannot be refuted (although I have heard some make ludicrous comments that Jesus was materially rich), and they seem difficult to swallow. After all, we know that all the Apostles except John died a martyr's death, as well as many others in the early church who met a grim earthly fate. That doesn't fit into the image or lifestyle that most Christians frankly want. We want "painless Christianity"; as Joe Magliato puts it, "We want to be overcomers, since it fits nicely with our self-image, but we don't want anything to overcome. No, that's painful."[31] We want easy living, prosperity and, of course, to serve God if and when we can.

While in America it seems to be the pervasive view that God *always* materially blesses believers, it is difficult to back that widely held view with Scripture. It is even hard to back that view outside of our own country or even our own time period. On the contrary to what we would all love to believe, the Bible actually speaks more of what we should expect: trials and tribulations. Anyone who has ever read *Foxe's Book of Martyrs*, a collection of the stories of the martyrdoms of many early church figures, and holds the "health and wealth" philosophy is going to have a real headache from the mental gymnastics it is going to take to reconcile their views with what many in the early church endured. For most in America however, poverty or persecution is far from the issue. More honestly, it can be said that most are materially blessed and spiritually poor or bankrupt.

Before I am painted into a corner of being one of those ascetic types who believes that we should all move to a monastery, or that I don't believe in any personal responsibility, let me balance the scales a little. First, I will quickly point out that we do see several examples of men of God in the pages of Scripture who were wealthy, some even extremely wealthy. Abraham, Isaac, Jacob, Job, David, and Solomon all possessed great wealth; and the Bible never condemns their possession of it. Solomon was clearly one of the richest men to ever live; and yet God used him to record some wonderful teachings regarding money, interesting if you hold a negative view of material wealth. Of course there are also numerous verses that teach about the blessings of God. Take Psalms 35:27, "Let the Lord be magnified, which hath pleasure in the prosperity of his servant," or how about Isaiah 48:17, "I am the Lord thy God which teacheth thee to profit." These Scriptures surely nullify or contradict others in the Bible, right? These are the Scriptures that are true and active today for Americans; Christ died that I might have victory over my middle-class status, right? Any apparent contradiction should be a quick reminder to dig deeper, for we should not forget that "all Scripture is God breathed" (2 Tim. 3:16) and does not contradict itself.

God *does* have a plan for you, including your financial position; and throughout the following, I will touch on some characteristics that the plan will have. Before we get too far down the road in discussing finances, let me reiterate the fact that a truly rich life has little to do with material riches at all. Money, however, is a huge factor in everyone's life and when managed and viewed correctly can enhance one's life in a number of areas. In this next chapter, we will touch on some of the main teachings regarding our finances in the Bible to help create a proper perspective.

CHAPTER 4

Mammon, Man, and Our Maker

As a financial planner, I have the high privilege to work closely with some wonderful people. As a fresh college graduate not too many years ago entering my field, I worked with just about anyone who could fog a mirror and had a distinguishable pulse. If they had two nickels to rub together, then I was really doing well. Like many in my profession, as my technical expertise grew over the years, the gradual effect has been that much of my expertise, technical in nature, is only valuable to individuals and families with slightly more than two nickels. I feel very fortunate for my experience with such a wide range of people spanning from modest means to significant wealth. Through this I have been involved firsthand with the fears, challenges, goals, and plans with very different people; and I have learned a great deal along the way. What has been most encouraging and interesting to me is that at the core, the Bible's message regarding money is able to deal specifically and individually with all people, regardless of where they may fall on the socioeconomic ladder. In contrast, if you were to go to the world and ask what the purpose of money is or what you should do with it, you would get ten million different answers. When examining the Bible, there are many clear principles and messages with virtually unlimited applications. I want to be clear that I am not imposing any kind of legalistic boundaries in this chapter but will be sharing with you truths which can give you the freedom to use money as God intended.

Some of the parts of the Bible that I am sure make so many uncomfortable are those which warn of the dangers of wealth. I know because they once bothered me and didn't fit comfortably with the ambitious financial goals that I had for myself. Also, as a financial planner I began to struggle with whether or not my helping people get "rich" was really more of a liability than a blessing. Instead of avoiding these Scriptures like so many, I think we should come to them humbly to see what our Lord is teaching; after all, it is for our benefit.

Warnings

> People who want to get rich fall into temptation and a trap and into many
> foolish and harmful desires that plunge men into ruin and destruction.
> For the love of money is the root of all kinds of evil. Some people, eager
> for money, have wandered from faith and pierced themselves with many
> griefs. (1 Tim. 6:9)

You don't have to look too hard at the headlines of the newspapers to find an example of what Paul is referring to here. One corporate scandal after another is just a public reminder of the fruits that the love of money produces. It is interesting to think about each of those most recent examples of corporate fraud. These "devious" individuals were at one time probably well liked by many, intelligent, powerful, and rich; but that wasn't enough. Now their lives, their families' lives, and certainly for those who proclaimed to be Christians, their testimonies are in shambles.

Benjamin Franklin once eloquently spoke of money's virtue,

> Money never made a man happy yet, nor will it. There is nothing in its
> nature to produce happiness. The more a man has, the more he wants.
> Instead of filling a vacuum, it makes one. If it satisfies one want, it doubles
> or trebles that want another way. That was a true proverb of a wise man,
> rely upon it. "Better is a little fear of the Lord, than great treasure, and
> trouble therewith."

What I believe most people want at their core is not wealth but happiness. Happiness or joy is one of the marks of one who is truly rich. I can't really speak from experience in saying that money won't buy you happiness, because my earthly wealth does not rank me anywhere near the Forbes 400, but hear the words of Solomon, arguably the richest man who ever lived.

> "Whoever loves money never has money enough; whoever loves wealth is
> never satisfied with his income." (Eccles. 5:10)

> "I denied myself nothing my eyes desired; I refused my heart no pleasure.
> My heart took delight in all my work, and this was the reward for all of my
> labor. Yet when I surveyed all that my hands had done and what I had toiled
> to achieve, everything was meaningless, a chasing after the wind; nothing
> was gained under the sun." (Eccles. 2:10-11)

We all can point out numerous people who have enormous wealth but are far from happy, and I can promise you that they would quickly strip themselves of that wealth if it could promise happiness. Unfortunately, while money will not buy happiness, neither will the ascetic lifestyle. Most would certainly agree with me that poverty or self-deprivation of all material riches is not the ticket to happiness either, not that many would ever really try anyway.

Let's look briefly at an account in the Bible that might make some of us with notable wealth break a sweat upon first reading it, but I will add some needed insight on this important matter. Mark 10:25 says, "It is easier for a camel to go through an eye of a needle than for a rich man to enter the kingdom of God." We could stop with reading that one verse and make the statement that being materially rich is a curse and we should sell all we have. As crazy as that sounds, some have taken that view. However, upon closer inspection and looking back to the beginning of Jesus's encounter with this rich young man in the book of Mark, he asked Jesus, "What must I do to inherit eternal life?" Jesus then asked him if he knew the commandments, and the man said that he has kept all of them since he was a boy. Jesus commanded him to go and sell everything and give to the poor and to then come follow Him. The man then went away sad because he had great wealth. It was then that Jesus made his statement that "it is easier for a camel to go through an eye of a needle than for a rich man to enter the kingdom of God." While I will address the other teachings of this passage, let it be clear that one teaching is that *it is difficult* for one to remain true to God with great wealth. As John MacArthur puts it, "the possession of material riches is usually a spiritual liability."[32] Puritan Samuel Willard agrees in writing that "it is a rare thing to see men that have the greatest visible advantages . . . to be very zealous for God."[33] There is a tendency to replace God as our object of devotion, a lessening of reliance on God. The great reformer John Calvin once wrote, "Wealth and honour frequently expose to vice; they too often puff up with pride, and lead to oppression, to the neglect of religion; and, despite of its great and glorious author . . . are you poor? Be resigned to the will of Providence: yea, be thankful that hereby you are less in danger of falling into wickedness."[34] This passage in Mark deals with these very issues; when confronted with a decision of incomparable magnitude, this young man chose to keep his wealth instead of embracing and following Jesus. Jesus put the young man's faith to a simple test, one in which you and I will never have laid out so clearly. Unfortunately, the young man chose reliance on his wealth for happiness and fulfillment at the expense of eternal life. While no one today has had a personal encounter with Jesus with such a test, many have failed to wholeheartedly follow Christ because of earthly wealth.

I would do a real injustice to this particular passage if I didn't finish its teachings. The disciples were even more amazed and said to each other, "Who then can be saved?" Because they, like many of us, thought that surely this man was wealthy as a result of God's blessing. If anyone can be saved, surely it is the rich. Jesus looked at them and said, "With man this is impossible, but not with God; all things are possible with God." What Christ is saying and imparting to His disciples is that it is God's work of saving a person. It does not depend on their efforts to merit favor; it is a gift, the very definition of grace. Jesus also indirectly was destroying the disciples' viewpoint that material richness is always a sign of God's blessing. Christ used this example of a camel passing through an eye of a needle, because a camel was the largest animal in the Palestinian area and the needle the smallest opening one could imagine, in order to show the absolute absurdity of the situation. We should view this passage as a strong warning of the entrapment of materialism and also as a reminder that God is the one who does the miracle of saving someone, not us.

We should all test ourselves to make sure that our wealth has not become the object of our service and devotion. The numerous warnings in the Bible are there because this is a struggle for most, an easy entanglement and barrier to a truly rich life. As Thomas Watson once said, "It is hard to carry a full cup without spilling and a full estate without sinning."[35]

Money as a Means

The Bible also gives a new perspective on money that we rarely think about. God in His amazing wisdom often uses money as a character shaper and revealer. As Ron Blue says it in his book *Generous Living*, "The Bible says that money is a tool, a test, and a testimony."[36] Through God's providential hand, He cares for us often through the provision of money. The economy is but a large-scale example of God's means to accomplish His purposes. Despite the common feeling that economic strings are pulled by politicians, the Federal Reserve board, and stock market analysts, it should not really be a stretch to realize that if God controls the movement of planets and destinies of men, then He is also in control of our economies. More than money's ability to meet out basic needs, God often uses it as a test; and we should use that opportunity as a testimony to Him and the rest of the world that we serve Him.

As we have already seen, Jesus often tests our devotion to Him with our money. The tests may come in the form of whether you should cook the books at work to get ahead, cheat on your taxes, or work eighty hours a week at the expense of family, friends, and church. Matthew 6:24 says, "No one can serve two masters. Either he will hate one and love another, or he will be devoted to the one and despise the other. You cannot serve both God and money." These stern words by Jesus in Matthew should be a reminder that God is a jealous God and will not share His glory with another. As Charles Spurgeon used to say, "Money is a good servant, but a bad master . . . If we make money our god, it will rule us like the devil." [37]

We should recognize that God wants our wholehearted devotion. You may get away with serving money for a while; but in most all cases if you are a Christian, there will be payback this side of heaven. If you don't believe me, just interview those who have suffered broken marriages, families, relationships, and careers. We should also realize that many times it is because of God's love for these individuals that He has disciplined them with these trials or allowed these circumstances to happen to give them a chance to see the error of their ways and bring them to repentance. Serving money, in other instances, results in terrible consequences due to the destructive nature of sin in general. While discipline is out of God's grace and love for His children, I would prefer it for everyone to not have to experience God's discipline or the other effects of this kind of sin and instead live in humble obedience.

Christ encourages and directs us in Matthew 6:19, "Do not store up for yourselves treasures on earth, where moth and rust destroy, and where thieves break in and steal. But store up for yourselves treasures in Heaven, where moth and rust do not destroy and thieves do not break in and steal. For where your treasure is, there your heart will be also." These verses should excite us about the reality of heaven and eternal life. They are also a reminder that we should focus not on the temporal things but on the eternal for they are the only things which are certain and lasting. I was watching a 2005 year-in-review news show on TV while writing this book and the show was a horrific reminder of the temporary nature of our earthy wealth. Hurricane Katrina's damage to New Orleans and the Gulf Coast was a grim reminder that regardless of how much we don't want our material things to become destroyed, stolen, or decayed this side of heaven, it's uncertain. However, if we place our allegiance with God and build our wealth in an eternal sense through stewardship, evangelism, and lives that honor God, those heavenly treasures have no end. If we keep this perspective at the forefront, with God's help we can continually pass the test of making Him our Lord.

God uses money as a means to shape and test our character because in the twenty-first century especially, it is the means to so many ends. Money affects nearly every aspect of our lives from our health care, to our children's education, to where we live, and often the people we are in contact with. While money doesn't intrinsically have value, it purchases experiences which do. It is for this reason that I chose my profession as a financial planner, because life is not about money, but money *can* affect nearly every aspect of life. I pray that you will recognize this simple truth and be on guard to recognize God's tests and His uses of money as means to not only provide for you but to build your character more and more in the image of Christ.

The Value of a Dollar

With constant bombardment from advertisers and the pressure to keep up with the proverbial Joneses, it is important to keep a true perspective about the value of material wealth. As Proverbs 11:4 and Zephaniah 1:18 remind us, "Riches profit not in the day of wrath," and "Neither their silver nor their gold shall be able to deliver them in the day of the Lord's wrath." The Apostle Paul refers to it all as rubbish when compared to knowing Christ. These scriptures bring to light the immeasurable value of a relationship with Christ and eternal life and the utter futility of material wealth. It may be easy to agree with that statement, but in reality we do value material wealth. After all, money affords us comfort and lifestyle choices that do make a real difference. The point of these Scriptures is not to say that money is worthless in a strict sense but that in view of eternity and of weightier matters, they *are* "worthless." In Matthew 16:26 Christ makes this statement clear as He poses the following question we should all keep in mind, "For what will it profit a man if he gains the whole world and forfeits his life (soul)?" The Bible makes strong statements like these because our tendency is to be so focused on the here and now and overvalue the temporal.

We are often like the rich fool in the parable in Luke who is concerned about building barns and storing up his wealth to live fat and happy. Luke 12:20: Jesus rebuked him saying, "Thou fool, this night thy soul shall be required of thee; then whose shall those things be which thou has provided?" In the grand scheme of things, it is obvious that wealth has no eternal value, although it may afford us present comfort, so we should ascribe a more accurate value to it instead of a headlong devotion like most seem to do. I can't say it any better than Paul when he said, "Godliness with contentment is great gain. For we brought nothing into the world and we can take nothing out of it. But if we have food and clothing we will be content with that" (1 Tim. 6:6-8).

Who Owns It

Possession may be nine-tenths of the law for civil matters, but God is clear in impressing upon His children the reminder of who it really belongs to. As the Puritan Thomas Manton once wrote, "God gives these good things to men, yet still reserves the property in himself; for by distributing blessings to the creature, he never intended to divest himself of the right." He also added, "We are stewards and must render an account to God."[38] The Bible in Haggai 2:8 also says, "The silver is mine, the gold is mine, declares the Lord of hosts." Most Christians and even most people agree that God is the creator of the world, but many don't think of Him as the possessor of it. "You are not your own, for you were bought with a price" (1 Cor. 6:20). So if you yourselves are not your own, then neither are your possessions your own.[39]

While these things are easily said, they have great implication and application when taken to heart. Recognition of God's ownership does a great deal in changing how we view money, and it should also serve in relieving the anxiety that wealth often produces. I can remember hearing about John Wesley, the founder of Methodism, who was away from home one day when a terrible tragedy was reported to him as he returned home: his house had just burned down. His response is a direct example of this ownership principle as he said, "The Lord's house burned. One less responsibility for me."

I consider it a privilege as a business owner to be constantly reminded that all I have comes from God. I can remember in my first few years in the business having no idea where my next dollar would come from or how I was going to pay next month's light bill. In those years and even today, I am learning more and more to trust God and His ability to care for His children. As He blesses and provides for me, it is very freeing to "give it back" emotionally ownership-wise to God, saying this is your house, your car, your TV, etc. If we can remind ourselves that He owns it, then we can more accurately make decisions or respond to events that happen concerning all that we have. If God chooses to destroy "His" house as he did with John Wesley, although still a terrible thing, we should be able to recover emotionally and submit to His will.

In watching the destructions that Hurricane Katrina caused, I was saddened to hear victims who were being interviewed who truly felt like their lives are ruined because their material substance had been lost. I don't mean to belittle a dire situation, but at the same time you do see examples of those who suffered the same loss but are coping and even thankful for what they did escape with – their lives, families, and friends. Recognizing God's ownership of "our" wealth can take great steps to lower our blood pressure; and more importantly, it is an attitude which honors God more by ascribing to Him the honor He deserves for taking care of all things. If we realize He owns it, we should faithfully be able to better steward it and give it back emotionally *and actually* if called to. I will address giving in more detail shortly, but let me interject here that giving to the church and to others is in obedience and recognition that "our" money is not really "ours" anyway. Regular giving helps us to keep this ownership principle at the forefront of our mind.

Good Money, Bad Money

Although it should be obvious by now, I still feel the need to deal head-on with the issue of whether or not money or the possession of wealth is good or bad. Puritan William Perkins makes a great point in writing, "These earthly things are the good gifts of God which no man can simply condemn, without injury to God's disposing hand and providence, who hath ordained them for natural life." Money is amoral, meaning neither good nor bad, yet it can be an extremely powerful force. In the hands of a Christian steward, it has the power to do wonderful things; yet in the hands of a self-absorbed materialist, it often can destroy. Money is a means which we all know can be used to accomplish a vast amount of things. Twenty dollars can buy a meal for a hungry family, or it can be used by terrorist to buy parts to make a car bomb to kill innocent people. So more than an object which intrinsically has worth or power, it only has power when directed by its owner. Money sitting in a pot on a deserted island won't accomplish anything; it is only when used as a means can it make a difference.

Money in most cases has a magnification type of characteristic when it comes to revealing a man's true character. If you take a godly man and increase his wealth, he will generally use it faithfully and will do great things with it. This magnification principle can also be extremely destructive, if in an opposite circumstance. Give a family who is self-absorbed and addicted to material excess gobs of money and they will literally kill themselves with it. If you need proof, just watch one of those "behind the scenes" types of documentaries on the lives of so many of our country's celebrities. Money will often bring out the best or the worst in people. We should guard ourselves however, because wealth can cause us to stray.

Interestingly, upon examination of Puritan writings, it reveals that those "religious prudes" had a very healthy view of money and wealth. The Puritans saw wealth primarily as a social good and not a private possession which falls right in line with the fact I have discussed that it all belongs to God anyway. They believed the uses of money included the maintenance of one's own affairs, the good of others, relief of the poor, maintenance of the church, and the maintenance of the commonwealth. Puritans believed in a simple life and saw hardwork as virtuous and treated prosperity as a gift from God. They were generous to those around them, and almost ironically, their disciplined lifestyle was very conducive to growing wealth.

Despite being so far removed from the Puritan's way of life and having to live in the midst of a consumer society, these principles remain what the Bible prescribes. The application of such principles at any level will start us down the road to a life that is truly much richer. To be sure, God does not condemn money; in fact, it is his dispensing hand which has made some rich and some poor. It should also not be overlooked that money in most cases is the result of one's vocation. Living in a capitalistic society, one could easily argue that one is paid for the value they bring to society; and those who are gifted with certain talents which specially equip them for some vocations are rewarded for their efforts. In that sense, money is not just a direct gift from God but a wage earned as a result of the talent He gave. It should then be no surprise that those who are hardworking and exhibit talents and attitudes that others value have the ability to create wealth. We would never think negatively about a gift of intellect that God gives a doctor as a curse, and the mere fact that society values that skill and will pay for it will undoubtedly make that person wealthy. No one in their right mind would fault God for that gift or think that capitalism has made an error; so we should also not look at wealth negatively, just cautiously. On the contrary, money can be a wonderful gift which can be a means to accomplish so many wonderful things; and we should use such a gift appropriately – to His glory. We should not have any guilt about making money; to do so is actually a part of good stewardship. As Puritan preacher Richard Baxter once wrote, "if God shows you a way in which you lawfully get more than in another way (without wrong to your soul, or to any other), if you refuse this, and choose the less gainful way, you cross one of the ends of your calling, and you refuse to be God's steward." Wealth and money *can be* God's good gifts.

In God We Trust

Command those who are rich in this present world not to be arrogant nor to put their hope in wealth, which is so uncertain, but to put their hope in God, who richly provides us with everything for our enjoyment. (1 Tim. 6:17)

If I have put my trust in gold or said to pure gold, "you are my security," if I have rejoiced over my great wealth, the fortune my hands had gained . . . then these also would be sins to be judged, for I would have been unfaithful to God on high. (Job 31:24, 28)

Yet another lesson and test God presents us with concerning money is to not trust in it. To be direct about it, God doesn't need money to take care of you, me, or anyone for that matter. The God who spoke and the universe was created is not bound by checking account balances or pension fund assets. You see, God in his wisdom, as we have discussed, has used money as His means of accomplishing His provision for many of us. In other parts of the world, this may not be the case. Unfortunately, we are so accustomed to dealing with money for the everyday expenses of life that there is a level of fear when it comes to "what if something happens to my money or my job?" We have transcribed our trust of our well-being from God, its rightful object, to money, the mere means by which He often works (at least in America). I am not saying that a total stock market collapse or a massive layoff of workers would not be extremely painful and a major obstacle, but what I am saying is that God's provision doesn't rely wholly on your investment performance or your employer's paycheck.

As John Calvin puts it, "we do God no small injury, so often as we distru that God will not give us food and clothing, as though that he had cast us out upon the earth by fortune."[40] We cannot dismiss Scriptures such as Philippians 4:19, "But my God shall supply all your needs according to his riches in glory by Christ Jesus," or one of my favorites:

> Therefore I say unto you, take no thought of your life, what shall we eat or what shall we drink; nor about your body, what you will wear. Is life not more important than food and the body more important than clothes? 31 So do not worry, saying "What shall we eat?" or "What shall we drink?" or "What shall we wear?" For the pagans run after these things, and your heavenly Father knows you need them. But seek first his kingdom and his righteousness and all these things will be given to you as well. Therefore do not worry about tomorrow, for tomorrow will worry for itself. (Matt. 6:25)

The Old Testament gives God many names, but one of the loveliest of the names is Jehovah-jireh (Gen. 22:14). It means "the Lord who provides." It is so much a characteristic of God that it is one of His names. The Bible says that man doesn't live on bread alone but by God's providential hand. God wants us to trust Him with everything. Recall the familiar verse of Proverbs 3:5 which says, "Trust in the Lord with all your heart and lean not on your own understanding." We should have confidence that the God who created the universe, who knit us in our mother's womb, and who has worked and continues to work numerous miracles, can take care of us if we trust Him.

On the flip side, if we feel more comfortable with our nest egg and employer's paycheck, no matter how big they are, then our confidence is grossly misplaced; and we might be setting ourselves up for a fall. Proverbs 11:28 warns that "whoever trusts in riches *will* fall." Thomas Manton stated the issue that this sin hinges upon,

"It is not the having, but the trusting."[41] A truly rich life is one in which little weight or confidence is obtained from our material possessions, but confidence that stems from and is placed in God and His plans for our lives.

I Would Be Content If I Just Had . . .

"If we live from hand to mouth, getting each day's supply in the day, we are as well off as Israel; for when the Lord entertained His favored people he only gave them a day's manna at a time"

"O Lord bless our substance. Enable us to use it for thy glory. Help us to keep worldly things in their proper places, and never may our savings endanger the saving of our souls" [42]

– Charles Spurgeon

"Give me neither poverty nor riches, but give me only my daily bread. Otherwise, I may have too much and disown you and say, 'Who is the LORD?' Or I may become poor and steal, and so dishonor the name of my God."

– Proverbs 30:8b-9

Another aspect of character building that God desires for his children is the peace of contentment. Ecclesiastes 5:19: "When God gives any man wealth and possessions, and enables him to enjoy them, to accept his lot and be happy in his work – this is a gift of God." We should pray that God would grant us contentment, give us the enjoyment of our lives; and we should practice contentment daily by exercising gratitude for what we have. I have at the writing of this book one son who is nearly three years old and who is a daily reminder of this contentment principle. I say that because anyone who has spent much time around a two-or three-year-old knows that if anything, most children at that age are not content. They busily move from here to there and want this and that. They often will ask for a certain kind of food and then change their minds, and it can be quite exhausting to say the least. I can't help but draw a connection between this two-year-old mind-set and the mind-set of most Americans today. We are a nation of avid consumers, hungry for anything new and trendy; and that mind-set is equally if not more exhausting to have and to be around. The issue of contentment is probably one of the most overlooked issues in society today, and it is paramount because it runs so deep within our soul. Contentment is a deeply spiritual issue because it truly reflects the fullness or emptiness of your heart. As John Piper paraphrased from Jonathan Edwards, "God is most glorified when we are most satisfied (in Him)." [43] The Bible says "if we have food and covering, with this let us be content." (1 Tim. 6:8)

Americans are some of the richest people on the face of the planet; and even most of the "poor" in this country have the basics of food, clothing, and shelter. It should be here that the message of contentment is most easily received because we are so blessed. On the contrary, we are the ones who are most hardened, cynical, and ungrateful for what we have.

I once heard a person make some statements regarding contentment that changed my whole way of thinking. They said that contentment is not about being "okay" with or "settling" with what you have, it is about being abundantly grateful for what we have. They went on to say that it is impossible to be truly grateful for something and in want at exactly the same time. When I got this concept into my mind and heart, it made sense; so I started doing this simple exercise. Anytime I was confronted with others who made more money than me, drove fancier cars, and lived in bigger houses, at the first inkling of jealously or discontentment, I would start reminding myself and thanking God for my income, my car, my house, my family, and everything else I could think of. An attitude of gratitude as I have heard it called is the secret to contentment and is an indispensable part of a truly rich life. I know that every person reading this book could easily fill an encyclopedia's worth of pages with things they should be grateful for. My prayer is that you will pray for this gift of contentment and gratitude.

Less Is More?

The Bible is full of apparent paradoxes. For instance, the Bible talks of mysterious things like if you love your life you will lose it, but if you give it up you will keep it; or what about the apparent paradox of not being saved by good works but through faith, but at the same time, faith without works is dead. Similarly, I believe the Bible teaches of God's sovereignty but man's responsibility; and while those apparent (explainable) paradoxes exist, I doubt most people in their day-to-day lives give much thought to them or ponder deep theological issues. However, there is another paradox which presents a decision almost daily about how we are to live. The paradox I am referring to is that you can live better on less than 100 percent of your money than you can on all of it. The Bible also speaks at great length of not only our duty to give but of the joy of being generous and the fruit of living in accordance to His will in this area. In my mind, these teachings are really where the rubber meets the road when it comes to walking in faith with our finances. Are we really to believe that "it is more blessed to give than to receive"? (Acts 20:35)

While I will not address the validity of the tithe and whether or not it applies as an obligation to Christians today, I will discuss the purpose of it. While some will disagree about whether or not a certain percentage applies, most all would agree that giving in general is commanded and that we should not live as if all the money God has lent us is just for our own use. Anyone who has attended a church for any length of time should be familiar with this regular giving; in fact, we are so used to the offering plate being passed down the pew that the meaning of this part of worship is often lost or even looked upon with disdain. Unfortunately, I think because of this attitude we are missing out on a number of ways God could use and bless us.

As I have previously discussed, the collection of the offering is an act of worship where we are giving back to God what is His. This isn't the "I feel generous today and liked the sermon" type of act. It is recognizing that God is our provider and He has supplied our needs. By returning a portion to Him, we are acting out of obedience and recognition of His ownership and provision. These are to be the "first fruits" of our labor, not what is left over after we have met all our needs. This give-first attitude recognizes His faithfulness to meet our needs and our dependence on Him to continue to do so. If we pay Him last, we are kind of missing the point and not recognizing this principle and trusting in His provision.

As I will continually repeat, God is not concerned with your money but is concerned with your heart. Because of this fact, I believe that your giving should be as regular as possible as the Scripture mentions (1 Cor.16:2), not twice a year or the big year-end tax-driven check. The reason is simple: it is not really about the money. The act of giving is a physical reminder of God's faithfulness and is a part of continual obedience and worship. There is no doubt that this is a serious test of faith for a number of Christians; the sheer statistics I have shared with you in previous chapters confirms it. Many people simply do not believe that you can live better on less than you can on 100 percent. I believe it is for this reason that while we are told not to test the Lord, God graciously told His people through the prophet Malachi that in this one particular area, giving, we are to test Him, "Bring the full tithes into the storehouse, that there may be food in my house. And thereby put me to the test, says the Lord of hosts, if I will not open the windows of heaven for you and pour down for you a blessing until there is no more need." (Mal. 3:10). Other verses are Proverbs 3:9, "Honor the Lord with your wealth, with the first fruits of all your crops; then your barns will be filled to overflowing, and your vats will brim over new wine," and Luke 6:38, "Give, and it will be given to you. A good measure pressed down, shaken together and running over, will be poured into your lap. For the measure you use, it will be measured to you." Let me stop right here and mention right away before any thoughts of "hey, this is a formula I can work for my benefit" enter your mind. As Joe Magliato put it in his book *The Wall Street Gospel*, "Tithing is not an investment package deal to finance our way to the top. To be motivated in this way will call forth God's remedy for greed."[44]

The story of the widow's mite in Luke 21 proves without a doubt that giving is not about the amount. "Jesus looked up and saw the rich putting their gifts into the offering box, and he saw a poor widow put in two small copper coins. And he said, 'Truly I tell you, this poor widow has put more than all of them. For they all have contributed out of their abundance, but she out of her poverty has put in all she had to live on.'" (Luke 21 :1-4) This sobering account should remind us that God is not concerned with the *size* but is concerned with the *significance* of our giving. Today we often attribute a great deal of honor to those who write the big checks, but this is contrary to with what God is concerned. In fact, in Matthew 6:1-4, Jesus stated that those who publicly make a show of their giving have already received their reward and commanded us to give secretly so that He may reward us. Our motivation for giving should be out of love and obedience, not to build our reputation or image in the sight of others. I am glad that many of the world's wealthy do give as they do with foundations, buildings, and charities bearing their name. I believe that much good is done with that money but unfortunately God is not as glorified in that public giving and the donor is missing a blessing as well.

It should also be noted that we are commanded to support our church and our pastors. The job of ministry is a full-time job and I'm sure almost any person in ministry can assure you, they don't do it for the money. We should support Christ's church in our giving; if we have a problem with how our particular church uses that money, then depending on your form of church government, you should either do something about it or find a better church. We should not, however, attend a church and not sup with our giving. There are many great parachurch ministries and other worthy causes, but it must be said that there is a primary obligation to support your own church family.

The Bible also delegates much of God's care of the poor, lame, and widowed to us, the visible body of Christ. In the book of James, it is written, "Religion that God our Father accepts as pure and faultless is this: to look after orphans and widows in their distress and to keep oneself from being polluted by the world." (James 1:27) By giving and caring for those who need it, we display God's love to them and our love for God. First John 3:17 while difficult to swallow gets at this very issue, "If anyone has material possessions and sees his brother in need but has no pity on him, how can the love of God be in him," or Proverbs 3:27-28, "Do not withhold good from those who deserve it, when it is in your power to act. Do not say to your neighbor, 'Come back later, I'll give tomorrow' when you have it with you."

These Scriptures mandate a duty which may appear hard to carry; but we should be motivated that what we do unto others is doing unto Christ; "He hath pity on the poor lendeth to the Lord" (Prov. 19:17) and Matthew 25:40 which says, "Truly I say to you, as you did it to one of the least of these my brothers, you did it to me." English Puritan minister John Robinson makes this insightful remark:

> God could . . . either have made men's states more equal, or have given everyone sufficient of his own. But he hath rather chosen to make some rich, and some poor, that one might stand in need of another, and help another, that so he might try the goodness and mercy of them that are able, in supplying the wants of the rest.

When confronted with the magnitude and scope of those in poverty, those who are hungry and in need, as well as those who have never heard the Gospel, it would seem that we should all sell everything we have and give it to the poor. Many times I have felt a great deal of guilt because of the material riches I have been blessed with and felt overwhelmed by the condition of others. If you have struggled with these same issues, that is a good sign that you understand God's heart, but I must point out that there will always be the poor, sick, and unevangelized. There will always be a more "altruistic" way to handle your money. God has given each man his lot, and it is important to understand God's greater plan in a way that is a little more complex than "sell all of your possessions and give to this or that." He doesn't need your money in the strictest sense; He is after your heart and devotion. God's plan for your life may mean you being in the upper reaches of society, a business figure in your community, yet to be a witness for Him. As I have pointed out, David and Job were very wealthy and did not strip themselves of their material riches. I'm sure David could have balanced the socioeconomic scales a little if he wanted to, but what would that have accomplished? God may be calling you to assist in His providential plan in a special way with your money. To be sure, guilt is not the result He is looking to produce in your heart. It is okay to be burdened by others' situation and desire to build God's kingdom, but at the same time we can't condemn His blessing us with material wealth and, in turn, possibly His plan for our lives. Recognize that giving and generosity are commanded, but also temper that with a greater understanding of His plan for your life and how He wants you to participate in His plans for others.

While we see the account of the first church in the book of Acts and its members selling everything they have and no needs were left unmet, in today's environment the repercussions of such acts are hard to figure. If I gave my possessions away, I probably couldn't be in business for myself and wouldn't be able to serve the people I serve, which would affect untold numbers of people. I think you get my point – we have to look deeper and pray about how we should live.

God's word also says that "whoever sows sparingly will also reap sparingly, and whoever sows bountifully will also reap bountifully. Each must give as he has made up his mind, not reluctantly or under compulsion, for God loves a cheerful giver. And God is able to make all grace abound to you, so that having all sufficiency in all things at all times, you may abound in every good work." (2 Cor. 9:6-8) God loves a cheerful giver and will no doubt bless those who are generous. Proverbs 11:24-25 says, "One man gives freely, yet gains even more; another withholds unduly, but comes to poverty. A generous man will prosper; he who refreshes others will himself be refreshed." As we have already stated, giving is not some sort of investment package deal; God's return blessing may not be material but may be joy, peace, relationships, contentment, or they may be eternal blessings (i.e., treasures in heaven). Whatever form, there should be no doubt that for the believer, God recognizes His children's obedience; and He will bless them in ways that can make them truly rich.

I will also add that many times we think of generosity as giving, but it also includes *sharing* what we have. I can personally attest to the generosity of others sharing things with me and the blessing it has been to my family. When you start to think of your possessions as His possessions and think about the joy or assistance you could bring to others by sharing what God has blessed you with, then these temporal things start to have real value. What good is it to have a garage full of fancy tools you never use? Let your neighbors know they are welcome to them or that you would even be willing to help. Wouldn't your swimming pool be a lot more fun when others can enjoy it too? If you have a vacation home, you could allow a church staff person or a missionary on furlough use it for a vacation they might not otherwise be able to afford. The bounds of generosity are endless when you start to think about it and are a great way to model the attitude which pleases God.

Giving acknowledges God's ownership of everything and our complete dependence on Him. It shows our willingness to obey Him and confirms that we love Him. Finally, it is the means by which He uses to care for others. He doesn't need our money to accomplish His care, but He has chosen money to be a means by which He does, a way we can participate so that our money does have true meaning. We should invest in the work of building God's kingdom and caring for all people, starting with His own. If we have been blessed with wealth, it is a special blessing to be able to give abundantly and share what we have and experience that joy; others may not be able to have that luxury. We should not hold our wealth in a tight fist but in an open hand, ready to give when we are commanded and called.

Life Stewardship

Finally, one of the main messages of the Bible concerning money is the concept of stewardship. By definition, a steward is someone who manages another's property or financial affairs. As we have discussed, God is the owner of everything and we are to manage His money in the way He would want. While that charge is hefty enough, the concept of stewardship concerns itself with more than just financial assets. Stewardship deals holistically with your life. As the Westminster Confession's catechism states, "man's chief and highest end is to glorify God and fully to enjoy Him forever." If we are to glorify God, and He owns us and everything we own, then stewardship by necessary consequence would suggest that it deals with all aspects of our life. Many people categorize stewardship as managing your time, talents, and resources in accordance with God's word. As Ron Blue and Larry Burkett state it, "Biblical stewardship is the accomplishment of God-given objectives using God-given resources."[45]

Since the scope of stewardship is so broad and deep, it should be noted that discipleship is the foundation of stewardship. It is impossible to have a balanced world and life view that can comprehend this concept of stewardship without understanding the God who commands it. The term "stewardship" has almost become a cliché that people use to mean giving or tithing. In reality, stewardship concerns our whole life and how we live it. Do we work just to make money so we can eat or should we possibly see all work as sacred? As Wilhelm Ropke, a traditional conservative economist, once said, "Life is not worth living if we exercise our profession only for the sake of material success and do not find in our calling an inner necessity and a meaning that transcends the mere earning of money, a meaning which gives our life dignity and strength."[46] Do we have children just because everyone else does and it seems like the thing to do? Do I have a talent or gift that could make a real impact for God's kingdom? Is my ability to earn a great deal of money only for the benefit of me and my family? You see, all of these issues are issues of stewardship. I encourage you to learn about the God of the Bible and then begin to think about what it means to "glorify God and fully to enjoy Him forever." Your journey in doing so will incorporate the true meaning of stewardship: if we are His, then we should manage our lives – time, talents, and treasures for His glory.

When the stewardship mind-set is in effect, it is much easier to make judgments about issues such as giving, mission work, professional issues, and the perpetual question of the standard of living that is right for you and your family. If we try and make decisions on these and other issues without this overarching purpose in mind, then the resulting by-product is usually stress and guilt. God will bless your efforts in striving to please Him, so we should always keep stewardship at the top of our mind.

In summary, there is much confusion in the world and in the Church today concerning the area of finances. This confusion stems from a number of issues, but not the least of which is the church's biblical illiteracy compounded by our sinful natures. God clearly warns us of the entrapments of wealth but does not condemn money itself. In fact, money is one of the main means by which God uses to test and shape our characters; and we should use that opportunity as a testimony for Him. In the grand scheme of things, we all know that we can't take our money with us so it really has no lasting value and, as a result, we should not place it highly on our scales of importance. We also discussed the ownership principle, which should not be difficult to understand. God made the universe and everything in it, including us; so therefore, everything in this world is property of God. The implication and application of this principle is overarching. As we shouldn't have had to explain, money and the possession of it is not in and of itself bad. It is God who disposes both wealth and poverty, and we must recognize that neither is result of the object's merit but of the will and perfect plan of God. I also explained that we should never replace God with money as our object of trust, for if we do, we do so at our own peril. We briefly discussed the topic of contentment, whose secret companion is gratitude. Another critical lesson we dealt with was the nature and aspects of giving which the Bible commands and prescribes as a life of generosity. Finally, as really an all-encompassing term, we discussed stewardship, which is not only about money but deals with every aspect of how we live our lives.

I will end this chapter with a reminder that the application of these principles is a daily exercise and one that can only be accomplished with God's grace and participation. As with all aspects of the Christian life, prayer, study, and fellowship with other believers are key ingredients to living a God-glorifying life. I also want to make it known that writing this chapter has been one of the most difficult things for me to do. It is not that the actual words, concepts, or books were difficult to find but that this chapter is a challenging faith statement that I wish to live by. My prayer is that this chapter is somewhat difficult for you to read as well; because if it is, then I have clearly conveyed the message that the Bible prescribes. Let us not forget, however, that by striving to glorify God in all that we do, particularly in our finances, He has promised to bless us. It doesn't take a genius to know that being truly rich is not about the size of your bank account; but unfortunately, many in their striving to have a truly rich life rarely go to the source of their life, which is God.

I will leave you with two excerpts that I think encapsulate a lot of what we have been discussing:

> Lord, save me from the evils that, so often go with riches; thou art giving me this wealth, help me to be a good steward of it, and not to make an idol of it.
>
> Lord, save me from becoming envious or discontented; let me be willing to be poor rather than do anything wrong in order to get money.[47]
>
> – C.H. Spurgeon

> Pray more to be kept from sin than from poverty.
> Look for opportunities for charity.
> Labor by faith to make God your trust and confidence.
> Ask for grace regarding what you have, so you aren't ensnared by it.
> Be sure your esteem for riches is below your esteem of religion.[48]
>
> – Thomas Manton

CHAPTER 5

Planning for the Trip Called Life

People don't plan to fail, they just fail to plan.

"Alice came to a place where there were many roads. She stopped and asked the owl for directions. The owl asked, 'Do you know where you want to go?' Alice said, 'No.' 'Well then,' the owl said, 'it doesn't make any difference which path you take now.'"

As a financial planner, I often feel like the owl in Alice in Wonderland trying to give directions. Studies confirm that most of us are not planners, especially when it comes to things financial in nature. Most people, busy in their everyday lives, barely stop to think about what they have going on tomorrow or next week; any thoughts of months, years, or even decades down the road are but fleeting thoughts. In this chapter, I will be discussing the practical, yet mysteriously positive, effectiveness of planning. There will be, like the rest of the book, a tilt or weighting toward those things that are financial in nature. My professional and personal belief is that planning not only produces positive results but is a part of seeking the Lord's will and an exercise of stewardship which leads to a truly rich life.

Recent studies have found that most Americans spend more time planning for their yearly vacation than they do for their retirement. To be quite honest, this is no surprise; after all, the common perception is that retirement is a long way away and it can wait. Interestingly, this thought is held by those who are not only twenty-five years away from an approximate "retirement age" but also by those who are much closer, even a few short years.

Let me dispel a common myth right away to prove that the vast majority of people aren't planners. There is a common misperception that wealthy individuals have their act together, are planners, and have done all of the planning they need. Many think that because a person is wealthy, they probably got to where they are financially because of careful planning and diligence. While this does characterize some, often inheritances, a great business sense, "marrying well," or just plain dumb luck has landed people in that upper echelon. A recent study done of those individuals with $10 million-plus net worths revealed that one-third of them did not even have a written will. While I can't say that these individuals had not done other planning, I can only guess that it is probably not their intention to die without a will. You may think a will is a minor issue, as it may be for individuals with small net worths; but for these $10 million-plus net worth individuals, they will essentially give millions of dollars in unnecessary estate tax to Uncle Sam if something isn't done prior to their visit from the grim reaper. This is a classic example of *all* people's propensity, even the wealthies, to procrastinate – even about important issues.

In a similar vein, Attorney Kenneth Feinberg was asked to dole out the $7 billion that went to the families of the victims of 9/11. It was his estimation that less than 25 percent of those who died had a will. This caused more than a few headaches for those involved; many lawsuits and infighting to determine the ultimate beneficiaries. I can only speculate that many of these people, especially those working in the World Trade Center, were affluent individuals. Life and death for that matter do not relent for your lack of planning, and terrible tragedies like 9/11 should paint a grim reminder of this fact.

Planning for things is really just common sense, right? In Luke 14:28, Jesus recognizes that any sensible person would plan for things as he says, "Suppose one of you wants to build a tower. Will he not first sit down and estimate the cost to see if he has enough money to complete it?" Of course you would! Any reasonable person would; unfortunately, most today actually don't plan at all for the important things of life.

Now let's go back and think about that "important" planning that we all have actually done for a vacation. You start by figuring out where you want to go, how long you will stay, what activities you want to do, and how much it will cost. If you can't figure out where I am going with this, it should be clear that this is a simplified example of what financial planning essentially does. Let's imagine that the trip you have in mind is a cross-country road trip from New York to Los Angeles. My question to you is, would you pick the approximate direction to go and just start driving or would you map it out? Most rational individuals would, of course, chart a course because of the possible time that could be lost due to wrong turns. Now this is not to say that there is only one way to get from point A to point B. Some may want to get there as quick as possible and drive interstate all the way with only bathroom and fast-food breaks. Others may want to take a more enjoyable drive with fun activities along the way. Again, this is a perfect example of financial planning: able to take into account one's objectives and at the same time avoid those costly mistakes.

For no other reason than the fact that you don't get to go back in life, it makes sense to plan. Think of your life like a long trip. I can't imagine anyone on a real trip who wouldn't stop to think ahead of time about things they want to get accomplished and do some planning to make sure the time was well spent; after all, you may not have that opportunity again. Why shouldn't we all live our everyday lives with this same type of "vacation" purpose? After all, there is no going back. For the Christian especially, in view of eternity, it is only sensible that we make the most of our time here fulfilling the reason God put us here, not wasting time on things that have no real value.

Planning is an extremely exciting tool and can be used to accomplish amazing things. My favorite example of this power is a popular 1979 Harvard Business School study of Harvard MBA graduates. The study found that only 3 percent of the graduates recorded their goals in writing. Another 14 percent had goals but didn't write them down, whereas 83 percent did not even have clearly defined goals. More interestingly, this 3 percent who had their goals in writing, ten years later, earned an astounding result ten times that of the 83 percent group!

Several things can be gleaned from even just a cursory look at this study. First, as I have stated, most people don't have clearly defined goals. More interesting is how profound of a difference it made for those who did! I am getting a little ahead of myself in my pursuit to persuade you, but I truly believe in the life-changing nature of planning. Let's begin the pursuit of planning by discussing the pivotal issue of goal setting.

Before I get pigeonholed into the category of one of those motivational types who would say something to the effect of "you can do anything you put your mind to," let me clarify something. I don't believe that we have ultimate control over our destinies or our accomplishments. God has certainly put the parameters of accomplishment on each of us, and we all kind-of intuitively recognize this. For instance, despite my determination, I couldn't set my mind on being a professional basketball player or a foreign-language expert and expect to accomplish it regardless of the plans I made; I simply have no aptitude for those things. So I do recommend a healthy dose of realism when considering your life paths. I don't mean to produce a feeling of being constrained but rather would just recognize that it is God's enabling which produces the end result.

Secondly, when caught up in the excitement of ambition, it is easy to put God in the passenger seat instead of the driver's seat. We must always allow Him to show us the path to take. While this is often difficult to discern at times, you can be certain that His plan will not run in conflict with other plans clearly laid out in His word. For instance, if you are a parent, it is probably not God's will that your new endeavor take away from that role; or if you have a great gifting in a particular area, forsaking that gifting is probably not part of His design either. Read and study His word; pray, and look for confirmation from others when making plans and setting goals. Comfort can be attained from the fact that God *is* in ultimate control, and He can and often does make dramatic changes in the course of His children's lives. This is obviously all somewhat of a mystery, but He does allow us to seemly direct our own paths. Proverbs 16:9 discusses this reality of our planning efforts, "In his heart a man plans his course, but the Lord determines his steps."

As I have mentioned, the road of planning starts with setting goals. I often illustrate this point to clients with this analogy: what is the most important piece or strategy to putting together a puzzle? Many people will quickly say finding pieces with similar colors or possibly finding the edge pieces – both helpful. Of course, with a little more thought, we would all agree that the box top with the picture on it is the most important piece of all. If you don't know what you are trying to create, what the end result is, you are destined to make numerous mistakes and waste valuable time and resources, not to mention frustration and bewilderment. With a clear understanding of what you are trying to accomplish, progress is more easily seen, as are mistakes.

My business partner Wayne Harris is one of the best goal setters I know, and I have learned and applied much of what he has taught me. One of the most helpful things I have picked up from him is that he believes that everyone's goal setting should be multifaceted in nature; for instance, setting goals for the family, physical, financial, business, spiritual, friendships, educational, etc. Before I started working with Wayne, I used to set personal, business, and spiritual goals but now see a real benefit in expanding that list to include *all areas* of my life where I want to improve. Let your imagination set the categories for you. Interestingly enough, almost all facets end up impacting the financial side of the equation in some way. Each area is extremely important and can be improved upon by a determined and disciplined will to work on it.

From there I find it helpful to set goals in each of these categories and add a time orientation, i.e., short-term, mid term, and long-term goals. Short-term goals are needed and serve often as a motivator, because results are often immediately measurable and felt. Midterm goals are often a little bigger or may just fall chronologically later, and finally long-term goals can often seem outrageous in size and often include such significant financial things as retirement/financial independence and legacy planning.

Goal setting is an invaluable part of the planning process; in this initial stage of goal setting, I am really not concerned with having polished detailed goals. This early stage should be more of a brainstorming exercise as to what you want to accomplish, approximately when, and in what general area of your life. I will be addressing primarily financial goals, but these principles can be used (with some variations) to assist in planning of any type. An example of a goal in this early exercise may be something to the effect of "you know I have always thought I wanted to teach economics to college kids when I retire, so I would probably like to get my master's degree sometime in the next five to seven years." This goal might be better summarized into two goals, one midterm and one long term: get master's degree and teach economics. These are by no means finished goals, but they accomplish what we are striving for at this stage – general direction.

So often our goals are limited by our own self-constrained ideas about what is possible. I have heard people say things like, "Well, I am going to stick with this job I've had since I graduated because I can't go back to school." I encourage you to think about what you truly want and feel called to do, keeping in mind that God should be consulted in all of this before making any decisions of whether or not this is in fact something that you are going to plan for and take action on accomplishing. Too often, we prematurely decide that something is or isn't possible. Also, way too often we decide what we are going to do without consulting God first, through prayer and study, to see what He may think – both should be avoided.

Once we have multifaceted, time-oriented goals, chances are they are still too obscure to be truly effective. What do I mean? Let's say by now that you have goals like, "I want to retire comfortably" or maybe, "I want to pay for my kid's college." Both of those at first glance seem like great goals; I would contend that they are great starting places to making great goals. The thing these goals lack is specifics. I like all of my goals to be **SMAC** certified. **SMAC** stands for **S**pecific, **M**easurable, **A**chievable, and **C**hallenging. Let's start with Specific.

Specific seems obvious, but so often our first try at goal setting will yield goals that use terms that are so obscure or general that they could mean different things to different people. For instance, paying for a child's college sounds great, but one person may be thinking Auburn University and another may have Harvard in mind, and, are we talking just undergraduate studies or graduate school as well? What about fraternity and sororities? Are they included in your "pay for college" goal too? I think you get my point. I find goals are most effective when they are specific enough that even someone who doesn't know you at all could read your goal and understand what it is you seek to accomplish. Being specific in your goal setting will assist you to achieve the "M" in SMAC as well.

"M" stands for measurable as in quantifiable. Once you have been specific in your goal, it is important to try and make your goal quantifiable in some way that you can measure your progress toward that goal. For instance, college cost at a certain university can be quantified in terms of "$15,000 a year for four years." This amount can then be projected using reasonable assumptions, and progress can easily be monitored. Often I hear, "I want to retire comfortably." This can be made more specific and then quantified into how much they project that would cost per year, and then progress can again be measured. You see, goals aren't just targets but also serve as measuring sticks to help chart and measure along the way. Of course, you may argue that goals other than financial don't follow this same criterion. Maybe so, but these do force you to think harder and make better goals, and by the way, in most cases these criteria can be accommodated.

Next we move to the "A" which stands for achievable. Here is where things may get a little hairy. I mentioned earlier that you should really shake off all inhibitions when making goals but at the same time still keep a level of realism. At this point in the process, it may not be appropriate to decide whether or not your goal is or isn't achievable. You may, however, be able to determine if it is within the realm of possibility. For instance, if your kids are seventeen years old and you haven't saved a dime for their college and you earn a modest income, it would take a lottery or some miracle from God to be able to "pay for child's college" unless your child's stay at college was just an overnight visit. This and other absurd dreams are not very healthy or helpful to have as goals, so just don't put them down. After all, if it is a miracle you are hoping for, then it doesn't really need a goal; there is nothing you can do to produce it. There will be things that are within the realm of possibility but may not be within the range of probability, but this can be determined later – leave that goal and continue to the next criterion.

Lastly is the "C" which stands for challenging. This should be obvious; but some people think that they can go through this exercise and get brownie points or something of the sort by making goals specific, measurable, and achievable although they would have probably accomplished these things anyway. For instance, it is not much of a goal for me to say that I am going to wake up in the morning by 7:00 a.m. and eat breakfast. This may be a goal for a college student; but for most, regardless of whether or not they have this goal, will do this anyway – why bother. The whole point of goals is to stretch you to do things that you probably otherwise wouldn't accomplish; so by their very nature, they should be challenging.

There are two things which I believe are pivotal issues which we must consider when setting goals and planning. The first deals with the verse in James 4:13-17 which says, "'Today or tomorrow we will go into such and such a town and spend a year there and trade and make a profit,' yet you do not know what tomorrow will bring. What is your life? For you are a mist that appears for a little time and then vanishes. Instead you ought to say, 'If the Lord wills, we will live and do this or that.' As it is, you boast in your arrogance. All such boasting is evil."

I think it is wise to keep this verse in mind as we plan our lives, keeping in the forefront that it is up to God what ultimately will happen. We should not be so presumptuous to think that we can plan and make it happen without God's blessing and participation. As the Scripture says, this is an arrogant point of view. Of course we also know that we must plan, so how do we deal with this? My answer is simply that we should strive to know God's word and consult Him in prayer when making plans, and we should commit those plans to the Lord and be willing to let Him redirect our paths.

The second issue I must mention is the idea of balancing our life. While I hope that I have made it clear that you should set multi-faceted goals, the balance I am referring to deals more with the issues of focus and time orientation. In our planning efforts, which are greatly needed because we so often *only* think of today, we can get a little too excited, go overboard, and get too fixated on the future. I am a big proponent of saving and investing for the future, but everyone should recognize that we aren't necessarily promised tomorrow. Not only that, but today is a day, just like tomorrow is a day. In planning, sometimes we get too focused on tomorrow and don't make the most of today. To make my point a little clearer, take the common example of a family with young children. Their goals for retirement and to fund their kids' college may call for investing every discretionary dollar they have to address these issues. With a laser focus on those goals, it is easy to lose sight of today. To be honest, who cares if you have a fully funded education account if you missed opportunities, such as trips or other experiences with your children along the way? Doesn't it make more sense to balance the scales and not place too heavy of an importance on the future and "live a little" today? Some opportunities, like doing special things with your children, will only exist for a finite period of time; they do "grow up so fast." My point is obviously to not let you off the hook from planning for the future but to temper your enthusiasm a little and shoot for a balanced life view with balanced goals.

Finally, once we have refined goals laid out, it is important to prioritize them in order of importance. This is often hard to do as we may have an equal desire to accomplish them all. However, it may not be feasible to accomplish them all, and something will have to give or take a lower priority. Prioritization is critical because most people have limited means and goals which would require an almost unlimited budget. If we are talking about all goals, meaning the multifaceted ones I suggested, time and energy might be the resource that runs in short supply. I will insert here that you should carefully consider these priorities as they might have a significant impact on the actual strategies that get implemented. For instance, I would highly suggest that having college funding for a child would be much less important than your own retirement/financial independence. The reason should be clear but is often made hazy because of emotions. There will be numerous options to pay for college when that time arises (some might not be ideal), but there is very little option for your retirement/financial independence if you don't adequately save. The only option would be to work longer or live on less, both of which may really not be an option due to expenses and/or health considerations.

Once you have finished this initial stage of goal setting, you have already accomplished more than most. In fact, something almost mysterious has already begun to happen. Once you have taken the time to decide what it is you want to accomplish and have identified areas in which you wish to improve, there is somewhat of a new sense of clarity and purpose that is hard to explain. Whether or not you continued through the rest of the formal steps of planning, which I would assume you would, I can only imagine that you are already much more likely to make those goals a reality. I will say, however, that if you don't continue on this process, it is far more likely that you will get off-track and your goals will go unmet than if you did continue with this worthy process. There is a saying that goes, "A dream without a plan is a fantasy, but a dream with a strategy has hope for accomplishment." Let's continue.

Now that you have your goals in mind and in writing (I can't stress that enough), it is time to proceed. Oftentimes this is the point in the process, especially if your goals are financial in nature, which you consult with a professional advisor, preferably a financial planner who can assist with the rest of this process. Many times you may begin this whole process with a planner, and they can assist with the goal-setting process as well. I usually like for clients to have already a pretty good idea of what they want to accomplish, because it is important for the client to come up with the general direction of things and be independent from what my view may be. It is often hard to not try and lead a person to a conclusion that you want; for that reason, goal setting is best done with prayerful consideration and communication with your spouse and family. However, a financial planner should have a pretty good amount of experience with a process to set goals and can be an invaluable asset in this early stage.

The next step in the financial planning process will be to gather all the data needed. This will include getting all financial documents such as tax returns, financial statements, investment statements, insurance policies, legal documents, etc., together so that the information can be put together in some usable format in which decisions and strategies can be more easily analyzed. This data gathering step may include getting together other information as well. Remember the example goal of "getting a master's degree." In this example we would need information on schools, costs, when classes are offered, etc. Essentially, in this phase, it is helpful to try and amass every piece of information that will be needed in the later step of preparing strategies. Goals have been established for where you intend to go, and now in this step you are figuring out where you are.

It's a little like going to the mall and knowing that you need to find a certain store. You know that you only need to go to that store, get something, and leave; so with a determined attitude, when you enter the mall, the first thing you look for is what? The map, of course, that shows the layout of the mall. Upon inspection of the map, and finding the store on the map that you wish to go to, what is the next thing that you are looking for? Undoubtedly the little arrow that says, "You are here." This is exactly what we are trying to accomplish in this step of the process. Once we have a clear view of where we want to go and where we stand, the rest becomes much easier indeed.

It is at this point that your goals should be reexamined. Often in light of where you stand, the "A" may not be achievable after all. If that is the case, then it may be time to adjust that goal downward or do away with it altogether. On the flip side, in light of your current situation, it may become apparent that your goal is not really "C" (challenging) which in turn you should adjust that goal or goals upward to where that criterion fits. This is also a great time to mention that all goals come at a cost. That cost may be financial, time, effort, etc. As they say, nothing in life is free; so it is important to evaluate here and at later steps as well whether or not your goal is truly worth pursuing. Sometimes, obstacles may be present that may prevent or change your mind regarding your goals causing you to change or do away with that particular one altogether.

Next, we move on to the part of the process which to me can be one of the most invigorating of them all; creating strategies to achieve the goals. I love goal setting and understanding where you stand is critically important, but it is really when you start to devise strategies that goals start to become real. I can remember setting a goal to write this book. It was kind of exciting to think about it; but when I started to break that goal down into a strategy of what it was going to take, I started to realize that it wasn't just something that I wanted to do but it was something that I could *actually* do. Often this part of the plan, again, especially if we are talking financial issues, is done by a professional. The reason is not that I don't think that only financial planners can use financial calculators, but it is because during this initial stage of laying out strategies to accomplish each goal that there may be multiple ways to accomplish a given goal. I am continually amazed at the number of different ways there are to accomplish similar goals. Slight differences in your circumstances may call for a completely different strategy than someone with similar goals. It is for this reason that most professionals, whether they are financial planners, attorneys, or accountants, are constantly pursuing continuing education; there are always new and possibly better ways to do things.

Once strategies for each goal are laid out, they are then coordinated to make sure that the high-priority goals get the most attention with less important goals getting their due attention. I will tell you that the coordinating of strategies is by far the most complicated part of planning, and I would strongly encourage the assistance of a professional in this endeavor as well. No strategy or decision should be made in a vacuum. If you decide to pay off your house in ten years, this will significantly affect your retirement savings plan, insurance plan, etc. It is for this reason that comprehensive and coordinated financial planning is so important.

Once the strategies are set and coordinated, then you move on to taking that first step toward accomplishing them by implementing those strategies. Again, in the financial context, this is best done with the assistance of a financial planner or advisor. With financial strategies, there are often complex products or investment management which requires a great deal of expertise to implement correctly. While I don't write off all that many "do-it-yourself" type financial gurus say, I do take particular issue with the notion that it is easy to properly invest or purchase financial products. I can personally attest to the numerous hours each week that I spend evaluating and understanding the ever-changing landscape of financial products, and, I can almost assure you that any quick "research" one may do on their own is not enough to ensure proper implementation. I will hopefully convince you of the other benefits of an advisor in another chapter, but it should be noted that this is yet another place that a qualified professional can add significant measurable value. Implementing a plan is not just a one-time series of acts but is a continual commitment to your plan, which involves practicing daily disciplines that I outline in the chapter "Blocking and Tackling."

The amazing thing, as author Richard Carlson points out, is "when you have a predetermined plan, something magical happens: Your plan helps you to draw out your inner strength, creativity, and discipline. In some mysterious way you are able to stick to your plan."[49]

Finally, as you implement and walk the path you have laid out, it is important to check your progress along the way. Let's consider the following example: if we were going to drive from Birmingham, Alabama, to San Francisco, and we had plotted our course and detailed our plan, it only makes sense that from time to time we would stop and evaluate our progress toward that goal. In the same way, regular reviews can serve as motivation for you as well as help you to stay or get back on track if there has been a setback along the way. As a part of this process, it is also helpful to again evaluate your goals and see if they are still valid, if they need changing or removing, or if you have new goals to add. As I hope you can see, planning is not a one-time event but more of a lifelong process. With financial goals in particular, I recommend at least an annual review to assess your goals and progress.

There are a few additional thoughts that I would like to add regarding planning. The first is that one of the main characteristics of any plan is that it should be flexible. As Larry Burkett once wrote, "Our plans should remain flexible because God may redirect our paths."[50] If you create strategies and plans which cannot be altered or ended without significant consequences, then we should truly examine whether or not that strategy best fits your situation. Flexibility means options and in the long run, one of the main reasons for planning is to have options and not ultimatums. With that in mind, flexibility should always be a top priority.

I find it also helpful to use your imagination a little and open your mind to the possibility of things when you are planning. For instance, as I will mention in the "retirement chapter," I love what I do and don't foresee retiring. However, it would be entirely irresponsible of me to not plan for retirement, because my health or situation in life or maybe just my desire might change in the next thirty years. I encourage you to also shake off these notions of "I'm too old to change careers" or anything of the sort which is limiting what is truly possible. I truly believe that many people settle in life because it is the easy thing to do. I think many can attest that a truly rich life is not one in which the person just accepts the status quo because it would take too much effort to change. If I can be blunt, that is just a lazy attitude. Whatever stage in life, there should be things to do and ways to improve. This does not mean that your goals have to be so monumental that a radical life change is required; it may simply mean doing something a little different or emphasizing something a little more. After all, it's your life, do what you please, but remember we will all have to give an account one day.

Unfortunately, we must plan for some of those not-so-pleasant possibilities of life as well. I outline in more detail the topic of risk management in another chapter, which should be carefully read and deals more with some of these risks, but it is also appropriate to mention here. Consider this: let's say that buying your three-story dream house when you are sixty-five is one of your goals. This may not be the smartest idea, because with a little realism, things like your health and ability to use three floors or maintain a home like that may not be feasible. I am not saying that in that situation I would say that it is unwise, but I would get you to think about it from a little more negative or possibly realistic viewpoint before making that decision or goal.

Estate planning is a perfect example of planning for a not-so-pleasant possibility. After all, who wants to think about the consequences of dying "prematurely" or the effect of leaving money to your heirs and the possible negative consequences of doing so? I can truly identify with those of you who are positive people and don't like to think about and, especially don't like to consider, negative circumstances in their planning, but at the same time you are only doing half the job if you only look at the positive side of things when making plans.

Another point that I hope you would take in consideration is, that if you are married, planning should be a joint venture. To plan what you are going to do or what the family is going to do without consulting and including your spouse is a recipe for disaster. As I write this, I am reminded of my goal of writing this book and how I discussed with my wife about how it was going to take a time and money commitment. I can't tell you how glad I am that I did that; because as I suspected, it did take a time and money commitment from us both. We both had made the decision and commitment together, and it made things much easier. I can't tell you how many times conflict arises because one spouse makes decisions and creates commitments that both parties must keep but only one spouse agrees with. Everyone knows that communication is crucial in healthy relationships and avoiding unpleasant issues; I would also add that by both spouses, or the whole family if appropriate, being involved in the planning process, it creates a new and wonderful sense of purpose.

I would commend you to encourage your spouse to read this book as a part of that process so that it doesn't seem like you are coming out of left field with some new view on life or some new enthusiasm to make changes. We all know that our natural reaction is to get a little defensive when somebody is "ready to make some changes around here." I also think it is critically important for everyone to be on the same page because it is a joint effort. Oftentimes a family's biggest liability is not a lack of systems or knowledge but simply a spouse who is a bit of a loose cannon or simply doesn't buy into the family's financial goals. Depending on how the roles and duties are split in the household also requires that each person knows what they should be doing and why, since silence or a demanding persona is laying the tender for a wildfire down the road. I don't like to bring it up, but it is also critically important to know where you are and where you are going in case something happens to a spouse such as a disability or death. All too often, widows especially are left with very little knowledge of what plans have been made.

I also want to encourage you by what the Bible says regarding our efforts to plan. Proverbs 21:5 says, "The plans of the diligent lead surely to advantage, but everyone who is hasty comes surely to poverty." Proverbs 16:3 likewise spurs us to "commit your works to the Lord, and your plans will be established." These are wonderful promises of God we can stand on and words of wisdom we can draw from.

This topic of planning always brings to mind Woody Allen's famous quote, "If you want to make God laugh, tell him your plans for the future." While I don't know exactly what Woody meant by it, to me it is a funny reminder that God is sovereign and controls all things at all times. I am also acutely aware of what I would call the law of secondary causes. This is simply the fact that God has laid a framework where personal responsibility is required. Simply put, if we throw up our hands and say that we trust God to take care of us and fail to plan for what we are clearly able to plan for, then we shouldn't expect anything different from what most would expect. Therefore, when it is in our ability and means to plan for the future, we should with the heart of a steward, chart our course. Of course, as I have mentioned, we should keep our hearts sensitive to hearing when and if our plans should change.

Since we have been given the apparent ability to live by design and not by default, I think it only makes sense to not drift through life like a rudderless ship. We should be purposeful in all that we do, and planning helps chart that course and keep us on track. By knowing where you are going and understanding what it will take, you will be better able to enjoy the trip. We all have the same twenty-four hours in a day, so we should use them wisely and try and enjoy them as much as possible.

I also like the wisdom of Warren Buffett as he says, "Noah didn't start building the ark when it was raining" and "What the wise do in the beginning, the fools do in the end." Things of significance almost always start with a plan; and unfortunately, for those who don't plan, the pain of procrastination and the ultimatums it creates are often very unpleasant.

I feel like before I end I must address a common objection that financial planners often run into when talking with potential clients. Many think that age and position in life change the need or priority of planning; but I truly believe that those criteria don't change its value, just maybe its accuracy. Let me explain. Those in the early stages of life would say that they are too young to plan for "retirement" or the "future" and can't bring themselves to develop goals for something more than a week away. The argument goes that it makes much more sense for someone within say, ten years or so to get serious about it, but not for someone so far away. That sounds logical, but the argument is really flawed. You see, those who are very close to "retirement" really have much less opportunity to have a significant impact on their situation because of that shortened time horizon. So in reality, it is really those who *have* the time that planning could most impact.

It is important to understand that the need to plan never really diminishes or wanes but is always there; the clarity of the outcome is just more vague with those farther away. To put it metaphorically, an advisor's first plan paints a long-term picture for those who are young in a manner that is somewhat impressionistic in art terms. Conversely for someone about to retire tomorrow, their plan is painting a pretty realistic picture of what is going to happen over the near term. Of course, planners aren't clairvoyant and there are always assumptions made, but the degree of accuracy is much sharper the closer you are to the goal. It's the same process, the same importance; just different degrees of clarity to the eventual outcome.

On the flip side of the coin, I often hear older clients who don't want to do planning because "nothing can be done about my situation. I have waited too long." This is a terribly fatalistic view and one that doesn't recognize that something is better than nothing. If you are going to have a "problem" down the road, it is better to know about it today and start working on it than to put it off until it is catastrophic. Other objections such as "I don't have enough money to need financial planning" or "I have so much money I don't need to plan." Both of these and really all objections are failing to recognize the emotional benefits of planning as well as often the actual material benefits of planning – not to mention the stewardship aspect. Yes, I will readily admit that different people derive different amounts and degrees of monetary value, but I have never come across someone who didn't need or couldn't benefit from some level of planning. If you are of meager means, you probably don't need the services of the smartest planner on the face of the planet but could benefit from sound basic advice from someone and go through the basic planning process. In contrast, the best financial planner/wealth manager on the planet may only be able to add a very incremental monetary advantage to a very wealthy person who has already done a good deal of planning; but that small increment may mean tens or hundreds of thousands or even millions of dollars over their lifetime, not to mention the emotional payoff of aligning your money with your values and objectives. I think you get my point; planning adds value in any facet of your life and especially in the financial spectrum.

In the American Christian worldview, we often promote a kind of legalism that focuses on what we *shouldn't do* as our primary way to glorify God: avoid the sins of commission. While we certainly should avoid these sins, I think we should be more offensively minded and use this mind-set in our planning efforts. As humans we get energy and motivation by drawing from the positive; what we should, could, and ought to do, and are often drained by the negative. For this reason and others, I believe we should strive to plan and live lives which eliminate sins of omission – good things we could have done but didn't. In this way, we aren't passive resisters of sin and evil, but champions of what is good and righteous. The actual result is by pursuing holiness intentionally, we are more able to (with the Holy Spirit's enabling) resist sin. So much of life is frame of mind and point of focus, and I feel confident that God will bless these pursuits in your life.

I hope that I have convinced you of the life-changing nature of planning and have motivated you to embark on a lifelong journey of planning and striving to live a richer life. My desire is that the rest of this book may aid in shaping your pursuits and goals and equipping you with practical knowledge which you can apply to your planning efforts. Then it is up to you, as B.C. Forbes puts it, "Plan your work and work your plan," and may God bless your efforts.

CHAPTER 6

The Imaginary Finish Line

The subject of retirement is one of my favorites to discuss because it is the financial "event" that is most talked about but also the one that I believe has the most misconceptions surrounding it. I believe it is especially interesting to delve into because with the baby boomers, some seventy-five million of them starting to retire this year, there is about to be a major shift in how many of us perceive and will live out our retirements. Everybody seems to have a little different idea as to what retirement means to them. For some, retirement means finally being able to do what they love; others are less excited but are tired of the daily grind and figure that it is simply what you are supposed to do. Interestingly enough, "retirement" as we know it is a relatively new phenomenon and is ever changing due to societal changes and things such as increasing longevity. In this chapter, I hope to share with you some food for thought with regards to retirement that might just transform your ideas and goals today and for the future. I will also share with you some of the pitfalls that are wrecking many retirees' dreams and keys of how to have a successful retirement and a truly rich life.

Before I get started, I feel the need to shake the current perception of retirement that is held by many today. I will do so by explaining the root of where today's idea of retirement came from and some trends that are changing that. To begin, let's go back about 120 years to the mid-1880s when some very important demographic changes were happening in America that made the traditional systems of economic security problematic at best and disastrous for many.

Prior to the Industrial Revolution, most Americans (nearly 80 percent) lived in small rural towns and on rural farms. Their sustenance and "wealth," if you would call it such a word, came generally from self-employed agricultural work or trades which supported it. The economic security of the individual came from the harvest of their own work and the interdependence on one another's work within the community, and one could make ends meet for themselves and their family as long as they were willing and able to work. With the advent of the Industrial Revolution, the work shifted from agriculturally based to that of being a wage earner in a factory. When one's economic income is primarily from wages, that economic security is now more dependent on outside forces, ones in which that person has little to no control, such as recessions, failed businesses, etc., and can cause serious problems to their financial security.

To no surprise, this shift during the Industrial Revolution also caused a migration from the farms to the cities because that is where the jobs were. Between 1890 and 1930, the percentage of the population living in cities doubled to 56 percent. Nineteen twenty was actually the "tipping point" in which for the first time more people were living in cities than on the farms.

This urbanization fueled another significant change in the fabric of America: the fading away of the extended family and the rise of the nuclear family. People used to live with, and in close proximity to, their extended family: parents, grandparents, cousins, aunts, etc. Today that is all but lost, and with it, the support from the family to members of the family that can no longer take care of themselves due to sickness or old age. Today we often applaud those we know who take care of parents; in the past, this was just an accepted part of life. This network of support provided security for all involved, but the shift to the cities and separation from family left most to fend for themselves.

Yet another significant change was coinciding with these changes during the early part of the twentieth century. Medical and sanitation developments created an environment where Americans began to live significantly longer. Between 1900 and 1930, the average life span increased by ten years, a staggering difference – one never seen before in the recorded history of mankind. The result was tremendous growth in this older segment of society which previously was almost nonexistent.

The result of these changes of urbanization and dependence on wages, decline of living with and around extended family, and increased longevity created new obstacles to economic security. Unfortunately, they were all about to be exposed.

On the morning of October 24, 1929, when the New York Stock Exchange opened, many people's futures started to change in a dramatic fashion. Within three months of the initial market free fall, the stock market lost 40 percent of its value; some $26 billion vanished. It would take twenty-five years for the stock market to return to its pre-crash level. America plummeted into a deep economic depression in which unemployment exceeded 25 percent and ten thousand banks failed; the GNP was cut in half. Two million adult men were unemployed and took up the life of hobos, wandering aimlessly. The situation for our nation's elderly was even grimmer.

I will take this opportunity to break here and make a simple comment: I don't think anyone who didn't live through that time period can truly understand what that era was like. Furthermore, I can certainly appreciate the fear, whether grounded in today's reality or not, that some elderly people have of the "big bad market."

Let's continue. The initial response to all of these woes was varied, from public outcry for extreme change in governmental policy to a more hands-off approach that saw this situation as temporary in nature. As this proved not to be a very temporary problem and the Depression drudged on, a new system would have to be adopted to deal with some of the issues of economic insecurity, mirroring some of the programs that were already widespread in Europe. It was a new president, Franklin D. Roosevelt, who would be the one to lead the charge. It was to be a social insurance program which would address the permanent problem of economic security for the elderly by creating a work-related contributory system in which workers would provide for their own future economic security through taxes paid while employed: Social Security.

> Security was attained in the earlier days through the interdependence of members of families upon each other and of the families within a small community upon each other. The complexities of great communities and of organized industry make less real these simple means of security. Therefore, we are compelled to employ the active interest of the Nation as a whole through government in order to encourage a greater security for each individual who composes it . . . This seeking for a greater measure of welfare and happiness does not indicate a change in values. It is rather a return to values lost in the course of our economic development and expansion.

> – Franklin D. Roosevelt
> Message of the President to Congress
> June 8, 1934

> We can never insure one hundred percent of the population against one hundred percent of the hazards and vicissitudes of life, but we have tried to frame a law which will give some measure of protection to the average citizen and to his family against the loss of a job and against poverty-ridden old age.
> – President Roosevelt upon signing the Social Security Act

While I do not want to sound like I am questioning the motives of President Roosevelt, I will add that there was increasing pressure to get older workers out of the workforce so that more productive younger workers would have jobs. He certainly did not want angry mobs of twenty-somethings raging in the street. That being said, President Roosevelt on August 14, 1935, signed the Social Security Act into law. One of the main features of this law was to pay retired workers a benefit after "retirement."[51]

Of course, one of the main questions to be answered was when did benefits begin? Policy makers took their cues from Otto von Bismarck, chancellor of the German Republic who had instituted the first social insurance program in 1889 and used the age of sixty-five. Interesting enough, he originally had chosen age seventy; but too few people were collecting benefits because they didn't live that long. After all, the life expectancy at the turn of the century was only forty-six-years-old! FDR and the

New Dealers liked that arbitrary number Bismarck had used and settled on sixty-five as well; life expectancy in 1935 was sixty-three years old. Like Bismarck, FDR didn't have many collecting checks and later moved the retirement age to sixty-two.

The passage of Social Security was a positive and well-needed piece of legislation at the time. It also, I believe, helped set this interesting precedent of age at which most all Americans feel they "must" retire. As Ken Dychtwald, author of *Age Power*, says, "Prior to this century retirement didn't exist . . . In the past, people didn't age; they died." However, for some strange reason, this age of sixty-two/sixty-five has become the finish line of productivity for many. The question that comes to my mind is why are we still using this arbitrary number of sixty-five to pinpoint the end of one's working life when life expectancies have increased dramatically and one's *relative age* has decreased proportionately?

To help you further understand perceptions regarding the aged near the inception of Social Security, it is interesting to look at what people were saying. In an infamous speech in 1905, Dr. William Osler, in his valedictory at Johns Hopkins, argued that men older than forty were useless to society, "All the great advances have come from men under forty . . . Take the sum of human achievement in action, science, in art, in literature, and subtract the work of men above forty, and . . . we would practically be where we are today."[52]

Contrast that with the prevailing thoughts of today. For instance, George Burns is quoted as saying, "Retirement at sixty-five is ridiculous. When I was sixty-five, I still had pimples." We live in a world today where the average age of a marathon runner is forty, baseball players continue their professional careers into their forties, and many Hollywood actresses seem to be having babies in their forties. This gives validity to the phrase "forty is the *new* thirty." Take the example of John Glenn who had to do it one more time and went back to space at seventy-seven years old. Or let's look at a more personal example; my dad and many of his buddies, who are in their fifties and sixties, still race dirt bikes nearly every weekend. Does it make emotional or financial sense to hang up your hat when you may still have thirty years or more left to live?

To be fair, Social Security surely was not the only cause of this introduction to the concept of retirement. After all, some states had pensions that paid piddly amounts, as well as some large corporations that offered pension plans before the advent of Social Security. However, what retirement meant and what it signified has changed dramatically since its inception and I firmly believe it is still changing.

What retirement meant in the 1930s was very close to what you might find in Webster's dictionary: to withdraw, fade away. Today's retirement definition for most would probably include some combination of terms such as recreation, relaxation, and focus on family. Tomorrow's definition of retirement, I believe, may be increasingly different for many.

Why do I keep making these speculations, you may say? Let me begin my case. First of all, I think it will have to be – two words: baby boomers. Happy to be home from the war, a fertility explosion occurred in America that produced seventy-six million children, nearly one-third of the U.S. population – between 1946 and 1964.[53]

Many demographers refer to this group as a pig moving through a python because of the massive hump that is present on age/population charts. Think of this, two-thirds of all people that have ever lived past the age of sixty-five are alive today.[54] The sheer number of baby boomers will influence every part of society, as they always have. When they start to retire, which is now, I believe many of the so-called norms will change.

One of those changes inevitably *will be* Social Security. Consider the following illustration:

> On January 31, 1940, the first *monthly* social security retirement check was issued to Ida May Fuller of Ludlow, Vermont, in the amount of $22.54. Mrs. Fuller started collecting benefits in January 1940 at age 65 and lived to be 100 years old, dying in 1975. She got a pretty good deal considering she only had worked for three years under the Social Security program. The accumulated taxes she had paid during those three years only totaled $24.75. Her lifetime amount she collected totaled $22,888.92 in Social Security benefits.[55]

This example was possible because of the "pay-as-you-go" system that Social Security relies on, which did not pose a problem in 1940. The basis and structure of this system relies on the premise that you would have more workers supporting the retirement benefits than those receiving monthly incomes. However, a serious strain occurs when you have more retirees and fewer workers, as you will have very soon.

John F. Kennedy realized that the system would have to remain flexible. In June 30, 1961, he stated, "The Social Security program plays an important part in providing for families, children, and older persons in times of stress. But it cannot remain static. Changes in our population, in our working habits, and in our standard of living require constant revision."

Federal Reserve chairman Alan Greenspan speaking before a gathering of policy makers in Jackson Hole, Wyoming, said he feared that the government may have "promised more than our economy has the ability to deliver to retirees" in Social Security and Medicare benefits and that we may have to "recalibrate our public programs so that pending retirees have the time to adjust through other channels."[56]

I make these statements not to put fear into those about to retire or those who already have but to simply make all of us aware of the fact that the status quo cannot and will not remain. As far as the fear that some have that "Social Security will go away," I can assure you that the lawmakers, who are politicians, will not do anything to endanger their electability. After all, the baby boomers have more money and political influence than any other group. The AARP is a goliath of lobbying power and will not be disappointed. That being said though, the younger generations should not expect the same deal our parents got. Things such as older ages for eligibility and qualifying on a needs basis could be options that we might see. I get particularly excited about privatization, but who knows. What we can reasonably expect is change.

I really don't mean to get entirely on the subject of Social Security and its viability but want to make the point that Social Security has set for many the date at which they retire and pays a substantial portion of many retirees' incomes. Social Security and the social norm will probably change due to the demographic changes, and once again Social Security's policies may play an integral part of that change.

What I would like to get you to think more about is the statement I made earlier regarding age. Does it make sense to retire (in the traditional sense), not just *financially* but *emotionally*, when your life expectancy is possibly another thirty years or longer? What will you do? How will you afford it?

Let's start with the question of what you will do. Michael Stein in his book *The Prosperous Retirement* states that "I have come to the conclusion that more retirements will fail for non-financial reasons than for financial ones."[57] In my experience, I would tend to agree. Recent statistics tell us that currently forty million retirees spend an average of forty-three hours a week watching television.[58] Surely, this isn't the idea of retirement that most had during their working years. Many men think that they will play golf every day, mow the grass twice a week, take a vacation every year, and do odd jobs around the house to stay busy and that will be it. Many of these men are reflected in the statistic above and end up watching forty-three hours a week of TV and driving their spouses crazy. Even TV watching may not be the worst idea for a week or two; but to be sure, it is not the ideal plan for the next several decades of your life!

I can't stress to you enough the importance of thinking through what you are going to do during "retirement." I hope in this thought process you will consider your skills and where they may still be needed, mentoring, charity, or mission work, as well as other things that you may really enjoy doing. As I mentioned in chapter 2, stewardship is not only of our finances but also of our time and talents. For many retirees, money may be a strain but time and talent are bountiful and I would encourage the stewardship of those resources as well. Others may have more money and time to give than ever before.

On a slightly different perspective, I also find it very important to have a plan for what you will do for another important reason: your health. In my own experience and in talking with other planners, it is quite a common phenomenon that those retirees who don't have a passion during retirement and who don't stay involved in activities fall victim to illness. A point I want to make clear is that these people who do fall into this category did not plan on being inactive; it just happened by default when they didn't have a real idea of what they wanted to do. I'm sure that most people know someone that this has happened to – a real tragedy.

I am not in the least suggesting that in one's later years they haven't earned the right to move at a more relaxed pace of life and enjoy some of the fruits of a long life of labor. I am suggesting two things however: your age is relative, and without a resolve to stay active and involved, the television will be your road to nursing care. I find that many people today are still hindered by the perception of old age and retirement that existed decades ago, and that translates into their lackadaisical attitude to this stage in their lives. To those who are hung up on these perceptions, I prefer a definition of old age I heard speaker Alan Parisse say at a financial planning conference: "Old age starts when your attachment to the past is greater than your excitement about the future." You can be old at forty and young at seventy; age does not determine mind-set, and we shouldn't allow a chronological marker to dictate our life plan or mind-set. I recently had the opportunity to see Zig Ziglar, the popular motivation speaker who is now seventy-nine years old. After about an hour and a half of nonstop entertainment, he ended; and I can assure you that there wasn't a person in the audience who wasn't blown away by his energy and enthusiasm about his career and his life. Why can't we all have a touch of what he has at that age?

I also think it is important to discuss working and staying active in this late stage in life, because for many, men especially, there is a real anxiety about it. If you work after sixty-five, are you viewed as a failure by the world? After all, most everyone does retire earlier. Or maybe you do want to do something but don't know what?

It is hard to explain; but many people, whether they loved what they did or not, did a certain job so long that it becomes a part of who they are and their co-workers are their "friends." To abruptly divorce yourself from this part of who you have become and this network of people can be traumatic. It is not at all uncommon for people to lie awake at night, not because of financial worries but of just "what am I going to do." Many experience thoughts and feelings of loneliness that they would have never expected; after all, "I didn't even like most of those people." Work can lay these thoughts to rest and provide a sense of purpose and connectiveness that is sometimes hard to replace. I have heard some retirees feel somewhat hurt or mad that their former co-workers don't keep in touch, but this is probably not intentional but just a result of having a busy life. How many retired co-workers do you call regularly?

I don't want to paint a negative picture that suggests that you will not have fun traveling with your spouse and playing golf or cards with your friends, because you very well may. I do think it is important to bring these other issues up, because not everyone has the same feelings regarding punching out for the last time. You should ask yourself these types of questions to determine which type of person you are most like so you can plan for the lifestyle that you want.

Now moving to the other question I asked earlier, does it make *financial* sense to "retire" in your early sixties or before? That question is another whole issue altogether. First let's look at the fact that seven out of ten people start drawing Social Security "early" at age sixty-two. While this does not pinpoint when the actual retirement date is for many, it is safe to say that it is probably sixty-two or earlier. With that established, does this make financial sense?

As I have been trying to make the point this entire chapter, much of what is our social norm of retirement is based on facts that have changed dramatically. Today's retirement is far and away different from that of thirty years ago with some of the main reasons being longevity, increasing health-care cost, fewer pensions, higher personal savings required, higher standards of living to support, and instability of Social Security, to name a few.

It is no surprise to most that we are living much longer today than was common just fifty years ago. Diseases and maladies that were death sentences to our ancestors are now either nonexistent or easily curable, so much so that younger people today have an invincibility complex that probably would have never existed a century ago. With scientist and doctors working every day for the next medical breakthrough, many predict that centenarians (those living to one hundred) will be commonplace in the not-too-distant future. Jeanne Calment died in 1997 at the age of 122; is it possible that these life spans of biblical length may again become commonplace? Some researchers estimate that a baby girl born today will have a life expectancy of age one hundred. When discussing life expectancy, I hate to bring it up, but women on average live longer than men. In case you haven't visited your local retirement communities or nursing homes, the lack of men can confirm this fact. Unfortunately (for men), the statistics state that women are much more likely to outlive their husbands by an average of seven years. This phenomenon of long life poses two issues: providing an income for a longer duration and rising medical cost.

Is it financially feasible to expect to have started your working career in your twenties and work thirty to forty years and then never earn another dollar and live another thirty-plus years in retirement? Maybe, but it will require discipline and understanding. To be sure, it also requires a great deal of money for most and a willingness to invest that money for a lifetime. To be more specific, it requires that your investable assets keep pace with inflation while at the same time generating income.

As we all know, inflation is the simple fact that things get more expensive over time. Using history as our guide and an understanding of today's economics would lead me to believe that 2 to 3 percent would be a close estimate for inflation in the future. This general estimation is because the Federal Reserve today has a laser focus on curbing inflation while at the same time our over promise/under tax political climate will always keep inflation somewhat of an issue. With that short lesson in inflation, here is what you really need to know: a $50,000-a-year retirement income today will need to be $105,000 twenty-five years from now with 3 percent inflation just to maintain the same purchasing power. This puts a whole new dimension on retirement that didn't exist when life expectancy after retirement was just a few short years.

A part of that inflation factor, which is really an issue unto itself, is that of rising health-care cost. While people are quick to complain (to which I am very sympathetic) about their health-care cost, let us be clear that without these costs, life expectancies would not be growing. Said another way, we are quick to complain about the cost of our medications or treatments but wouldn't dare do without them. Without getting into a debate regarding specifics of the health-care industry, I think it is fairly safe to say that those in that industry deserve to make a profit and have incentive to want to develop new techniques and medicines. If that is the case, I would imagine that health care would continue to get more expensive in the future. I also bring up health care as a specific item of importance because the vast majority of medical costs are incurred by the aging population which is exploding and will add to this increase in health-care cost. I also bring it up for those of us who are younger and take for granted the fact that medical costs are a big issue for those who are retired. A clear understanding of the risks and ways to insure those risks are of utmost importance to those in retirement and expert advice should be sought.

I will take this opportunity to also remind you that long-term care costs, those for custodial care, are also a major threat to retirees. If a need arises for long-term care, without insurance, it is easily possible to incur huge expenses to care for a loved one. These expenses often deplete the retirement nest egg that is needed to support the other spouse. This is also why life insurance can prove to be a critically important piece of the financial puzzle. If the ailing spouse dies after having spent needed retirement funds, often it is a life insurance death benefit that replenishes the investment account so the surviving spouse can maintain their standard of living. With the risk of needing care being incredibly high, it is devastating to not consider the possibility of long-term care expenses (either LTC insurance premiums or the true cost of care) in your retirement scenario.

Another issue to consider that makes early retirement today more difficult than in the past is the fact that standards of living are much higher than ever experienced. In chapter 1, I think I stated pretty convincingly that we are a consumer society and are accustomed to much more than the bare necessities. With that being said, I think it is a dire mistake to think that these appetites will be quenched at retirement and you can go to a bare-bones budget. If a reduction in standard of living is contemplated, it has to be a deliberate and, most of the time, gradual process in order to be effective. Many however do not plan to "cut back" at retirement but instead plan to "enjoy the fruits of their labor." They have aspirations of vacation homes and worldwide travel, which may be okay financially as long as you have counted the cost and have enough for this to be feasible. These higher lifestyles in effect make us more dependent on personal savings to support these expenses. In the past, Social Security from both spouses and some sort of company pension combined with a little extra would provide a comfortable retirement income. Today, Social Security income is a much lower percentage of your total income needed; and with no pension (will discuss shortly), this makes the majority of the heavy lifting fall to your personal retirement accounts and other personal savings.

Many people assume quite optimistically that they will only need 50 percent or so of their current income to maintain their standard of living at retirement. That certainly depends on a number of factors, including your income and amount of debt at retirement. For a rule of thumb, most financial planners would suggest somewhere in the neighborhood of 75-80 percent of your current income will be needed. The reason the assumed reduction from current income is possible is because hopefully most debt is paid off, as well as you now are no longer saving for retirement. Many retirees' commuting, clothing, and dining out expenses may reduce as well. On this last point, we all have seen older gentlemen down at the local coffee shops who are still wearing their business suit they wore twenty years ago. While I am not suggesting that you don't buy new clothes, it is probably not as important as it once was; and this saves money. The stylish gentleman sporting the crazy looking old suit may be wearing *that* suit because he likes it, but possibly because he didn't plan on living this long and doesn't have money for things like new clothes.

While this rule of thumb, known as the income replacement ratio, may be helpful for those who are far from retirement, those who are closer to collecting that final paycheck should do a mock budget. With retirement near, you should be able to estimate with some precision what your monthly expenses will be as well as what your income sources are.

Another significant difference in today's retirement is the fact that the traditional pension plan is on the endangered species list. At one time, company pension plans were part of the lifelong commitment that employers made to employees in return for a career long of servitude. Today these plans are becoming increasingly infeasible because of the frequent job changes of today's worker as well as the liability they present to the company. You don't hear about many people getting the gold watch today, but you do hear about pension funds trying to shuck their responsibility through bankruptcy proceedings. You see, the same demographic trends that daunt today's retiree are also a threat to pension plans. Because of these factors, most companies have terminated their pension plans in favor of shifting the investment burden to the employee. Often their plan of choice is the familiar 401(k) or some variety of it. In essence, corporations today are much more comfortable giving the employee money to which they can invest on their own rather than be on the hook for a lifetime of payments to a retiree and possibly their spouse. Pensions used to be an integral part of many retirees' income, which was comforting to many because this was a check that they would never outlive. There are still some companies today, most are your very large Fortune 500-type entities, which still offer these plans. For those of you who have one, many times there are tremendous planning opportunities that need to be analyzed prior to making a decision as to which option to take at retirement. *Please,* consult a competent financial planner prior to doing so; after all, most pension decisions are final and you may have to live with your decision for the rest of your life.

Finally, all of these factors point to the fact that one's personal savings is extremely important to have a comfortable "retirement," in the traditional sense of the word. Unfortunately, the personal savings rate in the United States is around 1-2 percent, or some even speculate it is negative, either way a far cry from where it needs to be. While I certainly hope that people come to their senses and come to the realities of today's retirement landscape, most probably won't, at least not in time. To be quite frank, I can't convince everyone of the need to save and invest more, but my hope is that I can convince you that it is important. Of course, with regards to the issue of personal savings, the question that everyone wants the answer to is "how much is enough?" Many people think it will take a nest egg of at least a million dollars or more. It may. As any good financial planner who has ever been asked this direct question with insufficient information would say, "It depends." Small changes in your circumstances, meaning a few years' difference here or there, differences in debt obligations, and slight changes in expectations can result in a pretty sizeable difference in the "nest egg" needed.

For many, I truly believe that their retirement will be much different than was previously planned; many because of financial reasons and many others for emotional or health reasons. I believe this is already taking place and will continue to in the future. A study done by the AARP in 2003 showed that 79 percent expected to work during retirement. It is my opinion that many of these will because they will have to. For those who either have to or want to work in the later stages in life, I do think it is important to have realistic expectations with respect to these late-in-life jobs. First, as of today, which is subject to change in the future, the fact is that there aren't that many new jobs available to the elderly. Second, many of these jobs in today's environment may pay considerably less than you may expect. I do speculate that this may change in the very near future and companies will want to retain top talent and will be flexible and offer competitive incentives to older workers, but today that is not the predominant case. Either way, working during your "retirement" years may help supplement your investment income or allow more years for your nest egg to grow before drawing on it and provide a perfect solution to a less-than-adequate nest egg. For others, it may provide that interaction and purpose that will give them a reason to get up in the morning and keep them young at heart.

I strongly encourage those nearing retirement to consider if working in some capacity might be a good strategy. One thing that I think a great point to ponder is; let's say you are five years from when you think you will retire. You may be stressed or don't like your job but feel you have to stick it out for five more years to make the numbers work. My question to you would be, what if you "retired" today and took a job you enjoyed, maybe for a fraction of what you are making today? How long would you "now" be willing to work? Many people may say that they can only put up with their present job for a couple of more years; but if they had another job that was less stressful and more flexible, they would be willing to work for several more. This type of planning is critical and may be the answer to many people's retirement dilemma.

Now that I have got you contemplating the possibility of working during retirement years, I need to address those of you out there who would say, "I love my job and will never retire." This is really my attitude toward my career today, and I find that many small business owners are the same way. They simply can't imagine not doing what they have always done and plan to "die with their work boots on."

I completely respect and am grateful that there are people who have those feelings; unfortunately, you are not off the hook for planning for "retirement" either.

Here are a few thoughts on the importance of planning for those "in love with their job" types. First of all, I am reminded from time to time that what you have loved in the past isn't always going to be what you love in the future. For instance, in my high school and college years, I "loved" some of the worst music you can imagine and just knew that I would be rocking to it when I was an old man. I was wrong. Financial author Mitch Anthony said it best in his book *The New Retire-Mentality*,

> Just because I love what I do does not negate the need to plan for financial freedom. Life can present us with vicissitudes that can radically alter our course: disability, a death in the family, divorce, and so on. We must plan ahead financially because we change our minds over time. What invigorates me today may bore me a decade from today. Investment savings are necessary to purchase the freedom to change course when we want.[59]

Plain and simple, planning allows for options in the future. If you are a business owner and plan to work in your business until you die and don't plan otherwise, chances are you will work until you die because there will never be an option. Age sixty-five is a bad time to realize that you really wish you had saved more and that you would really like to slow down and enjoy the grandkids. For business owners, planning cannot be emphasized enough. You just can't plan to sell your business for top dollar right away and walk away with a fist full of cash. After all, that business, in many cases, not only is your livelihood but also to those employees who worked for you. The business owner also has to come to the realization that competitive or market forces may make their business unprofitable and unmarketable. Many experts in the field seem to think with so many baby boomers looking to retire and sell their businesses, there will be saturation in the market which will drive down prices of small closely held businesses. I could go on and on to those of you who are business owners or to those who know them. It may be difficult to contemplate other options, but planning is of the utmost importance to them. I truly believe that if most business owners let that devil's advocate that they so often suppress come out a little, they would agree with me that they need to do something, just in case.

Another consideration for those who are the work-forever types is the inherent assumption that you will be *able* to work forever. While I have been making the case that many will live longer than many ever thought possible, no one is guaranteed a life of abundant health and energy. In fact, in understanding the human body and the reality of death, we all know that there is an element of slowing in one's later years; it may be rapid or gradual. You don't have to look far in your family or friends to have this grim reminder in living color, and it should serve as a motivation for you to do some planning, just in case it turns out that it isn't in the cards for you to run a marathon at seventy-five, like you may be thinking.

A term I have come to embrace in my practice instead of the term "retirement" is "financial independence." What this means is just what we have been discussing: saving and investing so that in these later years of life you can work because you want to, not because you have to. Financial independence means being able to slow down if desired, choose a different direction, or maintain your standard of living regardless of whether you can or choose to work. With this new goal, we already start to shift our attitude and goal away from the narrow traditional view of retirement to a broader and more exciting view that in all actuality will probably better align with what will really happen. Financial independence means having the freedom to choose an all-leisure lifestyle if you so desire and see fit or to continue pursuing other ventures which may or may not earn income. I am not saying that either of these paths is the right one for you; that is certainly up to you, but having that freedom of choice is usually only the result of proactive planning.

I would also like to add something to the discussion of "retirement" which I think is entirely relevant because it really goes to the core of where part of this concept stems from. There is a negative stigma of work that pervades our culture so much so that it is not at all uncommon to hear people make comments and use terms such as slave to the daily grind, working for "the man," just punching the clock, another day another dollar. With this mundane drudgery, no wonder people want to quit. I do however want to remind you that God has ordained work and not as a punishment. If you will remember, God's command to Adam to subdue the land was before Adam's fall into sin. Now certainly there did come a curse which would make man's work less fruitful, but it is interesting to remember that God did not make man to just roam around and pick fruit from the trees. He created man and work, and both where good. To hold a negative view of work is unhealthy and can produce a life view that can produce a number of negative consequences.

I prefer Pablo Picasso's statement, "Never permit a dichotomy to rule your life, a dichotomy in which you hate what you do so you can have pleasure in your spare time. Look for a situation in which your work will give you as much happiness as your spare time." I certainly recognize that not everyone will have the choice to do something they love. I also recognize that God can be glorified in the normal and even mundane actions of some people's occupation. I will contend that when the specifics of someone's situation permit, it only makes sense to have an occupation that not only pays the bills but where there are also intangible benefits of satisfaction and enjoyment. I know many men who have unselfishly done occupations they didn't enjoy for their families' financial well-being; there are often seasons in everyone's life when we have to "pay our dues," but my prayer is that you will seek, if able, and that God will bless you with a job or career that can be the blessing that He originally intended it to be. As Truett Cathy, founder of Chick-fil-A, says, "learn to love your work and you'll never have to 'work' again."

In summary, retirement today and in the future should not be thought of as a lapse into dormancy. The retirement of decades ago is far and away different from the retirement or financial independence of today and in the future. People are living longer and healthier lives thanks to advances in medicine and nutrition. These new longer-life assumptions should help to spur change in our thoughts and plans when it comes to how we are to spend our lives. I think that present-day view of retirement as a time of unending leisure is a difficult one to pull off financially and emotionally for many. The need to plan in order to have options in the future is one of the main lessons of this chapter. Personal retirement savings is where the bulk of future income liabilities will fall; and with the current savings rate at incredibly low levels, people are going to have to start saving and investing hard and fast. Most importantly in my mind is the concept of stewardship that we are all commissioned with: how can my time, talents, and treasures be allocated at this stage in my life?

While I could have gone into detail in this chapter about how an investment plan should be structured and details of how a traditional "retirement plan" could be laid out, I will save that mostly for a professional financial planner to assist with. I did want to leave you with some food for thought that you can be chewing on prior to your planning for this later stage of life, instead of those "gold watch" types of ideas that many people have concerning the traditional "retirement." Hopefully you will adopt a more realistic and fulfilling goal of financial independence which can lead down many exciting paths. Finally, I encourage you to talk to people who are in this later stage of life and especially to those you view as "doing well" late in life. In doing so, like me, you will pick up on some jewels that will enable you to plan and with God's help live out a truly rich life and finish strong.

CHAPTER 7

Blocking and Tackling

Wealth is not acquired, as many people suppose, by fortunate speculations and splendid enterprises, but by the daily practice of industry, frugality, and economy. He who relies upon these means will be rarely found destitute, and he who relies upon any other will generally become bankrupt.

– Julius Wayland

It is not uncommon that if you were to ask most people what they thought it would take to be financially successful; they would tend to mention something like having a high-paying job, inheriting money, marrying into money, or maybe even some grand investment scheme that would be certain to hit a home run. A recent study done by the Financial Planning Association and the Consumer Federation of America showed that 21 percent of the one thousand Americans surveyed believed that winning the lottery was their best chance for accumulating wealth.[60] In fact, very few people, at least at first thought, would mention any of the boring fundamentals such as saving, investing, debt management, etc., as keys that would lead them to financial security. But it is these fundamentals that can be attributed to the large majority of those people whom we could comfortably categorize as financially successful and which we will be discussing in this chapter.

As far as the strategies that most others would mention, here are my thoughts. How much you get paid is irrelevant if you spend it all; with life expectancies increasing, you may have to wait until you're seventy to inherit, and that is assuming there is something left over; never marry for money, you will pay for it for the rest of your life; if the investment scheme is "surefire," well, I will address this in the investing chapter.

All athletes know that focusing on the fundamentals is what success is all about. The blocking and tackling, so to speak, is what every play or strategy relies on. When we try to focus on things that others are doing or what might happen, we often abandon those things which we can control and those things that contribute most to our success. In finances, it is very easy to let emotions take control over our activities and lead us into focusing on the wrong things. This is specifically true with regards to investing, which I will address in detail in other chapters. As the saying goes, public successes are the result of private accomplishments. It is the development of daily disciplines, a purposeful daily walk, which leads to financial success and a truly rich life. I also believe that in many cases it is the testing grounds for your faithfulness to be able to handle more.

Today's financial headlines are full of shady CEOs who have embezzled, misappropriated funds, etc. I would guess that any CEO who ran his company like most people run *their* financial lives would either be guilty of the same or go bankrupt; at the very least, if full disclosure was given, they wouldn't have many investors. My goal in this chapter is to get you to focus your attention on, above all other financial advice, the fundamentals. If you don't develop these disciplines or habits today, you will be forced to develop them eventually. As Warren Buffet has been noted saying, "Unsuccessful people do in the end what successful people do in the beginning." The pain of self-discipline is mild as compared to the pain of regret; and regardless of your age or stage in life, these principles can make a huge difference. I will also advocate some methods that can help those of us who lack some of that needed self-discipline.

As I have mentioned, financial success is normally a result of the practice of daily disciplines regarding one's finances combined with someone's ability to earn money. Financial success or independence is a hard-to-define term and one that doesn't have a corresponding dollar amount attached to it. In the recent past, there used to be the prevailing thought that $1 million was the threshold to be "financially successful" and it was supposed that only white-collar professionals could obtain such a status. I can tell you from working with many people that the dollar amount does not determine "financial success" any more than having a convertible will make you young again. I have met people who have worn short sleeves all their lives, saved, invested, and made prudent decisions with their lives and money who have enough money to take care of all of their needs comfortably and I would deem financially successful. On the otherhand, I have seen and heard about individuals in the upper echelons of society who despite having multi-million-dollar net worths are but a financial hiccup or two away from real trouble. These "affluent" individuals who have amassed a large, by normal standards, portfolio of investments often have correspondingly large standards of living which will never let them be financially secure. I say all of this to make the point that financial success is a relative term and can be achieved in this country at nearly any income level. I am not saying that everyone has a shot at becoming a millionaire by age fifty or that retirement can mean thirty years of leisure; but to be sure, honing the basic skills of earning, saving, investing, and spending wisely will pay big dividends over time.

To start the process of living a truly rich life, in a financial sense, you first have to know where you stand today. A cash flow statement and a balance sheet are two of the main diagnostic tests, so to speak, that can give you an immediate snapshot as to your financial health and probable future financial health. A cash flow or income statement that shows more money being spent than made will lead to a net worth that is eventually very negative. A budget that is positive will eventually lead to a balance sheet that is in the black. Let me first define both of these terms as we discuss them in more detail.

A cash flow or income statement may sound like some super technical analysis, but let me be clear. I am not concerned with format or any adherence to some accounting standards; what is important is that you have on one statement, preferably one page, where your money is coming from and where it is going. Without an understanding of this, it is very difficult to do any kind of meaningful planning. To make a cash flow statement, list out all income sources and then all of your expenses or outflows, both fixed and variable. While this may seem unnecessary for some, I believe it is extremely helpful in identifying issues and opportunities. Many people may not realize how much they spend on certain expenses that they don't really even consider significant or, on the flip side, not recognize that they are not really saving very much as a percentage of their total income – both causes for closer examination.

The second statement I mentioned is a balance sheet. This is one I use annually as a measuring stick of financial progress. A balance sheet is constructed simply by listing on one side of a page every asset your own: bank accounts, investment and retirement accounts, value of home and other property, etc. Now on the other side of the page list your liabilities, everything you owe: mortgage amounts, car loans, credit card balances, etc. You can calculate your net worth simply by subtracting your liabilities from your assets. A net worth that is growing is extremely important for those who are prior to "retirement." Ideally, debt (as a percentage of net worth) should be reducing year to year and assets should be growing year over year. A balance sheet can also be a way to quickly identify problems that will impact the income statement or effect cash flow. If you are adding to debt significantly without a corresponding asset to show for it, problems lie ahead. This "net worth" focus will also discourage things such as new car purchases and other purchases which quickly depreciate in value or have little "real" value.

My purpose in mentioning these statements is simply to make you aware of these tools that everyone should employ from time to time to evaluate where they stand, where there is room for improvement, and what hurdles they might have to overcome.

With those diagnostic tools in hand, let's look at the first fundamental with which we should try to hone. The first fundamental is what I like to call your offense; it is your ability to earn money. While career coaching is beyond my skill set and the scope of this book, it should be no surprise that a great deal of your financial situation will be contingent upon your or your spouse's ability to earn an income. I truly believe that God in his wisdom, providence, and grand plan for everyone has instituted the concept of work. Our occupation also plays a big role in who we get to interact with, ultimately what problem we solve, service we provide, or product we make for the rest of mankind's enjoyment – a noble task. As I have also mentioned, it is through our work that God provides for our needs by earning money. It only makes sense in my simple mind that if my occupation is noble and commanded by God (almost regardless of what it is) and it is the engine, so to speak, of my financial life, then it makes sense to be as good as possible at what I do. We are blessed to live in a free market capitalistic society where, for the most part, you get paid in relation to the benefit you produce for someone else. If you make your employer a lot of money, you will make money. If you are the best at some particular task or job, you will more than likely get paid more than someone who is mediocre. If you don't like your job, you have the freedom to look for other employment. If you own your own business and fill a need of society, it is possible to make a very good living. The thing I hope to get you to think about is that, at some point and time, nearly everyone has to take the initiative to find a path, a job, a career, a business that can accomplish not only your income requirements but possibly a greater purpose. For the most part, there is not going to be somebody telling you what you should do, if you should change, whether or not you should go back to school, etc. These are going to take your own initiative; and by the way, these types of decisions are not just for young people. For those of you who have already found the career, job, or business that you feel fits all of those needs, you should strive to do your best not only for the capitalistic payoff but because we are to do our work as unto the Lord.

Unfortunately, I have crossed paths with people who have "dead-end" jobs they hate, and they refuse to do anything about it. They refuse to look for other jobs which would fit their situation better, refuse to get educated so they are qualified for another job, and most financially have little hope of improvement because their "financial engine" is set on idle. On the other hand, I have the high privilege to work with some of the most successful people in their fields. It is uncanny that most like their jobs, are fulfilling their family's financial needs, are performing a task that is obviously valuable to somebody, and their ability to earn an income (regardless of their portfolio size) is their biggest asset. Most would also tell you that they got to where they are through hard work, sacrifices, perseverance, and personal initiative. This is not to say that they nor I don't recognize God's directing and blessing of these actions; but to be sure, their financial status would not have come from sitting around complaining about their sorry boss.

The breadwinner or breadwinners of your family are your biggest asset. Think of it this way, the ability to earn $50,000 a year is roughly financially equivalent to a $1.25 million asset. If you can improve your skills, be better at what you do; your economic value to your family will increase exponentially. However, while the ability to have a great offense is well and good, it is of little effect if you don't have a good defense.

It is commonly said that you can make all the money in the world but if you spend it all, you are still broke – thoughts of M.C. Hammer come to mind. It is fair to say that many people today are like NBA basketball: all flair and no defense and they often run out of money before they run out of month. To be successful financially and even in many other areas, a defense has to be established. Your defense will be multipronged and will, for simplicity's sake, be divided into prudent spending, saving, investing, and debt management. You may say, "How in the world can spending be a part of a good defense?" Let's discuss it briefly.

As they say, "despite the high cost of living, it's still popular." Whether we want to admit it or not, it costs money to live. We all have the essentials of food, clothing, and shelter as well as the nonessentials of entertainment and other luxuries. It should make sense that how we spend money on these items can make a tremendous impact on our financial situation. Thomas Stanley, author of *The Millionaire Next Door* and *The Millionaire Mind*, writes that "frugality is the cornerstone of wealth building."[61] Even one of the richest men in the world (worth $42 billion in 2006),[62] Warren Buffett still has frugality so ingrained in his personality that even his personal car tag "thrifty." Now I am sure that some of you may be reading this and think I'm about to go off the deep end and suggest we all start cobbling our own shoes and growing tomatoes, which is not the case at all. I am suggesting a somewhat more thoughtful process of purchasing than what we are probably accustomed to, which will not only lead to saving money that you would have otherwise wasted, but will keep you from buying things you really didn't need in the first place.

One of the first lessons I have learned and applied is the concept of planning expenditures. I will go ahead and tell you that my wife is the one who taught me this lesson and continues to drive the point home on a regular basis. If you are going to need to buy a car for instance, don't wait until you are in dire straits and "have to buy one." This puts you at a point of desperation and one in which you have little room to carefully consider your options. You should understand how the business of whatever it is you are trying to buy works. Should you buy a brand-new, just-released car, or should you maybe buy last year's model program car or maybe even a used luxury car which may retain its value better over time and be a better car than a new economy car? Does it make sense to buy all of your clothes "in season" or to get them 75 percent off at the end of the season and wear them next year? If you do this continually, you will never have to buy clothes at full price. The point I am trying to get across is not that you should be "cheap" but that with a more planned and thoughtful approach you can save real money and own the same things. Also keep in mind, with cars for instance, that they are used the day after you buy them. Make sure you aren't paying a premium for little things like "having the latest and greatest" because, as we have all learned, everything is quickly dated. You can buy the new top-of-the-line computer and pay top dollar because you had to have "the best" only to see it next month on the "specials" ad in your local newspaper. Unless you are going to get a new computer every month, wouldn't it have been wise to wait a month or two or buy the next model down and save a bundle? Let's talk designer fashions for a minute; is it really necessary that our kids have a $35 T-shirt with a certain logo on it? Wouldn't an almost identical shirt be a fraction of the cost and serve the same purpose? I fully realize that cost is not the only consideration when considering a purchase; there should be a "value" judgment which takes into account what you are getting (features, benefits), cost of available substitutes, quality, life of the product (time you will use or enjoy it) in addition to price. In this I am not saying that buying nice shoes, clothes, cars, etc., are not wise purchases; but I am saying that they may or may not be upon considering all of those factors. You see, I am not telling you to abstain from any purchases. I will let you make that personal decision of stewardship; but what I am saying is that when you do purchase things, you might as well be smart about it. For those of you who are retail business owners, please apply this principle in your own life; and don't worry, the average American consumer won't take my advice, so your profit margins are safe.

I am sure you will agree with me when I say that we all buy "stuff" we don't need, we don't end up using, and we wish we could take back. That little thing called buyer's remorse, that sinking feeling after you have purchased something you probably shouldn't have is normally the result of an emotional purchase that could have been avoided with planning. You see, we are emotional beings; and as author Jonathan Pond puts it, "the longer you think about some nonessential luxury item, the more you will convince yourself that you absolutely, positively need to have it."[63] It is for this reason that window shopping is a precursor for real shopping. If you don't want to be emotionally handcuffed to that next shiny gotta-have, then don't travel down that road that leads you to it. It is for this reason that I try to avoid stores and places that I know will make me discontent, rob me of my appreciation of what I do have, and start me down the road of justifying a purchase I really don't need or truly want to make. It is kind of like a person on a diet avoiding the doughnut shop; why go to a place that only sells what you don't really want or need?

Yet another strategy for avoiding unneeded purchases is very simple yet highly effective; it's called waiting. I know this sounds a little silly and overly simple; but whenever you find yourself emotionally engaged in any purchase, either something you need or something you just want, I recommend a little "cooling-off" period. It is hard to say how long this needs to be and would certainly depend on the amount of emotion involved and the other circumstances of the situation. Let's take a car purchase for instance. Say you are thinking about maybe needing a new (new to you) car in the next year or so. You happen to be out driving and see a car lot with cars that tickle your interest, so you decide to stop (maybe a violation of my previous advice). You get out *to just look* at a nice car, a salesman lets you drive it, and before you know it you are discussing financing and checking the trade-in value on your car. I can assure you if you don't have a predetermined "cool-off" period for major purchases like this and get out of there and give yourself time to think about it, absent from the pressure of the salesman and view of that good-looking car, there is no doubt in my mind that you will have just purchased that car. Hopefully you got a good deal and you liked it; nevertheless, you really didn't leave yourself a way out emotionally by committing early and not leaving a cooling-off time to more reasonably reflect on the situation. This scenario plays itself out in big ways every day in the car and real estate business, and anyone who has ever subjected themselves to one of those time-share presentations can relate to the emotional pressure to which I am referring. My idea of a cooling-off period is not new or fancy but can be extremely effective in helping you lessen the chances of making a decision you will regret and in most all cases will not keep you from getting what you want. Waiting can also help or enable you to take advantages of those "sales" or price reductions due to buying at times when the rest of the world isn't. Maybe you do buy that new car; but wait, make sure that it is exactly what you want, and get it at a year-end sale for thousands less – probably well worth the wait.

While we are on the subject of spending, it may be of some surprise to you that I don't endorse any specific method of cash management. There are those out there who yell and scream about how bad credit cards are and how you are an idiot if you use them. We will discuss debt a little later and I certainly recognize the temptation that credit cards pose for some but at the same time they offer some great benefits for those who are responsible enough to pay them off at the end of the month. I tend to use a credit card for nearly every purchase I make and almost never use cash. Credit cards can offer consolidated reporting of your spending, can assist with irregular income flows, can offer cash back or other perks as well as insuring some purchases and protecting against loss or theft of your card. I am aware of studies which show that consumers who use credit cards spend more than if they used cash and I do agree there is something psychologically that isn't quite the same as using cash, but I also leave the option open if you are the type of person who can handle the temptation and responsibility.

As I mentioned, there are some proponents of an all-cash type method of managing day-to-day expenses. This may be a great way to help minimize weekly expenses on things like eating out or other normal purchases which are easy to splurge on too often. If this sounds like a method that works for you, go for it. I will highly recommend that you not carry a lot of cash on you, however. I can remember when I first got married; my wife and I had just read a Dave Ramsey book and were using the all-cash envelope system because it seemed at the time the "only way" to do it. We subsequently had a good amount of cash in my wife's purse which was stolen out of her car and quickly recognized that all-cash may have some drawbacks. The key to this whole decision is really knowing yourself and your spouse and coming up with a way that accountability can be in place and will work well for all involved.

On a similar note, I often have people ask me about how they should handle the family finances, meaning how many accounts, which accounts do what, etc. Again, here I am going to suggest that you have to find something that works for you. How do you know if it works for you? Are both parties happy with the situation, and is there some level of accountability? Are the bills getting paid and the investments, giving, and savings getting done? If so, then it is working; if not, it may mean reevaluating things.

My wife and I only use one checking account plus a brokerage account that serves as both a savings and investment account; it has worked for us for a number of years but may need adjusting in the future. On the flip side, I know another couple who handles their money well and they have numerous accounts, one where all of the bank drafts come out, one for all other household type expenses, and each have an account for their individual weekly expenses as well as a brokerage account. To me it sounds crazy and difficult to manage, but it works for them, which is all that matters.

Now let's deal quickly with the budgeting issue. Some people are very big on budgets and contend that budgeting is what you should focus on and learn to master. I understand their comments but also recognize that most people's hair stands up on the back of their necks when budgeting gets mentioned. It is for this reason that I tend to have a somewhat different focus and back into a budget. With that I mean, once you decide what you need to be doing with your money, e.g., giving, investing for financial independence, investing for kids'college, paying for insurance, etc., and you are doing those things, then, whatever is left, you can spend as you please. For some people, this may force them into a traditional budgeting-every-little thing mentality; but for others whose means exceed their needs, it is a little more of a positive and freeing idea.

I am not saying that I don't do budgets, I do them quite often with clients and myself; but what I am saying is that instead of trying to fit each thing in each section and subsection, you focus on doing the hard things like giving, saving, and investing and the rest can take care of itself. If you are the type that likes to manage each penny and allocate it appropriately, then, by all means, go for it. I tend to find that my approach is a little easier, at least mentally, for many people to handle. I am also used to working with more affluent families where this approach is more plausible than counting each nickel and dime. As I previously mentioned, I do recommend you doing a cash flow statement which is essentially showing where you are *actually* spending money today, not just where you *want* to be. To do an effective budget, you must first start with this statement and then make adjustments. If you just start with some pie-in-the-sky numbers, your budgeting efforts are sure to end in failure. There are so many resources which deal with budgeting that I will stop here. The point is there should be some system, just like with the day-to-day cash management, which works for you and your family. Just like a diet or a fitness regimen, it doesn't matter how good your system is if you can't stick with it – choose one that can provide benefit and work for you.

Now that we have discussed some diagnostic tools to help you as well as the benefits of thriftiness, avoiding impulse buying, and managing the day-to-day expenses, we can move on to the final fundamentals: saving, investing, and debt.

I think it is safe to say that the general consensus among people in the financial world is that the rate of savings of Americans has slid down the mountain of materialism to a point where it is almost nonexistent. The savings rate was nearly 12 percent in the 50s, 10.8 percent in the 70s, 4.9 percent in the 90s, and today, excluding company pensions, it is around 1-2 percent.[64] Some studies even suggest that due to the recent housing boom, the savings rate is negative when you factor in the fact that many have robbed the equity out of their homes for purchases. Interestingly, the rest of the world has healthy rates of savings with South Koreans saving 25 percent of their incomes, the Japanese saving 12-15 percent, and Europeans, in general, saving approximately 10 percent. [65] This spend-all-you-make mentality in America is what creates that "perpetual earn-and-consume treadmill" that I described earlier in this book. It should be apparent that spending all you make will only lead to missed opportunities and strapped to a job by the need to just keep up your expenses.

I mention that saving is one of those fundamentals that all must adopt and incorporate, not only in their lifestyle, but in their mind-set as well. Savings can mean regularly monthly/weekly setting aside of money or it can mean not spending all of that year-end bonus or tax refund or both. The point is to create a habit of putting current income aside for a later use, whether it is for long-term things and can be invested, or for having money set aside so you can respond in giving when a need arises. Savings is obviously closely related to the topic of investing, both setting aside money for a later purpose, and the point of both is setting your standard of living appropriately so that saving and investing is a regular part of how you handle money. The two best ideas I have regarding making this habit easier are these: regular bank drafts and saving a portion of income increases.

First let's discuss bank drafts. In my experience, both personally and professionally, if you wait until the end of the month and try and save what is left over, there will be nothing left over. In contrast, if you pay yourself first, meaning save first (before other expenses), then you will always ensure that it gets taken care of. The means that works best and requires the least discipline is some sort of automatic draft, whether it is from your checking account or deducted from your paycheck before you even get it. The only discipline this requires is setting it up; once you have done that, your savings and regular investing are on cruise control.

One thing I want to mention is a psychological block that most people tend to have. Many times, regardless of how crazy it sounds, people don't want to start saving until they can do a specified amount, such as $500. If they don't feel like they can do that amount, they would rather wait until they can, instead of just starting with $100 now and increasing it later. I don't know why this phenomenon exists; but trust me, it does. I promise you that it is far easier to increase your monthly savings and investing than it is to start. Once that emotional momentum is going, it is much easier to save a little more. Chances are if you don't start saving now, you probably won't.

Now let's talk about that other easy method of saving that works wonderfully. Again, I am not introducing any groundbreaking idea that hasn't been told before, but that doesn't negate the fact that it works wonderfully and the fact that most people don't do it. The idea is simple: save part or all of your pay raises or increased income. It should be simple; you are already living on one amount and any additional should not be "needed" so it only makes sense that it would be easy to save, right?

Unfortunately for most people the answer is wrong. You see, especially when the raise is anticipated, most already start to spend in view of that new income; and it is not at all uncommon for that new spending to exceed the eventual raise received. This is the reason that I often hear well-paid professionals say things like, "I make twice as much as I did five years ago, but I have no idea where it all goes. I mean I don't feel like I have increased my standard of living that much."

However, just because others don't do it doesn't mean it can't be done. In fact, I can attest to many people who do utilize this technique to the effect of significant savings and investments over time. Just do the math, say you make $100,000 and you save 10 percent or $10,000 annually. Now let's assume that over a five-year period you got annual raises of 6 percent. So now, five years down the road, you make $133,822. If you saved half of your raise every year in addition to the $10,000 you are already saving and enjoyed the 3 percent increase in pay to keep up with inflation, your savings over that time period would not be $50,000 (or $59,753 if still saved 10 percent) but would be $66,911 not including interest or return that would have been earned on that money which could accentuate the power of this type of strategy. Obviously, if you have larger pay raises or bonuses or implement this over a longer period of time, this type of strategy can produce astounding results. Again, as I mentioned in the last section, if it is a monthly pay raise, then you should be able to automate this decision via a payroll deduction or a bank draft.

It should also be noted, as author Richard Carlson states, that "if you raise your standard of living to match your current income, it forces you to keep producing at the same level, whether you want to or not."[66] So if you don't take my advice and continue down the path of raising your standard of living every time you make more money, it makes it increasingly difficult to ever be able to achieve financial independence. Many people suggest that your retirement income should be around 80 percent or more of your current income to maintain your standard of living. Just think however if your standard of living is well below your income and you have been saving a large percentage; then it is possible to live off much less and financial independence is much more possible.

Now that we have dealt with saving in general and some specific strategies to help in your efforts, it should be noted that we are kind of getting the cart before the horse. After all, as I mentioned in the chapter on planning, you should be saving and investing with purposes in mind. Before we move on to the fundamental principle of investing, let's discuss some of the main reasons for just plain saving. First and foremost, I wouldn't be much of a financial planner if I didn't throw out some rules of thumb that everybody uses like, "You need to have three to six months worth of expenses in short-term savings." This savings is what many deem "emergency funds." I agree that everyone should have some amount in this type of setting. Of course, I will add that it all depends on your specific situation. If you are like me and own your own business, even six months of expenses might be too little; or if you have an uncertain job situation, you should certainly have more in this short-term bucket.

It is normally my suggestion to have this money in a money market fund or some short-duration investment that has immediate liquidity and little risk to principal; after all, you don't want to have to sell an investment at a loss when you are in need of money. If you and your spouse both work and have steady jobs, maybe three months' worth of expenses is adequate. Often, people think that having such a large amount of money is "too much" to have "not earning much"; but it should be remembered that the purpose of this money is for emergencies like the furnace going out, loss of a job, short-term disability, etc. Having money earmarked for this type of situation can help you avoid cash flow problems and the need to take on debt to fund them. I can also attest that while we are not to place our trust in our money, it does offer some mental comfort to know that it is there if needed. I will mention that as a person gets more comfortable with investing, and if the situation is right, possibly some of that "large" emergency fund can be invested and offer some more potential for growth, of course recognizing the trade-off of the added risk.

Other purposes for just regular savings would include things like having money set aside so that when needs or ministry opportunities present themselves, you can be prepared to give generously and not grudgingly because it may "take away" from something else. This predetermined generosity can make the joy of giving much greater. Also, savings can help fund those things which are too close in time to invest for. Often, people save for vacations, Christmas and birthday presents, or anything else for that matter that would put a cash crunch on you if you tried to pay for it all in one month. Again, the purpose is to avoid debt when possible; and to be honest, in most cases, much of what we do use debt to finance could have been planned and saved for. As I write this, my wife has been saving for months to go visit her sister in California and also to tile our shower in our downstairs bathroom, great examples of things most Americans would have just put on the credit card. I am getting ahead of myself in discussing debt, but I think you get the point with regards to savings.

While I will go into greater detail in a following chapter, I feel I must address the fundamental of investing as a daily discipline here. You see, I have run across several people and even some clients who are always wanting to know what the next great stock tip is or when it is a good time to invest. If they were less concerned with these details, of which there will always be varied opinions, and just invested regularly, they would have a lot more money. This is a perfect example of focusing on the wrong thing at the expense of the right thing. I feel like just repeating the old Nike slogan – Just Do It. There should be no argument against the fact that investing over a long period of time can produce positive results, and those returns can compound which, as I will show you in the investing chapter, can produce tremendous results. Again, in most cases you invest for specific purposes such as retirement, education, etc. As I mentioned in the chapter which addresses planning, you can invest for any financial goal which has a time frame that is long enough to reduce the possibility of losses. While I find that many people don't have a problem investing for retirement and college for their kids, they often don't invest for the unknown.

While weddings, college, and retirement are all sort of expected and planned events which have a corresponding time frame, I find it helpful to have some money invested for the unknowns of life. Let's say you are thirty-five and you are investing for all of the things I just mentioned; it is also a great asset to have money invested for the unknowns as well. Who knows, ten years from now you may want to start your own business or take a year and do mission work or buy that cabin at the lake. I don't know what it could be. To be certain, if you don't invest for these unknowns, the opportunities won't exist. I recognize that many people don't have enough money to save for all of the things they need to, plus unknowns. Point taken. However, some people do and should take my advice; and others, with the help of an advisor, should discuss the allocation of your investment dollars across all of your goals, including "unknowns." My partner Wayne Harris is the one who introduced this idea to me when we first started working together, and I can attest to the opportunities and freedom that it has allowed many of our clients to have.

To just briefly summarize, it is a good idea to have money going into what I would call three buckets. One bucket is a short-term vehicle and contains your "emergency fund," another midterm bucket invested for midterm goals and may include money invested for the unknowns of the future, and, finally, money earmarked for the long-term goals of financial independence and/or possibly college funding.

Also, just like saving, a good deal of your investing should be automated through payroll deductions or bank drafts so that the question of "Is now a good time?" doesn't paralyze you from investing at all. Of course, year-end bonuses, tax refunds, and asset sales are also great opportunities to prefund these future goals. Since I am not going to touch on it in the investing chapter and I would think it is obvious to everyone, if you have a 401(k) or employer-sponsored retirement plan at work, especially if they have some sort of matching arrangement, you should take as much advantage of this as possible. As an example, if your company matches your contributions up to 6 percent of your salary, it is a very tough argument to try and justify not putting at least 6 percent of your salary in; after all, that is a 100 percent return on your investment with no risk.

Lastly, I must mention the all-too-common topic of debt. It is safe to say that credit is vastly available in America; and unfortunately, many cannot handle the responsibility. To prove this point, the *Guinness Book of World Records* actually records an American who has 1,262 credit cards. Almost just as amazing is when I was in college without a dollar to my name and no job, I got credit card applications in the mail with limits as high as $10,000 – and I had no income. Without reiterating the statistics I have already shown about the dire situation of most Americans, I think we can agree that most Americans have the instant gratification and "I will pay for it later" mind-set. In fact, you can watch car commercials which advertise that new BMW with a lease payment of only $350 a month or that Jet-Ski will only cost $75 a month. Being only concerned with today and this week at best, most Americans will buy, never asking what it will really cost in the end. It is for this reason that Charles Spurgeon once wrote, "Money borrowed is soon sorrowed."[67]

I will take this opportunity to warn you of the dangers of debt. The Bible is not silent on this issue, but at the same time debt is not prohibited. I could go on and on about how credit card interest can compound into infinity and how buying and financing that new car every five years will cost you millions down the road, but I think most people are aware of this. I really feel like if one focuses on the other fundamentals such as prudent spending, saving, and investing and being able to track one's progress with balance sheets and income statements, the mind-set of taking on debt is destroyed and the actuality of debt is lessened to a great degree. You see, debt is really just a by-product of not doing these other fundamentals. If you focus on these others, the by-product will be a healthy amount or no debt at all over time. I do understand that many people, even those who may read this book, have not had that mind-set in the past and have unfortunately taken on more debt than they should have and more certainly than they would have liked. For them, I will just say that you have to have a plan on how to deal with it. If the situation is dire and you sound like a radio caller on the Dave Ramsey show, then you may have to take drastic actions. If your situation with regards to debt is much more manageable, then debt reduction can coincide with saving and investing. Of course I would suggest meeting with a qualified professional to assist with this type of planning as I have with all of the other types of planning. There is certainly no doubt that debt is literally a liability to your wealth building, but it can also be a major liability spiritually and emotionally as well. It is for this reason that a healthy respect for debt is in order, and it should only be incurred when it is economically reasonable or absolutely required.

I will add here that keeping your credit score high is important, regardless of what some "experts" who hate debt may say. Your credit score will enable you to obtain debt at a good rate when needed or desired, as well as affect your costs of things like home and auto insurance. Having lines of credit can also serve as a great asset and even a sort of "emergency fund" for those who are responsible enough to have them.

So there we have it. It is all about the fundamentals. If you can focus on these, there is little doubt that wealth will accumulate and not for the purpose of just storing up money but for living a truly rich life. Most of all, developing a habit of these disciplines will create a lifestyle that has much more opportunities and freedom and hopefully translates into better lives for your children as you teach and model these habits to them. Remember, just like the pro athlete, you should never get past the fundamentals and start putting too much focus on other aspects; just hone the basics. You should major on the majors and minor on the minors. After all, there are professionals who are better equipped and trained who can major on your minors while you are busy living a truly rich life.

CHAPTER 8

The Flight Attendant Hand Jive

A couple of months ago I boarded a plane headed to Philadelphia on business. Like everyone else, I got seated, got out a magazine, and put on my headphones. Like always, once we started pulling away from the terminal, the flight attendant started the familiar routine of pointing out exits and putting on masks – you know the drill. For some reason, I started observing those people around me. One guy, obviously a nervous flyer, fidgeted and swiveled in his seat to locate the emergency exits. Another conscientious observer, a mother, watched intently and even pulled out the pamphlet from the seatback to get the lay of the plane; but the overwhelming majority was completely oblivious to this potentially lifesaving information. In my experience, people act this very same way about most other risks that they face. Of course, there is always the exception, the conscientious mother or the nervous guy; but most have that "it's not going to happen to me" attitude. Admittedly, air travel is pretty safe, but the point remains the same: we should pay attention and act accordingly when "lifesaving" information is being disseminated – so pay attention and listen up.

I recognize that for most people, risk management and insurance are just about their least favorite things to discuss and probably their least favorite things to spend money on. Because of this, we continue to strengthen our procrastination muscles by putting it off or ignoring risks altogether. In fact, we may say we are "thinking about it" or considering alternatives or some other disguise for the real issue, which is often our disgust for paying for insurance. I must remind you, however, that no decision in this area of finances *is a decision*. A decision to "think about it" will work the same as a "no" decision when it all boils down to it. I will give you a "get-out-of-jail-free" card on past offenses, but risk-management issues are something that you and your family cannot afford to put off or look away from anymore.

While I, like most people, don't enjoy looking at life's future with a negative point of view, I find that it is incredibly important that we are at least realistic. As a financial planner for a number of individuals, protecting their wealth is as much a part of what I do as anything – and there are many risks. Unfortunately, trials and tribulations should be expected, and even the "unexpected" should be expected or at least considered in your planning. The reason this is extremely important to point out, besides the fact it is one of the cornerstones of a solid financial plan, is the fact that most people in their optimistic (when concerning themselves) worldview seemingly ignore risks; others are in some kind of state of denial. There are some who psychologically believe that if they ignore risks, then they won't happen, and by recognizing them, they are encouraging them to happen. A simple example is that regardless of horrendous symptoms, many men will not go to the doctor, claiming they are not sick; and they will certainly not go to the doctor for a routine checkup for fear of the doctor finding something. When you think about it, how crazy is that? Only a small portion of the population seems to actually identify with Murphy's Law, "If something bad can happen, it will." In this chapter, I hope to bring to your attention *some* risks that can't be ignored and some basic recommendations as to how to handle them. I will also briefly lay some foundational rules of insurance.

An interesting point to bring up is that youth, or self-perception of youth, drastically causes one to underestimate risks and have faulty assessments of their reality. I say this to hopefully catch the attention of the younger reader who may be about to skip this chapter because they don't think it applies to them. Ernest Hemingway is quoted as saying that "every young man believes he will live forever." I, as well as most people who can remember their youth, will certainly agree; and this phenomenon is not isolated to the male gender, although possibly exaggerated in it. I can remember as a kid growing up in my neighborhood, riding skateboards and bicycles, searching for the next death-defying feat to accomplish while not once recognizing the death-defying nature of any of it. I would jump ramps, scream down hills, etc., and never thought of the consequences (this was before kids wore helmets!). Even when carnage did find me, I somehow blocked it out as a "freak accident" and went on as normal. Many other people I know had similar childhoods. Young adulthood may have changed the activities, but the recognition of risks seems to still be greatly reduced and only has my older age slowly revealed a scarier world. When I was younger, I can't recall people dying of cancer or car wrecks; but today's Sunday school prayer request list seems to be forever full of loved ones that have had a tragedy or are dealing with a serious illness. The fact of the matter is that those things were happening then at a similar rate as today; we just didn't notice. We, everyone, young and old, must see the world with open eyes and not have some enchanted view of how life will be for us. Only God knows what is in store for you and those around you; but you must be a good steward of your life and financial assets, for yourself and those who depend on you.

While the history of insurance can date back to the third and second millennium BC, when Babylonian sailors would insure their ship cargo against piracy or shipwreck, the principles of how it works remains the same.[68] Whether you are insuring your home against fire or insuring an athlete's right arm, the financial mechanism that makes insurance work is the idea of risk pooling. It works like this: everyone, who shares a similar risk, accepts a small loss so that in the event of the insured risk (a big loss) taking place, the pool of money is used to pay that loss. It is this concept, when used in conjunction with carefully formulated statistics and the ability of the insurance company to invest those dollars, which allows insurance companies to cover risks that would otherwise be catastrophic and impossible for the average individual to recover. So all of that is to say that insurance is a wonderful financial tool and the world is much better for it. (I have to state that for all of those people out there that hate insurance.) Now let's move on to some basic principles of risk management.

The first rule of insurance that can really be applied across the board is simply this: you insure the things you can least afford to have happened. I am not talking about minor inconveniences like losing your cell phone but catastrophic risks like dying. Thankfully some risks are required by law to be insured such as liability coverage for automobile drivers and fire coverage on your home. For these types of risks, there is not a way to personally recover from such a loss other than through insurance. I would also include disability, death, and medical expenses to the list of possibly catastrophic risks that *must* be covered.

You see, insurance is not supposed to be a profitable deal for the insured, a so-called "good investment", as I have heard said many times before. Essentially you are excepting a small reoccurring loss (the premium you pay) so that you never have to experience a catastrophic loss. Over time, hopefully it has been like throwing your money down a hole; that just means that you didn't have an unfortunate event take place! However, if you do have a claim, there probably could have been no investment in the world that could have produced as good of a return as that "terrible ole insurance." That is the reason why you don't have to "believe" in insurance, as I often hear; it is simply the only reasonable economic method to transfer many risks that can be financially devastating.

Now, in this chapter I certainly don't have the time or willpower to write concerning every type of insurance available. For instance, I will not comment specifically on whether or not you should insure your cell phone, buy pet health insurance, or take the extra insurance out on the rental car. The reason is twofold: first, you probably don't really care and you probably already have your mind made up on these types of things; second, they are pretty insignificant in the grand scheme of things anyway. Since I have mentioned the cell phone insurance, I will note that if you are terrible about losing things or being careless with them, this insurance was really created for you, even though you are probably not the type to buy the insurance.

Another great maxim I have heard regarding insurance is "Control the things you can and insure the things you can't." Death, disability, illness, and litigation are just some of these "can't control" type of events.

The second basic concept is what I like to call "probable vs. possible." Here is how this concept works. First, ask yourself the first insurance question: can you afford for this risk (event) to happen? If no, then you should probably insure it. If the answer is yes, you can afford for the risk (event) to happen, albeit inconvenient, then you should apply this probable-vs.-possible rule. This will give you a little guidance when it comes to what I would call these more ancillary insurances. Simply ask yourself if the risk you are considering is probable or just possible. Virtually all things are possible, but that doesn't necessarily warrant insurance coverage. A great example would be if an insurer sold lightning-strike insurance that would pay some amount if you got hit by lightning. Essentially this is like buying a lottery ticket; it is possible that the event could happen, but not even close to probable. If it is probable, meaning statistically significant chance of happening, then you should then consider the financial effect if it did happen. A great example of this might be cancer insurance. If you have a family history of cancer, this may be more probable than for a person without a family history; but what would be the financial effect if you were diagnosed with cancer? Do you have sick leave at work, disability insurance, comprehensive health insurance, any savings? You see, for many, cancer insurance might just be a way to profit from an unfortunate illness, not a way to recover a loss. I will discuss this concept further later in the chapter, and I am not weighing the validity of cancer insurance in any specific situation. Take these principles and apply them to all of your insurance purchases; it can help you make prudent decisions as to what should be an insured risk and what risks you should bear on your own.

Now unfortunately, there often exists a little dilemma regarding insurance, particularly life and disability insurance which is this: you need insurance the most when you can least afford to pay the premiums. You see, the time period when you and your family are most vulnerable financially is when you are young, with kids at home, with a great deal of debt, and probably near the beginning of your earning potential. You have a great deal of responsibility, but the budget is tight. I am sorry that this is the time I have to remind you of your convictions and priorities and make sure you do the prudent thing. In most cases, buying the correct amount of life insurance or disability or both is not a question of really busting the budget but more about having to trim a little on the extras that we are so accustomed. No one can make these decisions for you; and often, the people who will be most affected, possibly your children, don't have much of a say in financial matters anyway. I can promise you that if your kids had the intellectual capability to make the decision for you to buy life, health, or disability insurance, they would.

Now let's get a little more specific as to individual risks and how to best manage them. First, we will discuss an area of planning I have a great deal of experience in: life insurance. Life insurance planning can be one of the most difficult insurances to plan for and implement correctly, not because of the complexity of the product but because of the numerous assumptions you have to make in considering how much one needs. I will start by saying you can toss any rules of thumb like "ten times your income"; these are a lazy attempt at solving a tremendously important issue. Most people will need the aid of a professional advisor or at least a financial calculator to figure what amount of income you want to replace for your family, how much debt needs to be liquidated or serviced, and take into account available resources and reasonable rates of return and portfolio depletion. This will generally be a good starting place for how much you need.

I will pause here and mention that I often am surprised that men who love their wife and children will often say things like, "She can get by on this amount of income or she will probably move home with her parents or remarry." Whoa! The point of insuring your life isn't just so your family won't starve; it is so they can have a quality of life that you want them to have. The loss of a loved one will be enough to recover from emotionally without having to deal with serious financial issues. What I believe is really happening in these conversations is there is a little bit of denial that death is a real risk; I mean, after all, I can still run a six-minute mile, right?

So once you come to grips with reality and you get a good starting place with the amount of life insurance that you think you need, it is time to start thinking a little bit bigger in scope. For instance, do you have business expansion plans or plans to buy something new or incur a new debt? Maybe you might inherit some substantial money in a few years and estate taxes may be an issue. Perhaps you know that you are going to make partner in a few years and your income will double or that you and your wife are trying for more children and your family size may double. Take these broader aspects into consideration and realize that it often makes sense to get a little more insurance than you presently need, just in case your insurability changes in the near term. I would hate for a client who is young and healthy to buy a small amount of insurance and then in just a few years, after his family size, income, debts, and lifestyle have grown substantially, to be diagnosed with skin cancer or some heart issue and can't get more insurance to cover the new increased need. If you had just looked a little more into the future and made some realistic assumptions, you might have been able to prepare more prudently. A simple way I often explain this to younger clients is this. Do you remember when you were little and your mom bought you a new pair of shoes or pants? Did she buy them to fit just right for you then, or did she buy them a little bit big? Of course she wisely bought them with "growing room," also a wise tip for life insurance.

Once the appropriate financial need is recognized, the proper type of insurance is the obvious next question. This is a much more difficult decision. For the large majority situations, term insurance is without question the smart and cheap thing to do. Thanks to increasing life expectancies, improved underwriting guidelines, and fierce competition, term insurance is unbelievably cheap for most people. Term insurance, just like the name implies, is for a term, or period of time, and the major question regarding it is how long of a term should you buy. While that is always subject to analysis, I would always get you to consider the unfortunate possibility that you may not be insurable after you get this particular policy. So if you absolutely need insurance for thirty years and you are comfortable with the prospects that you may not be able to get more insurance in the next ten years, then by all means, don't buy a twenty-year term – buy the thirty. Of course, consider costs and projected resources.

There are however many times when permanent life insurance may be a good option. Many people often say that they don't believe in permanent insurance. Again, it is just a financial tool; and if the economics and math work, it should not be dismissed because of a negative stigma. Many financial professions often use permanent insurance where there are multiple needs to protect and accumulate or where there is a low toleration for investment risk but a desire to maximize a legacy to a succeeding generation. Permanent life insurance or cash value life insurance, as some may refer to it, is an incredible financial instrument with unique tax characteristics, but should only be utilized within the context of a comprehensive financial plan and the assistance of qualified advisors. Despite the misinformation that many radio and TV personalities spew, permanent insurance is an irreplaceable tool for any good financial planner who works with wealthy individuals or in estate planning. I would warn you, however, to maintain a healthy skepticism of some life insurance agents who are not financial planners and are pushing permanent life insurance. Not that many of these people aren't well-meaning, but I have rarely seen permanent insurance that has been properly sold and where the client knew of precisely why they had bought it, except in cases where that person had an experienced financial planner and had made the purchase within the context of a comprehensive financial plan.

Moving on, while death is bad financially for a family, disability can be worse. Again, we have a wonderful way of dismissing this risk as some far-fetched possibility when in reality the probability of being disabled for ninety days or longer during your working career is about one in three. Just think about that for a minute; if the breadwinner becomes disabled and can't bring home a paycheck, the bills still have to be paid and that individual is still going to need to eat their next meal. For those husbands I mentioned before that said their wife would get remarried if they died, hopefully that won't be the case if they get disabled and can't work. With very little imagination, I am sure you can visualize how devastating a disability, permanent or temporary, can be to a family.

If you are fortunate enough to work for a large company, chances are you have some group long-term disability coverage; don't take my word for it, you better check. There are several issues with group disability coverage that you should be aware of. First is the definition of disability; most will have a definition that will declare you disabled as long as you can't do the duties of your job and aren't working anywhere else. While this maybe fine for many people, if you are a professional of some type, doctor/lawyer, this could be a limiting factor.

Without getting in to a lot of details regarding disability insurance, there is another more obvious issue with group insurance. Most group insurance will pay around 60 percent of your *base* salary up to a maximum of some amount. Recognize that if your employer pays the premium for you, or if you pay for it on a pretax basis, the monthly benefit will be taxable to you. In many cases, a little quick math will determine that you would be taking a *significant* pay cut if you became disabled. Depending on the burden that may put on you and your family, or, if you don't have any coverage at all, it may be sensible to purchase individual long-term disability coverage.

I will warn you right now, when you find out how much individual long-term disability coverage costs, you may start to get second thoughts; it can be expensive. It is expensive for a reason: the probability of you becoming disabled during you working career is significant. So if you really don't think you can afford the premium right now, just think if you became disabled next month, what could you afford then? It is my view that this is one of those liabilities that can't go unfunded.

Again, with disability insurance policies, the devil is in the details; so an experienced financial planner or disability insurance agent is needed to get a proper plan. They can explain proper coverage amounts, the definition of disability outlined in the policy, taxability issues, and coordination issues with existing coverage. I mention all of this because all too often, a successful person will come to see me and I ask them if they have addressed the risk of disability, they assume they have it all covered because they have group coverage through work. A risk of this magnitude deserves a thoughtful look and decision that is made with the help of a professional.

A close cousin of long-term disability is the need for long-term custodial care. With a rapidly aging population, the threat to society and the risk to the individual that long-term care poses is staggering. The wonderful advancement in the practice of medicine that has dramatically stretched the length of life arguably has not necessarily improved the quality of life for many elderly people. Granted, in many cases I would rather deal with some inconveniences of health than be dead. Doctors and medical advances have taken illnesses that were previously fatal and made them chronic. According to the Health Care Financing Administration, 80 percent of the sixty-five-plus population have one or more chronic diseases, 50 percent have two or more, and 24 percent have problems so severe as to limit their ability to perform one or more activities of daily living.[69] Because of this phenomenon, some have speculated that the average twenty-first-century American will actually spend more years caring for parents than for children. Currently more than twenty-two million households actively provide some type of elder care, and this figure has tripled over the past decade.[70]

The risk of needing some sort of long-term care can't be ignored. The chance of needing long-term care if you are over the age of sixty-five is 43 percent.[71] This is a risk not only regarding your health but possibly your family's financial security. Caregiving is usually attempted first at home by a family member, usually a spouse or a child. Costs of equipment, additional assistance, and loss of income from the caregiver can make even staying at home very expensive for you and for your family. The move to a caregiving facility such as an assisted living facility or a nursing home can be extremely costly. In many cases, don't forget the other spouse is still living and depends on the retirement nest egg to provide for them for the rest of their life. Even a sizeable nest egg can be quickly eroded when care is needed. When these types of expenses mount, where does the money come from to pay? The retirement portfolio that the other spouse still needs? Sale of an asset? From the incomes of children who may have their own families and children to support? It is a tremendous problem, but, thankfully, there can be a solution.

Before I move on to that solution, I breezed past the issue of children having to pay for their parents; so let's go back. While I certainly recognize the Christians' duty to care for their parents and would never recommend shucking that responsibility, let's address the problem that it causes. With the baby boomer population aging, many of whom are unprepared for their own financial future, we are approaching a time when many of their (the baby boomers) parents are in need of care. These boomers have kids in college and high school, are in their peak earning years and trying to make up for lost time in their retirement savings and now having to deal with parents who are in need of long-term care. These boomers are often referred to as the sandwich generation, sandwiched between their kids and their parents. The financial ramification of such a sandwich is untold but is real to a growing number of people. While there is little way of escape for those already in this predicament, there is a solution for the rest of us. That solution lies in the ability to insure such a risk.

To start discussing the details of long-term care insurance (LTC insurance for short), let me first dispel a myth that is commonly held. That myth is that Uncle Sam, better referred to as Medicare and Medicaid, will pay for your long-term care. In reality, it is important to understand a few pivotal characteristics about these government programs. First, Medicare is designed to cover medical, acute care. Crudely put, what this means is that if you have a medical issue which is treatable and curable, Medicare may pay, excluding deductibles and such. It is not designed to pay for *chronic* or custodial care. Also crudely put, custodial care is for ailments which will not get better with treatment. To say it more simply, Medicare wasn't designed or intended to pay for long-term care and thus *will not pay for it.*

Medicaid, however, will pay for long-term care. It is very important to understand that Medicaid was designed as a medical insurance program for the indigent. When they mean poor, they mean poor: less than $2,000 of assets (excluding home value). Of course everyone knows of someone who has beat the system and made themselves poor and qualified for Medicaid which paid for all of their long-term care. Just realize that the government isn't extremely dumb (they may be dumb), and today there are ramifications and potential risks to such planning. While I could discuss this aspect further, let's just leave it at that. "Medicaid planning," is not the way most individuals should want to cover such a big risk; and there is a better way for those in the middle and upper class.

LTC insurance is still relatively a new product in the insurance world; and to be honest, many carriers are still trying to figure out how to assess the risks they are taking. On top of that, many speculate that companies have been pricing policies to take market share in this new area, not to pay claims. Whatever the case may be within the workings of these companies, the good news is they are trying to figure out a way and, for the time being, are doing a great job at covering this terrifying financial calamity. Policies are structured with a lot of different bells and whistles, and even the basic structures of the policies are varied. Some contracts are reimbursement policies, meaning they reimburse paid or charged medical expenses, while others are indemnity and pay a stated amount upon qualifying as needing assistance with the normal activities of daily living. Most policies today include benefits while the insured is being cared for in their own home – no longer just "nursing home insurance" like it was so aptly named in the beginning. There are many variations and features which are all important but are beyond the scope of what I am trying to accomplish in this brief introduction to the subject. What is important to understand is that unlike much insurance, but similar to life and disability insurance, you do have to qualify medically. To keep it simple, don't assume anything about whether or not you can or can't get LTC insurance. Simply ask a professional and when in doubt apply and at worst, get turned down.

Having to qualify medically for LTC does pose quite a dilemma for clients and financial planners alike. The dilemma is this: when do I buy LTC insurance? Do I buy it when I'm fifty or do I wait until I'm sixty, sixty-five, etc.? I will tell you up front that I or any other financial planner, who understands their liability in giving advice, would never tell someone dogmatically that they are too young. If we did, that would end up being the client who became disabled and whose cost of care ravaged their family's nest egg. Of course, no one, including the financial planner, wants to see money spent on insurance premiums when that money could be put to use elsewhere. The decision is always going to have to be made by you, the client, and only after careful consideration of the current cost, the rise in premium for waiting until an older age, and the potential risk of needing this type of care or becoming uninsurable during the "waiting period." It is a decision that is often difficult but one that I would encourage you to consider as rationally as possible. Decisions like this one are not the time to be flexing your optimism muscles.

There is so much to discuss on the topic of long-term care, and the details are beyond the scope of this book. However, this is what is important to know: long-term care costs are a real threat, and insuring that risk is the sensible approach for most people. Also, as if I haven't already said it enough, a qualified financial planner should be sought when considering it. Remember as well, that all of these risk-management decisions, but especially this one, should be made in light of an overarching financial plan. The structure and amount of your other assets as well as your estate-planning goals will weigh heavily on the correct LTC insurance decision.

In discussing and calculating the risk of long-term care, be careful, as I have to remind myself, that this is not only a financial risk but a lifestyle or quality-of-life risk. According to a study by the National Alliance for Caregiving and the AARP, one in five American adults provides unpaid care to another adult.[72] The cost of care will often determine your quality of care and quality of life. Your ability to pay for care will greatly affect the rest of your family's quality of life or lifestyle. It is easy to get into crunching numbers and forget about the realities of this risk – keep them in mind, but remember, it's not all about money.

The last main risk I will discuss in this chapter is one that is a growing concern for many people in the United States: the risk of becoming somebody's lottery ticket via a lawsuit. To start us off in this topic, let's review some urban legends which serve as wonderful examples of actual American justice.

Kathleen Robertson of Austin Texas was awarded $780,000 by a jury of her peers after breaking her ankle tripping over a toddler who was running inside a furniture store. The owners were understandably surprised at the verdict, considering the misbehaving toddler was Ms. Robertson's son.

Nineteen-year-old Carl Truman of Los Angeles was awarded $74,000 and medical expenses when his neighbor ran over his hand with a Honda Accord. Mr. Truman apparently didn't notice there was someone at the wheel of the car when he was trying to steal the hubcaps.

While these examples have been found to be fictitious, there are countless suits like these that would stretch the imagination of any reasonable person. There are some ninety million lawsuits filed by Americans each year, which is about one every three seconds in the United States. While those numbers may not accurately reflect the risk of lawsuit to the average or even wealthy individual, it does show that we live in a litigious society. Add to that the fact that the United States is the only country in the world which permits contingent fee litigation. In all other countries, it is unethical for an attorney to take a case on a contingent fee basis. In addition, in many countries, the plaintiff must post cash with the court to handle the defendant's fees and costs if the plaintiff is unsuccessful. No wonder every year, one out of ten Americans is sued for some reason. There are currently around one million lawyers in the United States, each licensed to file lawsuits. A large percentage of these lawyers (estimated to be as high as 36 percent) are either unemployed or "underemployed". The economic incentive for these underemployed lawyers to file suits and force settlement is simply irresistible.[73]

Living in Alabama and being from Mississippi, I can honestly say that there arguably isn't a worse place than the South to live when it comes to the risk of liability claims. Our court system and the lawyers it has attracted make anyone with financial assets a possible target. Just a short time ago, you wouldn't have imagined seeing the numerous TV ads or billboards with attorneys advertising their legal services, many with no up-front cost to the plaintiff. Everybody is looking for a lottery ticket, which could come in the form of a slip on your front steps or a fender bender at the grocery store. I do understand that not all liability lawsuits are frivolous, but the sheer number of them suggests that many are. What this means to the rest of us is that our wealth and our families' financial security and lifestyles could be in danger.

If you are a professional such as a doctor, lawyer, accountant, or if you have some big title, an unscrupulous attorney has already placed a target on your back. For instance, there are some 13.9 malpractice claims for each one hundred doctors. Four out of ten medical doctors have been sued. The average obstetrician in New York has been sued eight times. Nationwide, the average jury verdict is 1.33 million, and in New

York it is three times larger than that.[74] Due to the nature of the medical profession it is understandable that doctors are sued for issues arising from their practice; but their liability, like everyone else, doesn't stop at the door of their practice. For this reason, it makes sense to protect your assets.

When I suggest protecting your assets, I am not suggesting that you not pay someone you have wronged or shuck your responsibility in a legitimate situation; but I am suggesting that you have much more control over the issue and not get taken for everything you own, especially on a frivolous claim.

"Asset protection" planning is really just prelitigation planning designed to help resolve a future and unforeseen issue in the most favorable way. In many cases, it is less expensive and disruptive to buy peace, i.e., reach a favorable settlement, rather than fight on principle. A good asset protection plan is not some bold "you can't get me" type of plan, and shouldn't be, but rather a number of decisions that were made for a number of reasons, with asset protection as a kind of added benefit. For instance, having large amounts of money in IRAs serves the purpose of retirement planning while at the same time protecting those monies from creditors. If you live in a state with a homestead exemption, it may make sense to pay off your mortgage (not necessarily a bad financial move either). Separating risky assets like rental property into separate entities away from your personal assets is yet another example of a common technique that makes sense not only from an asset protection planning standpoint but on a number of other fronts as well. Things as simple as ownership/title changes in conjunction with adequate homeowners/auto liability coverage and an overarching umbrella liability policy are a good start for managing this risk. There are, as you may imagine, a litany of techniques that also include things like trusts, LLCs, life insurance, and of course, those offshore accounts everyone likes to talk about.

I reiterate, the purpose of this type of planning should not be overtly "you can't get my money" as this is not viewed favorably by judges or juries. These techniques are used to achieve other purposes, but of course, with the understanding of this protection benefit. It only makes sense to discourage a greedy TV lawyer from pursuing settlements over your basic liability insurance coverage and stop the bleed over from one set of assets to another. After all, if you are an ambulance-chasing attorney, why pursue something that is going to be a nightmare to try and get, when there will be more "victims" whose target hasn't done adequate planning and will be much easier to cash in on? I am not condoning this type of legal practice but just recognize that it exists. The goal is to be able to structure a more favorable settlement and have more control over the issue. Hopefully, you will never get sued and the other benefits of the techniques you used serve you in other ways. A qualified attorney and a financial planner can work together with you to address this increasing risk and discuss the other "main" reasons for doing this type of planning.

Unfortunately, I do have to provide yet another warning with regards to this type of planning. There are "professionals" who travel around and give seminars, some even "endorsed" by credible associations, who would sell their "asset protection system." They are pretty convincing people and may even correctly discuss some of the techniques. My main warning to you with regards to these circus acts is that they often have software or pre-done forms for you to draft your own legal documents and to do these complicated strategies on your own. Any attorney worth their salt would tell you that these documents provide a false hope that they will accomplish what you intend them to. It only makes sense that any legal document should be specifically written by a qualified attorney in that field for each specific situation for each particular state. If it is important enough to go to the trouble to do this type of planning, then it is important enough to make sure it is done properly. It should be also noted, as I have tried to make clear, that if you are engaging in this type of planning for the sole purpose of defrauding creditors or potential creditors, then your plans will probably not hold water in the courtroom and may make a judge or jury just downright mad.

As a Christian, I want to make it clear that I am not advocating skirting responsibility here; but I am recognizing that the risk this imposes and the potential consequences of a lawsuit, for whatever reason, can be devastating to your family if you don't proactively plan.

In summary, part of living a truly rich life is planning for potential snares and pitfalls that you may encounter along the way. I mentioned some of the main risks to plan for and some basic principles to help guide you. It was no accident either that I repeatedly mentioned that the help of a qualified professional should be sought. This recommendation is not simply to promote my profession or allied professionals self-servingly but to emphasize to you the value that can be provided by these professionals. Finally, I should mention that there are an uncountable amount of risks that face us all, and, of course, it would be impossible to insulate ourselves from all of them. New risks such as identity theft are popping up every day. We should develop a new thought process of how to manage our risks the best we can and take advantage of the instruments and laws that are available to us today. Once we have done what we can, we should live free of worry and trust that the Lord will take care of the rest.

CHAPTER 9

The Psychologically Impaired Investor

Perhaps one of the most interesting, complicated, and critical areas of financial dealings is that of investing. Investing is also one of the areas where I see the most self-destructive behavior and the most damage done to families' financial futures. In this chapter I hope to make the case that the biggest threat to the average investor is *themselves*.

As I am sure you know and have heard, everyone has their own slant on how to get rich in the market; and while I am not about to handily dismiss all of these, before you give them any validity, I would ask you to first consider the source. For instance, if the investment advice is from a book, magazine, or TV, then I must ask you to remember the maxim, "Don't believe everything you read or hear on TV." The fact that it is widely distributed doesn't make it true and after all, our media's main motivations are self-promotion and the almighty dollar so the more extravagant the claim, the more spotlights and attention they will draw, the better they like it. TV programming is driven by ratings and magazines and books driven by circulation and the end goal is to make money and thus they will provide and propagate to the consumer what sells. CNBC would have a pretty low viewership if they got on and said that stock picking should be left to the professionals and that the market is too difficult to predict, so stop trying! That doesn't sell! They have to tell you the breaking news or hottest stock tip of the summer or the possibility of the chairman of the Federal Reserve getting a cold which will make him cranky which could affect interest rates! They provide news, then analysis, then analysis of the analysis; and it is very easy to get caught up in all of these very "important" matters.

While I would love to jump right into planting seeds of wisdom regarding the fundamentals of investing, I feel the overwhelming need to first plow the ground a little. You see, many economists, investors, and even financial academics are of the belief that investors are rational and make the best possible choice after review of all available information before deciding to buy or sell an investment. In reality, both individual and group psychology have a lot to do with how and why we make the decisions we do.

To aid me in my pursuit of "ground plowing," I will introduce you to a topic you are probably not familiar with: behavioral economics. With utmost confidence, I can say that nearly all of an individual's investment decisions, and all types of financial decisions for that matter, can be explained by behavioral economics: a combination of psychology and economics to explain why and how people make seemingly irrational or illogical decisions when they spend, invest, save, and borrow money. The study of such things has been around for some time now but has been brought to the forefront of the financial world by Amos Tversky and Daniel Kahneman, psychologists whose paper on the subject won the Nobel Prize in economics in 2002. I mention it in this chapter simply because its effects seem to be exaggerated due to the anxiety-producing world of investing.

I am sure many of you at this point are thinking, "This doesn't apply to me" – I will certainly let you be the judge. I challenge you though and am confident that many of these issues, if not all of them, affect your decision making in some way. You see, although we would like to think that we are intelligent individuals and we *always* make rational decisions that are in our best interests at all times, the fact remains that we are inherently emotional and oftentimes our emotional decision making is *not* in our best interest. Many psychologists and researchers would even suggest that even those analytical types out there still make emotional decisions; they simply put their analytical muscles to work to justify the decision they have already made.

At this point you are probably still skeptical, so let me begin. I will briefly discuss several of the emotional biases classified and how they plague our investing decisions. The first emotional bias I will address is one that will undoubtedly chafe your pride a little (it did mine). Simply put, you're not as smart as you think you are. Said more sophisticatedly, it is referred to by psychologists who study this sort of things as *overconfidence bias or grandiosity*. Don't believe me? A 1981 survey of automobile drivers in Sweden showed that 90 percent of them described themselves as above-average drivers. Other studies have been done where factual questions were asked to a group of respondents and they were in turn asked to give the percent of confidence that they had in their answer. Interestingly enough, the questions that were answered incorrectly had percentages of confidence in those answers that were exceedingly high.[75] Authors Gary Belsky and Thomas Gilovich, in their book *Why Smart People Make Big Money Mistakes*, use this question to prove this point: How do you pronounce the capital of Kentucky? "Loo-ee-ville" or "Loo-is-ville?" How much would you bet on that answer: $5, $50, $500?[76]

I will answer the question in just a minute, but let me continue. You may ask, "How does that translate into financial decisions or investing?" I submit to you that part of the reason why more than two-thirds of small businesses fail or why can't-miss real estate deals end up missing is this little thing called overconfidence.

Back to the capital of Kentucky question; how much did you bet? Well, unless you pronounced the capital of Kentucky as "Frankfort," then you just "confidently" lost a large amount of money. This bias is the reason that people, despite not really planning for their financial futures, think they will be peachy and the same reason that most people, when they invest money, think it is a sure winner. Overconfidence explains why nearly every investor became so smart in the mid to late 1990s and was shocked when the market turned south. It is also the same bias that drives those investors who, despite no formal training, decide that they are going to plan their own retirement and manage their investments themselves using some online brokerage site. Surely no one would risk their financial well-being over a small cost of an advisor if they thought for one second that they couldn't do it themselves. The problem is they think they can. Most people infected with this inflated confidence likewise think they are better at identifying the next hot stock than everyone else even though everyone has access to the same if not better information than they do and some are highly trained professionals.

By the way, bookstores are full of books for people of the overconfident type, the do-it–yourselfer; so be careful on what advice you take. Online brokerage and trading sites continually have TV and print ads showing some successful-looking silver-headed retiree sitting at his computer in his home library trading anxiety free and making easy money. Trust me, that is definitely not reality TV! The do-it-yourselfer, overconfident type is chock-full of optimism which is a main cause of people exaggerating their talents and leads people to underestimate the possibility of bad outcomes which they have no control over. Now we can understand how so many are victimized by the "big bad stock market."

Overconfidence is just one of many biases that hinder our decision making, and the consequences of this inflated self-image can be catastrophic to your wealth and overall well-being.

Unfortunately at the same time, most people tend to stay overconfident because of another bias called *confirmation bias*. Simply put, people remain overconfident because they have a convenient way of suppressing or forgetting their failures and clinging to their successes, or put another way, "Heads I win, tails it's chance." Psychologists' research shows that people attribute their success in any situation to their own ability and disregard failure due to poor circumstances or "chance." Now I am certainly not trying to destroy any healthy self-esteem mechanism that God has put in you or diminish the fact that sometimes things do just seem to go against you, but I think a healthy dose of reality is in order for everyone from time to time. The fact is that many people invest money in the market with no real strategy and if it goes up, then they think they are pretty smart and if it goes down, then it was just some anomaly. This is potentially very destructive behavior. This is the same attitude that keeps the amateur day trader burning through money when a reasonable person would stop. This is not financially or emotionally healthy, and it is certainly not good stewardship.

Another emotional bias that most investors portray is the tendency to compartmentalize money; some refer to this as *mental accounting*. While this can be beneficial in some instances, and for the most part, isn't as terrible of a wealth destroyer as others, it is very prevalent and it does somewhat hinder good investment strategy. For instance, let's say you have an investment account, IRAs, and a 401(k) – oh yeah, don't forget your CDs at the bank. Rather than seeing the whole investment picture, people have the tendency to look at the individual performances of each account. It is this mental block that causes people to not pay off high credit card debt when they have money sitting in savings; they simply have an aversion to seeing the big picture. Most people have a tendency to say, "My CDs are my money my grandmother gave me, and I don't want to use them to pay off this debt." To the person with this issue, it makes sense; to an outsider looking in, it seems ridiculous.

Due to differing tax treatments and performance characteristics of different types of investments, this can become an even bigger problem. Let's assume you have a person in their fifties who is preparing for retirement and they have two accounts: one is tax qualified like an IRA and the other is simply a brokerage account with no tax advantages. Their investment plan calls for an allocation of 60 percent stocks and 40 percent bonds. Since bonds produce interest which is currently taxed at ordinary income rates, it might make sense to hold them in the IRA so that there is no present tax due and since it will be taxed at ordinary income rates in the future anyway. The stocks, whether dividend paying (which is currently taxed at a special 15 percent tax rate) or just appreciating, might be held in the nonqualified account since the appreciation is deferred until the stock is sold and if held for a year is at the low long-term gains tax rate. While all of this may make complete economic sense, most investors would never do this; and even most advisors are afraid to do this because they fear that clients may see the "all-stock" portfolio fluctuate much more wildly than the bond portfolio and have the tendency to compare the two accounts instead of seeing how they are working in tandem. So what they do instead is hold 60 percent stocks and 40 percent bonds in each account, possibly a sub par solution.

You may be affected by mental accounting when asked how your investments are doing; you say, "Terrible, my IRA is down 12 percent," while at the same time you have some old bonds that are doing great and your 401(k) at work (which is allocated differently) is holding steady. Compartmentalizing money can be helpful at times, but it is important to remember to think more "big picture" in most cases when investing.

Kahneman's Nobel Prize-winning research dealt with another very interesting bias referred to as *anchoring*. What he found is that depending on how the situation was framed, either positively or negatively, affected the perceived probability of an outcome.

Example 1: you choose the best situation

a. 80 percent probability to win $4,000, 20 percent probability of winning $0
b. 100 percent probability of winning $3,000

Example 2: you choose the best situation

a. 80 percent probability to lose $4,000, 20 percent of not losing anything
b. 100 percent probability of losing $3,000

In the first scenario, even though (a) had a higher expected value (80% x $4,000 = $3,200), 80 percent of those surveyed chose the safer choice (b). In the second question, 92 percent of the participants picked the riskier option (a). What these questions show is that depending on how the situation is framed, people have very strong differences in the choices they will make. In fact, one of the main findings of Kahneman's research was that investors fear losses nearly twice as much as they value gains.[77]

It is this phenomenon that leads investors to overvalue certainty and be willing to pay a high cost for it, which explains the recent demand for companies in the annuity business to offer "guarantees" on investments. Being a planner throughout this last bear market, I can't tell you how large a demand that was created for investment products that have "guaranteed" returns of some kind or protection from losses. While I am glad that many of these products were created, because they do fill a need for some clients, many people are willing to pay extremely high costs to get those "guarantees," which in the long run are probably to their detriment.

At this point you may be wondering how this framing effect they referred to as anchoring works in the real world. Simply put, it states that people tend to anchor their predictions in the present. If things are currently bad, the prediction will be bad; if the current conditions are good, the predictions will be positive. If you asked a person in 1999 what their expectation of the market was several years in the future, they would have said 20-plus percent; after all, we were in a "new paradigm" or a "new economy." If you asked today, in January of 2006, the same question, the answer would be far different. The danger is not in some hypothetical question but in how investors decide when and how they are going to invest; you can be sure that it has a great deal to do with the present situation and little else.

Take another "anchor" that is common with investors. Very often, an investor does not want to sell a stock anywhere below its all-time high stock price; they have anchored that number in their minds. At the same time, I would speculate that none of them can recall what the earnings of the company were at that time or any other relevant information related to the stock price. You see, our mind and our emotions lock onto some piece of information, anchor to it, and that is what steers our decision making, regardless of its validity.

"Adding to the effects of anchoring is the role of regret – a powerful, often paralyzing force. Research shows that the regret people feel after taking an action that has costly consequences is far more intense than the regret that comes from the costly consequences of not taking action."[78] The fear of regret explains why you may still be hanging on to that stock that has fallen for fear that it might actually turn around and come back. This phenomenon is what is commonly referred to as regret aversion which is where investors avoid actions that may cause a feeling of regret, such as selling a stock and "realizing" the loss or the fear of selling a stock when it is high for fear that it might go higher. What this phenomenon causes is the investor to sit in the stands and chew off their fingernails with anxiety and leaves little opportunity for any proactive change. People have a tendency to regret taking an action more than inaction. Many times it leads investors to "deer in the headlights" type of reaction where they think if they ignore the problem it will go away. Unfortunately, not making a decision is a decision; and much like the deer that doesn't move, your problem might get worse in a hurry.

Another close relative of this psychological glitch is "cognitive dissonance" which is simply ignoring that there is a problem when the circumstances clearly show there is. The consequences of denying a bad investment mistake can be worse than the initial mistake. It is much better to confront the problem and take an action, something that is sometimes easier said than done.

"Availability bias" is another factor that most of us have messing with our decision-making ability. Said simply, "the more you hear something, the more you believe it." Unfortunately, the media again plays a major role in our emotional health and affects our decision-making ability when it comes to investing. As Peter Lynch says, "a bull market must scale a wall of worry, and the worries never cease."[79] It is very difficult to convince yourself that now is a good time to invest when CNBC and the news keep barking negative news 24-7. In fact, studies show that the negative bias in media is 17:1, negative news to positive.[80] With that being the case, it is no wonder that people invest at the wrong times. Peter Lynch is right in saying that "people are advised to think long term, but the constant comment on every gyration puts people on the edge and keeps them focused on the short term."[81] For that reason, "small investors tend to be pessimistic and optimistic at precisely the wrong times, so it's self-defeating to try to invest in good markets and get out of bad ones." He further goes on to say that "the stock market demands conviction as surely as it victimizes the un-convinced."[82]

This issue wasn't such a big influence fifteen years ago when the most you would hear about the market was a quick one-minute recap of what the Dow Jones did sometime after sports on the evening news. Just think about it, until the 1990s, no one followed the market closely and there certainly weren't TV stations and entire networks devoted to it. Think back at the magazine stands fifteen years ago. How many personal finance magazines were there? Not many. The media jumped on the unprecedented climb of the market during the 1990s, and it became en vogue to "follow the market". All this and I haven't even mentioned the effect of the Internet on disseminating information and disinformation.

Today's investor who wants to not be affected by the emotional pull of the media would almost have to lock themselves in a closet; it is everywhere. I am not suggesting that you avoid all market information, but what I am saying is be aware of the effect it has on your emotions and your decision making. Just because everybody is saying that some sector of the market is going to do really well over the next three years doesn't mean it is going to happen. Likewise, just because things look grim in the short run doesn't mean that you should go to cash.

This "availability" bias is closely related to "familiarity bias" where investors are much more comfortable with risks that they have already taken as opposed to a new risk. Studies show that given two investments, a familiar but riskier investment and one unfamiliar but safer, subjects will choose the familiar one. This phenomenon might be part of the reason that American investors truly believe, without consulting any research or reason, that the U.S. market is safer and superior to foreign markets. The unfamiliarity causes many to not invest and diversify overseas despite research that proves that doing so is beneficial. And if you think that it is just because we might truly have the better market, how would you explain that those in other countries feel the same way about their familiar market?

I almost feel the need to put this paragraph in bold all capital letters, because I have yet to run into a retiree from a big company that this issue didn't exist. What else can explain why people hold such a large amount of their retirement money in their company stock? If you ask them to invest half or 75 percent of their money in any other single stock, they would think you had lost your mind. On the contrary, many are perfectly comfortable owning their company stock and if anything are skeptical of the rest of the market despite much less overall risk. I will address diversification in detail later in this book, but please realize that familiar does not mean safe. Enron, WorldCom, Tyco, HealthSouth, and Lucent employees will be happy to steer you straight on this one – just ask them.

Another investing bias is referred to as the house money effect. Much like a gambler who has just won and is "in the black", many investors after a significant investment gain are willing to be much more aggressive with that new money because it is "house money" and not really theirs (at least in their minds). The euphoria of the winnings often turns to just plain moronic decision-making ability; and as you can guess, many quickly lose their "winnings." Why else do you think casinos are willing to put "winners" up in the swanky complimentary suite? They know that people will play very loose with their new winnings and eventually give most, if not all of it, back to the casino. I am using a gambling example, but this same type of behavior is very common with many investors, or even business owners for that matter.

The other side of that same coin is a phenomenon I call the "snake bit effect," where an investor is much less averse to investing after losing money. It is important to remember that the game hasn't changed since you lost; your attitude has just shifted to a much more pessimistic or possibly realistic level. To be honest, this bias is one that I worry about with a new client. Even though I have hopefully done a good job at counseling that client about our investment strategy, I truly hope and pray that the first couple of months will go well; because I know that people have a tendency to doubt the wisdom of our strategy if it mounts any losses early on. While there is nothing I can do to control the markets, this is a phenomenon that I see regularly; and I don't want an early negative experience to shift that client's risk tolerance to an unnatural and unwarranted level of conservatism.

Another interesting fact about how people's minds work is a phenomenon called heuristics. Simply put, the brain often handles large amounts of information and complex ideas by using rules of thumb, shortcuts, or even stereotypes. These rules for decision making are called heuristics. Here is an example of how this might work. Consider Joe who lives in a town where there are only two types of occupations. The vast majority of the population has jobs that can be categorized as manual labor, and a very small fraction of the population are lawyers. With that information, answer the following question about Joe who lives in this town.

> Joe drives a luxury car, wears glasses, is short and portly, loves to drink scotch, and enjoys a good game of golf. Is Joe (a) a manual labor worker or (b) an attorney?

Now many people would probably say that Joe is an attorney; and by doing so, they are ignoring the *main* fact that the vast majority of people in the town are *not* lawyers. Your brain, in handling those details about Joe, quickly and almost without detection made a connection to some of the stereotypical aspects of a lawyer and ignored the main fact that most of the people were manual labor workers. Investors commonly do the same thing when presented with enormous amount of information (the main facts); they make a decision based on a stereotype or shortcut previously established. This is why many today, regardless of the potential of IBM or Microsoft stock, think they are good investments and would invest in them without hesitation.

The human brain is also interesting in its ability to look for and find patterns, even where none exist. Numerous statistical researches have been done on what some call representativeness, and people's ability to find interesting patterns through historical data to support some new investment strategy. The problem is that while a "pattern" may have existed for some period in the past, there often is no support that it will persist in the future. Let me give you a perfect example. Let's say that we went mining through historical stock performance data and found that the third Tuesday of every other month over the last five years has been an extraordinary day for small drug company stocks. While that may be an interesting fact, meaning it did occur, it has no predictive value whatsoever because it cannot be accounted for by any other reason than chance. Our minds and our greed often significantly undervalue chance or randomness when viewing events, particularly investments.

A close cousin to representativeness is what some refer to as gambler's fallacy which is the self-perceived ability to predict when a trend will change. Give yourself this quick test. Let's say I have flipped a coin fives times in a row and it has come up heads all five times, what do you think it will be on the next flip? Most people would say that it is probably going to be tails, but the probability of that event does not rely in any way on the previous flips and therefore is still fifty-fifty. Nevertheless, our hunch is strong and if we are right, we will pat ourselves on the back and if we are wrong, we quickly forget about it.

Lastly, as far as patterns that may have some support in the market, some reasoning behind them as to why they occur, I wouldn't get too carried away about them either. Chances are that others have the same idea and will exploit that idea so much so that the opportunities quickly go away or change altogether. Put away your crystal ball; trust me, it's broken.

Now if these internal psychological factors weren't enough, they are accentuated by group psychological factors as well and can trap even the most intellectual of us, as it did to Sir Isaac Newton in 1720 when he lost his shirt in the South Sea Bubble. It is after this that he lamented, "I can calculate the motions of heavenly bodies, but not the madness of people." What he fell subject to is what many deem herd mentality or "the madness of crowds," and it is the result of social pressure. Michael Horwitz, PhD, CFP, in his article "Mob Mentality" gives this example. Let's say you are walking down the street and all the sudden everyone else is running in the opposite direction, what are you going to do? You don't stop and take a comprehensive view of the situation; you spin and start running in the opposite direction too. You run not because of "social pressure" in the strict sense but of "social proof." You don't know why they are running, but surely they know something you don't; they must have information that warrants such a response. When information is limited, "herd mentality" can be a positive factor (if people are running the opposite way on the street, by all means, turn and run!); but it can also be detrimental to your investments.[83] The Internet bubble of the 1990s, the so-called tech wreck, was a perfect example of herd mentality; everyone was relying heavily on the information of others. When Internet stocks were "in favor," life was good; but when the tide shifted, the aftermath left many in its wake to which they are still trying to recover. Try to not rely too heavily on the ever-changing emotions of other investors; as Sir Isaac Newton found out, the madness of crowds is impossible to predict.

I am not predicting another mania just around the corner; but if history comes around as it has in the past, we will probably experience another "bubble" in the market in the future. Bubbles or periods of rampant speculation in the market are not unique to the last few years with the "tech wreck" of 2000 and 2001. I point this out to just give more confirmation that this emotional frenzy does happen, and it does happen on a large scale from time to time. The first documented case of frenzied speculation happened in Holland. While the pilgrims were settling on our shores in Massachusetts, people in Holland were bidding increasingly higher prices for tulip bulbs – yes, flower bulbs! This "tulip mania" episode of the mid-1600s incredibly had people taking out loans on their home to purchase bulbs they didn't intend to plant. They were buying them for the sole purpose of selling them to someone else at a huge profit. Prices soared to modern-day equivalent of tens of thousands of dollars *per* bulb. Like all bubbles, it eventually burst.[84] This bubble was followed by France's Mississippi Bubble in 1719-1720, then the South Sea Bubble that got Newton in 1720, the Roaring '20s U.S. bull market that was followed by the "great crash" in 1929, the Japanese "bubble economy" in 1984-1989, and then the still-painful Internet bubble of the late 1990s. Why didn't people see the handwriting on the wall with these? As investing legend Benjamin Graham puts it, "Uncontrolled optimism can lead to mania, and one of the chief characteristics of mania is the inability to recall the lessons of history"[85]

It would seem easy to just ignore what everyone else is doing; because after all, you aren't really concerned with their investments, you are concerned with yours, right? In reality, neuroscientists have found that real pain (physical pain) and social pain caused by going against the crowd so to speak are felt in exactly the same places in the brain. Dr. Eisenberger and Lieberman in their 2004 study on the subject showed that taking that contrarian investment view, buying while others are selling and selling while others are buying is about like having your fingers hit with a hammer routinely.[86] While it may be somewhat painful on your own to go against the crowd, a levelheaded advisor might just be that word of confirmation needed that you are doing the right thing that could make taking such an action bearable.

Emotional biases are often increased dramatically when certain "liquidity events" take place. What I mean by a liquidity event is some time in your life when a lot of money becomes liquid or accessible; for instance, at the death of a spouse, retirement, a divorce, sale of a business or a property, a lawsuit settlement, or at the termination of a trust. It is during these times especially that you should be aware that you may not be in the right frame of mind to make a rational decision about your money, and it is normally the time when most people want to make the biggest decisions with their money. I suggest two things to help reduce the chance of a big mistake: first, prior planning should be done and second, a cooling-off period.

If you have been planning for the event a reasonable amount of time before it happens, it allows for clearer, less emotional decision making and can drastically help reduce the anxiety produced once the event does happen. You can already have a plan in place as to how to handle the money or have already set a period of time that you will wait until you will make any important spending or investing decisions.

If you have not planned ahead or if the event was unexpected, as deaths can often be, it is very, very important that you do not make irreversible decisions early on. This sounds like common sense, and it is, but you would be surprised how many recipients of estate assets who want to move, buy and pay for a new house, give the kids money, and invest in some property all within six months of receiving the inheritance. Even without financial counsel, I can promise you that their decisions would be different if they just waited until the emotion was less apart of the decision.

Rushing into decisions not only leads to increased anxiety which is burdensome but also results in big mistakes.

Another reason to avoid a cascade of financial decisions, besides possibly an irrational state of mind, is what I will call a lack of mental endurance. Research shows that individuals seem to tire as a result of multiple decisions, and their decision-making ability begins to deteriorate. So whether or not you may be making rational decisions at first, most people faced with multiple decisions end up making sub par decisions the more they continue making. The lesson to take away here is clear, especially with application in the world of investing. The fewer major decisions you can make in a short period of time, the better. This is also yet another straw placed on the back of the day-trading/stock-picker mentality.

I spend so much time explaining these psychological issues not to destroy all confidence you may have but to hopefully prove to you that 99 percent of people are emotional decision makers. Even the most analytical thinkers probably only use their analytical skills to justify their emotional decision. The 1 percent that are truly analytical you will probably never meet because they are at home ironing their underwear. I also believe that in realizing your biases and setting guidelines for decision making beforehand, you can prevent these costly errors. Besides the fact that I find these types of studies intriguing, it is these types of biases that I try to avoid myself, in my own practice and in my own financial life. Don't be fooled for one second that your advisor or broker isn't susceptible to all of the aforementioned phenomena; they too are human and emotional beings. Amateur investors are not isolated in this type of behavior. Studies of brokers and professional institutional investors show that there is much more excessive trading in their accounts than is justified on rational grounds. I will make sure I add the caveat that a good advisor has an investing philosophy and strategy that recognizes their own emotional weaknesses and doesn't rely upon "picking a winner" or "timing the market" as their primary means of achieving investment returns.

I will help end my argument with this final nail in the coffin. While I will mention the following study in the next chapter in more detail, I feel I must go ahead and mention it here for those of you who think I am giving the average investor a bad wrap. A study was done from 1984-2002 by the Dalbar Institute which showed the following staggering facts:

> From 1984-2002, while the market returned 12.2 percent, the average equity mutual fund returned 9.3 percent, but the average investor return was only 2.6 percent. In more detail, a study in 2004 found that the systematic investor earned 6.8 percent, and the market timer lost 3.29 percent. The average fixed-income investor actually outperformed the average equity investor. [87]

I will explain further in the next chapter some of the other causes of these dismal returns, but the main reason can be linked directly to emotional decision making.

Emotions will generally tell you what you most want to hear – obviously the wrong thing to listen to when investing money.

It should be noted, however, that our emotions are not all bad and do help us make decisions, just not always the right ones. Without an emotional response, a completely analytical thinker will oftentimes be paralyzed by the information, what I like to call analysis paralysis. So that being said, it is our emotions that eventually get us off the sidelines and help us to take an action. We just need to make sure it is a correct action.

Over the last year, I have become somewhat of a fan of watching these high-stakes poker tournaments on TV. I want to be clear. I am not a fan of people who gamble away hard-earned money, but it is the similarities between poker and investing that I can't seem to get away from. Successes in both are ultimately driven by the numbers, but emotion plays a big part. It is no surprise that the same people end up at the final table in these big poker tournaments; it is because they are able to stick to a strategy, allow time for the numbers to work in their favor, and avoid the mistakes that are driven by emotional decision making. Of course, the element of bluffing adds a little different element to the mix with poker; but most of the time decisions are made on a very clear-cut system of decision making: drawing odds, pot odds, etc. Investing is really very similar, especially in that just like these poker tournaments, those who don't follow a strict set of investing rules end up making emotional bets, which in the long run allows the few people who do stay the course to end up with most of the money. The good news for investors is that investing for the most part is not a zero-sum game, and it is possible for everyone to make money as long as the underlying companies make money. I also enjoy watching poker because it allows you to see how quickly players are willing to adapt their strategy in an irrational manner in the heat of the moment. It is very common to get a strong hunch that your luck is about to turn, the very same type of hunch that investors think is going to make them their next big winner. True investing is not gambling, but what many people are doing in the market is very similar to a poker game among ten-year-olds.

The case I am trying to make I think is pretty clear: investing is serious business and it demands a clear objective, direction, and conviction. We are emotional beings – unfortunately, when bombarded with tons of information and disinformation, it is no wonder most people do so poorly. If you are aware of this, I believe that in your humbleness you are more likely to rely on the advice of professionals and/or after careful consideration of your options on your own. One of my favorite quotes from the most successful investor of all times, Warren Buffett, is, "The market, like the Lord, helps those who help themselves . . . But unlike the Lord, the market does not forgive those who know not what they do."[88]

CHAPTER 10

The Raw Materials in the Construction of Wealth

There is the risk you cannot afford to take, and there is the risk you cannot afford not to take.

– Albert Einstein

There are two rules to investing. The first rule is don't lose. The second is don't forget rule number 1.

– Warren Buffett

In my dealings with clients over the years, I have found that a large percentage of the individual investors really have very little understanding as to what they are investing in or how in the world they are going to make money in doing so. Simply put, they know that they are *supposed* to invest and they know that over a long period of time they are supposed to make money. While both of those statements are true for the most part, it is important to understand why it makes sense to put your hard-earned money in the market or any investment for that matter. Knowledge of investing can help you to feel more comfortable in what is now a necessity of life and can help you be a better investor which ultimately pays dividends in all areas of your life. I have read many investing books, many of the do-it-yourself genre, that like to put investing into a sort of "can't-miss" box and make it seem as if anybody with half a brain can "beat the market." I have to confess that this chapter doesn't quite tell that story, nor is it going to make you into any kind of expert on the subject. Frankly, investing and the markets are extremely complicated and can't be fit into neat little boxes that are easy to understand. There are many components which are all in a constant state of flux, and there is even a small degree of variability that even the smartest academic has a hard time putting their finger on. Investing, however, *is* a necessity for nearly everyone's financial future; and there are some fundamental keys that can take you from being an anxiety-ridden victim to someone participating in an exciting producer of wealth. In this chapter, I will lay out some basic components in the market, a few more investments which you should be familiar with, and finally discuss the financial markets in general. While money isn't the sole determinant of a truly rich life, poor investing or not investing in most all cases (at least in this country) is not a path that leads to a rich and fulfilling life – we must at least learn the basics.

Before I get into the meat of the coconut, let me first answer an objection before it even gets brought up in your mind (especially for you conservative types out there). Why is it wise to invest in the first place? A short answer which might not suffice is, it just makes sense to allow your money to work for you. More specifically, it is because of a little thing Albert Einstein called *the greatest mathematical discovery of all time*: the power of compounding interest. The concept of compounding interest is simple; it is kind of like rolling a snowball for a snowman. You can start with a small amount; as it gains size, it begins to continue to grow exponentially because each new increase begets more increase– astounding. To accentuate its power, let's consider the following examples:

The Manhattan Indians sold New York City in 1626 for $24. Had they invested that $24 and earned 7 percent over those 338 years, it would have grown to *$2.8 trillion.*

Francis I of France paid Leonardo da Vinci $20,000 for the Mona Lisa in 1540. Had he invested the same amount and earned 6 percent, his investment would be worth *$1 quadrillion* (that's a million billion) today.

Those examples may seem a little ridiculous, but the math holds true. You can develop your own more realistic example by using a simple rule that shows the power of compound interest: the rule of 72. The rule of 72 simply states that if you take an interest rate and divide it by 72, the result is the number of years it will take an amount to double if it grows by that rate. For instance, if an asset grows at 10 percent annually ($10 \div 72 = 7.2$), it will double in 7.2 years; or if your asset grows at 7.2 percent, it will double in ten years. This little rule can quickly show you a more realistic example of the power of compounding interest. To harness that power does not only make a lot of sense, but in today's world, it is a necessity.

Compound interest is an extremely powerful force. If you do a few calculations you will quickly see that the number of years an amount compounds has a large effect on the end result. This is why I would encourage everyone to invest as much as possible as soon as possible in order to take advantage of this powerful force and would warn anyone of the consequences of waiting. Let's look at an example to make this a little clearer. Let's say you have two individuals; one is Diligent Dave and the other is Procrastinating Pete. Both have thirty years until retirement. Diligent Dave decides to invest $5,000 a year starting now and invests for only ten years, for a total of $50,000 invested. Procrastinating Pete, however, decides that retirement is a long way away and he would rather wait so he doesn't start investing for ten years. Starting in year eleven to thirty, he invests $5,000 a year for a total of $100,000 invested. Both investors have good market returns and earn 10 percent annually. The question is simple, who has more money in the end? Pete invested twice as long and twice as much but got a slow start. Would you guess Diligent Dave had the most? Over the years at various financial talks, I have used this example; in most cases people correctly pick Diligent Dave as the winner, but few have guessed that his investment would have grown to $536,095 while Procrastinating Pete's $100,000 investment only grew to $286,375 (that's nearly twice as much!). I hope this simple example makes the point; compounding is tremendously powerful, and getting started early can't be emphasized enough.

Some might try and use this example in a negative fashion, as I have heard many times in the past, and say, "I'm Procrastinating Pete, so I've blown my chance." While I would agree that you don't have the same opportunity as you would have had early on, it should be noted that ol' Pete still did pretty good and almost tripled his investment. The power of compounding interest is why people are wisely drawn to investing.

Another reason that we *must* invest is because of a little thing some people refer to as the silent tax: inflation. By definition, inflation is a protracted period of rising prices. When we abandoned the gold standard as our backing of our currency and gave the government the ability to help smooth out the variability in the economy, we also built into that same system an inherent inflationary environment. While the Federal Reserve seeks to keep inflation low and economic growth sustainable, nevertheless, inflation still persists. Even with inflation low, we must have our dollars invested to outpace inflation; otherwise, our buying power is declining.

I find we all tend to dismiss inflation to some degree because it is so gradual. I mean do you really notice or care that milk went up 25¢ over the year? Most people don't, but over time it shows up in a substantial way. Do this exercise that I learned from my partner Wayne Harris. Ask yourself or someone you know who is in their fifties, sixties, or older this question: What did you pay for your first house? Now with that answer in mind, recall what you paid for your last car. It is not uncommon for older individuals to have paid more for their last car than they did their first house – a glaring example of inflation. You see, a 3 percent or so change from last year is nearly unnoticeable; but over a longer period of time, that 3 percent compounding annually, say for thirty years, and your dollar's purchasing power has been cut to less than half of its original value, just $.41. This little thing called inflation is yet another major reason why investing is not only desired but has become a necessity.

Let me make it clear that when I refer to investing, I am not talking about "playing in the market," as some are accustomed to do; this is no game. If you want to do that sort of thing for fun, go for it. I would caution you however and suggest that you only use a small amount of "disposable" money which is not relied upon for a future goal. Generally speaking, those who do that sort of thing are not investing but are speculating; and I tend to agree with Mark Twain who said, "There are only two times in a man's life when he should not speculate: when he can't afford it and when he can." While the person "playing" in the market may own some of the same stocks that a serious investor owns, as Benjamin Graham, "the father of value investing," puts it, "intention more than character will determine whether the security is an investment or speculation."[89] My intention with this chapter is to teach you about managing your *serious* money, the money you will depend on one day for the needs of life.

As we start this discussion regarding investing, it is pivotal that you understand the relationship between risk and return. Essentially this concept works like this: the more risk you are willing to take, the higher the expected return. Now, of course, the opposite is also true: the less risk, the less potential return. The goal in all investing is to get as much return for as little risk as possible. This rule, while very easy to understand, is really one of the keys that so many other things hinge upon. I also bring this up now simply because everyone I know wants a huge potential for return with very little risk, and these two factors are diametrically opposed to one another. Now that we understand this, let's take this very basic foundation and build on it.

Let's start by defining and discussing some of the main types of investments. While this may seem very elementary for some, I often find that even those who know these facts somehow lose sight of what comprises these investments once they get enthralled in the emotion of investing. In the next several pages, we are going to primarily deal with the fundamentals of stocks and bonds. Once you have a firm grasp of how these investments work, an understanding of other types of investments will be much easier. This chapter will be just a basic primer on a very complex subject, but I believe a basic understanding of this subject is critical for nearly every person. With that, if this topic sparks your interest, I strongly encourage you to read other great books on this enormous topic; but be on guard and have healthy criticism for any "beat the market" type of books out there. We will start by discussing the three main asset classes available to retail investors: stocks, bonds, and real estate.

The first investment that is paramount in having a basic understanding of is a stock, or as some may call it, an equity. Contrary to what many people think, a stock is not just a name on the page of the newspaper that has numbers that change every day. What the name represents is an ownership portion of a company – a business. As Warren Buffett continually explains, there is no fundamental difference between buying a business outright and buying shares of a company. Many times I have people ask me about what I think about a certain stock, trying to solicit a hot tip or recommendation from me, to which I often reply that I don't know anything about that particular company. I normally will ask, "What do they do?" to which the person asking either doesn't know what they do at all or if they do, it is probably limited to an advertisement they saw or at best a ten-second spiel they heard on CNBC. Ask yourself this question, why in the world would I invest in a stock, i.e., buy a company, that I didn't know anything about? I may not be being completely fair; chances are many people, despite not knowing the company's business that well, can rattle off to you a short history of the stock price. However, I tend to agree with Peter Lynch when he said, "To my mind, the stock price is the least useful information you can track; and it's the most widely tracked . . . What the stock price does today, tomorrow, or next week is only a distraction." As Peter continues, "If you follow only one bit of data, follow earnings."[90] You see, a stock represents ownership in a company; as a stockholder, you own part of that company. As an owner, you are entitled to any dividends paid which represent earnings being distributed and you also participate in the growth of the company as it does well. If you don't think you are *really* an owner, just get together several millions, maybe even billions of dollars, and buy a majority of the stock outstanding of one company. I can promise you that within a short amount of time you will get a phone call from the management of that company, ready to tell you anything you want to know. I'm sure they will be very curious as to what you want because management's job is to grow shareholder value – they work for you now.

It is because of this truth that almost intuitively it doesn't make sense to trade a stock frequently over a short period of time. After all, the company you bought last month probably hasn't changed its business model drastically, if at all, over that time period, and any day-to-day operation of that business is the same. Also, if there is a change taking place with that business that hopes to be beneficial in the long run, it takes just that – a long run to work itself out. As Buffett puts it more frankly, "Calling a trader an investor is like calling a person who engages in frequent one-night stands a romantic . . . Time is the friend of the wonderful business and the enemy of the mediocre."[91] Of course, you might say that the stock price is reacting to what the *expectation* of the company's performance is in the future, to which I would agree, and that is why it takes more than a cursory look at a company to know whether or not it is a good time to buy or a good time to sell and whether or not it is fairly valued.

You see, the stock price is just one of the signs or indicators of what might be going on inside a company. I liken a *true* stock evaluation to that of a medical exam. A doctor doesn't just look on the outside (the price) but examines the inside, how things are working. The physician knows that a person can look fine but be internally coming apart and that those internal functions will eventually show themselves externally. In the same way, when looking at a stock, while it might be of some value in knowing a stock's price, it is important to be able to examine the inner workings of that company to determine the company's health, value, and potential. For example, many a dot-com company traded at extremely high prices; but a closer look would have revealed that they carried a high amount of debt, had very little cash flow, no earnings, and their prospects for ever justifying that high stock price were nonexistent. If only we didn't so quickly judge books by their cover and took the time to dig deeper.

To be quite honest, it is probably well above the heads of most individual investors, and even many advisors, to analyze a company's financial position or make any kind of determination as to its relative value or future prospects. There are people who can do this type of analysis, but they probably have MBAs from top business schools or are Chartered Financial Analyst (CFA®) charterholders and carry their calculators with them. In most cases, this rare breed of people probably works at investment companies. You can have one of these people do the legwork for you, as I will discuss shortly. Let me also add that it is not sufficient to know all the inner workings of a particular company, but you must also realize that it functions within an economic and competitive framework. What this means is that you probably also need a good understanding of all of that company's competitors as well as the macroeconomic forces and how they will affect your company of interest. A good company that has strong or strengthening competitors or is in a weak economy is not necessarily a good investment. Also, a great company is not a good investment if you pay too high of a price for it. The point I am making should be clear; it is not easy to pick a winner every time, and for the most part it should be left to professionals.

Now that we understand a little about what a stock is, let's delve a little deeper into why we buy them. Of course we buy them to make money, but how does that really happen? Two ways: through earnings that are distributed as dividends paid to the stockholders and through any capital appreciation that is generated through growth of the company. Depending on what kind of company it is will depend on the mix of these two components. For example, a newly started pharmaceutical company is probably not going to pay a dividend, but instead they are going to reinvest any earnings into the company to hopefully grow the company faster in the future. In contrast, a well-established company in a mature market may distribute a good amount of its earnings as a dividend. Which is better? It depends. A dividend generally is a good assurance that the company is really making money, and the income it is generating is generally pretty stable – companies don't like to have to lower a dividend. Capital appreciation (the stock price increasing), on the other hand, is all dependent on future growth of the company and is only realized when the stock is sold.

What amount of return can you expect from a stock? Just like any company, it could go bust or the upside could be limitless. A fairer question is what is a reasonable expectation for stocks in general over the long run? The short answer can be summarized like this: stock returns over the long run are better than returns on cash, better than inflation, better than returns on bonds, and better than real estate returns. It is often commented and recognized that stocks perform well when bonds are doing poorly and vice versa. While many bonds do offer a safe-haven during tough economic times or times of panic in the market, it should not be assumed that bonds have a negative correlation with stocks (meaning move in opposite directions), as this many times is not the case. I will address reasonable return expectations in greater detail very shortly.

Another major building block and asset class is that of bonds. Once again I find many people think of a bond like a stock; it's just a name on paper and they think it's safer but they aren't quite sure why. A bond is simply a debt instrument, or said another way, you are loaning a company or government money in exchange for payment of interest and eventually repayment of your principal. Bonds are generally issued in denominations of $1,000 and they pay a fixed amount of interest for a period of time and at the end of the period they pay your principal portion back. As a bondholder, you are a creditor of that company and you have a priority position to get paid if that company goes into bankruptcy – for instance, you would get paid before a stockholder would get any of their value. It is because of the more steady payment schedule and priority of claims protection that bonds are "safer" than stocks; and because of that, the potential return is less, as we discussed earlier.

There are some other very important things to understand about bonds that can be somewhat cumbersome to grasp. First is the concept of credit risk; just like you wouldn't lend money to your local crack addict, it probably is not a good idea to lend money to a debt-laden, poor-cash-flow, start-up company with bad credit. Bonds can go into default, meaning that your money is probably gone or just technical default where they can't pay you the interest payments they owe on time. It is for this reason that credit quality matters greatly. The old risk-reward lesson we previously discussed comes into play here. To compensate you for the additional risk you are taking, companies with low credit quality will generally pay higher amounts of interest.

The next thing to understand about bonds involves interest rates and specifically, the relationship between maturity length and other types of risks. To make these issues clear, consider this example. You may feel okay about loaning a company money for a year or two for a given interest rate because the time horizon is pretty short. Your fears of default during that short time period are pretty low, and the economic landscape seems pretty manageable. However, if you were to lend money to that company or municipality for say twenty years, then a few other things come into play. This longer maturity brings into question inflation fears. If inflation rises over this period of time, then, in effect, you have lost purchasing power; so to compensate you for this risk, you will require a higher amount of interest. Secondly, default risk is greater the longer the time period. Thirdly, the issue of the interest-rate risk or the risk that changes in the prevailing rate of interest in the market will negatively affect bond prices makes investors in longer maturity bonds generally want more return for that added risk.

You see, short-term interest rates are a way the Federal Reserve helps to influence the volatility and overall direction of the economy by controlling the money supply. As they adjust interest rates up or down to achieve the desired effect, it directly impacts the bonds that are currently issued, as well as the supply and demand for different maturity lengths. Let's look at the following example: let's say you just bought a 6 percent corporate bond that matures in ten years. Assume that inflation is taking off and the Federal Reserve raises interest rates 1 percent to curb inflation. Because of this, other companies are now offering ten-year bonds that pay a coupon of 7 percent. You could hold your bond to maturity and get your 6 percent interest and your $1,000 of principal back after the end of ten years. The issue arises, however, if you need your money back before the end of ten years as you will have to sell your 6 percent bond in the market. The problem should be obvious – who would want to buy your 6 percent bond when they could buy a new bond at 7 percent? To compensate, you would have to sell your bond at less than $1,000 to make up for the lower interest payments; and thus, *it is possible to lose money if you sell before the bond matures*. This lesson can be summarized in this statement: When interest rates rise, bond prices fall; when interest rates fall, bond prices rise.

What return can you expect from bonds? As with all answers, it depends. If you buy a bond at par, meaning $1,000, and hold it to maturity, then your rate of return is what the coupon interest payment is (a 7 percent bond will result in a 7 percent rate of return). If you buy it on the secondary market at above or below par ($1,000) and sell it before maturity, then it depends. Overall, bonds are great income generators and offer stable returns that are superior to cash and inflation. As I mentioned earlier, many people commonly notice that bonds perform well when stocks are faltering and perform poorly when stocks are booming (be careful with this generalization). There are obviously volumes more that can be said about bonds, but my point here is to get you familiar with how they work in general. There are a thousand and one flavors of debt instruments which vary in just about every regard; but for the most part, this quick explanation covers the fundamentals.

Next, a good argument can also be made that another major building block and asset class is investment real estate. Real estate can be invested in several different ways as a part of an investment portfolio. The main way I will mention here is what is called a REIT, or real estate investment trust. Directly owned investment real estate (i.e., the rental house or fixer-upper) can be an incredible investment if you have the time, energy, and expertise to do it correctly. If it seems like something that is of interest to you, I would recommend that you read and talk to a professional real estate investor to learn more. I would also caution you, as I do with all investments, that diversification is crucial and all of your investable resources should not be allocated to any one asset class. I feel I must make this caveat as many real estate investors forego all other investments, because "real estate is such a great investment."

What I am going to explain a little more is specifically REITs or real estate investment trusts which can be used in a more traditional investment portfolio. The short story on the workings of a REIT is this. You and other investors' money is pooled to invest in real estate properties, these properties are leased out, and the cash flow is paid back to the REIT shareholders in the form of a dividend. A REIT can be traded in the market on an exchange which allows you to buy and sell shares at any time or it can be a private REIT which is not publicly traded. The difference between the two is simple; the publicly traded REIT has liquidity (meaning you can sell at any time), but for that added convenience, it is subject to the daily whims of the market. While publicly traded REITs are a good investment and diversifier, they do trade much more like a stock (small company stocks to be specific) than the real estate which actually underlies the investment. Private REITs, on the otherhand, are very illiquid (often with holding periods that are up to ten years), but their value is not very correlated to the stock or bond market. Some may argue with that statement, as economic pressures that effect the markets often do effect real estate prices, but the connection is much weaker, or at least, much less visible with non-traded REITs.

There are many different types of REITs that differ greatly in returns and liquidity, as well as the type of properties they are invested in ranging from prisons to high-rise office buildings to retail shops. Real estate in an investment portfolio can be a great tool for diversification because many of the factors which drive its returns are fairly unrelated to stock market performance. REITs are also great income generators via their dividends. As I have said with the others, this is just a quick two cents about REITs; they can vary greatly in quality and operation and should be evaluated closely.

Many would add that commodities such as oil, gold, cotton, etc., are also considered an asset class; but I have not included these in this chapter because at this point, they are not readily available to the average investor. These commodities are most often traded by companies that utilize them as a part of their business, and expert knowledge in each individual commodity is needed as they can exhibit high levels of volatility. I think it is a wise recommendation that this area of the market should not be entered into directly by the average investor at this point in time. New investments are being created continually and maybe in the near future they will merit commodities inclusion as an appropriate asset class – for the time being, it's best to stay away.

There are also a number of "alternative" investments which some include as an asset class and building block unto itself. While these are available and often used with highly affluent individuals, these investments remain a small part of a portfolio and are not readily available to the mass public. Many of these investments, specifically hedge funds, utilize investment strategies that are often highly sophisticated, high risk, and unique to that particular investment. Because of the breadth and depth of the subject of alternative investments, I will leave it at that.

Now that we have the basic building blocks that make up "the market," let's discuss what "the market" really is. The market is just as the name denotes; it is a place where things are bought and sold. When people discuss "the market," they are probably referring to the major U.S. stock markets which are composed of the NYSE (the New York Stock Exchange), the AMEX (the American Stock Exchange), and the NASDAQ (the National Association of Securities Dealers Automated Quotation: it's an electronic exchange). Of course this narrow definition of "the market" is ignoring the regional stock exchanges, bond markets, commodities markets, futures market, options market, or any of the international flavors of these same markets. The world's capital markets are enormous and provide an amazing opportunity for investment.

Let's quickly deal with the basic theory of how a market works. In a very simplistic sense, it is where buyers and sellers both come ready to transact business. A seller comes to sell something – a stock. Buyers are present and make bids to purchase the stock, and obviously the stock will be sold to the highest bidder. The rules of supply and demand drive the prices in the market, meaning if there are more sellers than buyers, the sellers will be willing to drop their price to unload the stock; in contrast, if there are more buyers than sellers, the opposite would be true. It is important to keep in mind that this process is not independent of the underlying security's intrinsic value or other considerations that the buyers and sellers are well aware. Case in point, if a stock's (company's) earnings have gone up more than everyone expected since the original purchase, then the seller would probably ask more for the stock than when they purchased it and buyers will be bidding higher based on that information. In summary, the pricing of a security is a result of the underlying company's financial position *which drives* the supply and demand situation in the market. Theoretically, the supply and demand for a given stock should be in line with the stock's intrinsic value, but it isn't always. Said another way, it is important to know the companies you are investing in and to understand the overarching economics involved in the market to have a chance at making a correct decision.

It is also important to remember that the supply and demand relationship to your underlying security depends upon the relative attractiveness of alternative investments. If I could buy a stock with similar characteristics for a lower price, that will have an effect on the price of all stocks that are similar. Author Jonathan Pond makes this insightful and almost comical observation regarding the market, "In order to buy a share of stock, someone has to sell that same share, and both the buyer and seller think they've made the right decision."[92]

I fully realize that in my effort to explain the market in simple terms, it quickly can become cumbersome. This should not instill fear or dread, but rather a healthy respect for it and the professionals who operate in it.

Let's continue with some observations of the market. I am about to make two statements that I understand appear contradictory but I hope to reconcile them shortly so please give me some latitude. The first observation is that the markets are pretty efficient. What this means is that a stock or any other security's current price reflects all available public information. With that being said, that is why I am often very skeptical of the brother-in-law's stock tip that was based on last week's news. If indeed that was a real piece of news, even one that wasn't anticipated by those following the stock, the stock's price quickly compensated and reflected that new information. There are millions of people with trillions of dollars invested in securities of all types and most securities prices are extremely sensitive to new information and there is even a heavy amount of speculation as to what the news will be before it is reported. It is hard to be the first to the party. With that in mind, a stock's price is usually fairly close to what is viewed as its proper value, meaning a $2 stock is probably $2 because that is what people think it is worth, and a $65 stock is worth $65 based on all information available at that particular point in time and the market's future expectation. Of course there could be a healthy amount of debate about these statements; but I can be sure that unless you are an extremely sophisticated investor or an investment analyst, chances are if you have a different value for what a particular stock is currently worth, it is probably nothing more than a shot in the dark.

Now, with that being said, my second observation is that the market is also inherently emotional. It is easy to get caught up in all the math of the market and forget that underlying it all is emotion. Why? Because people run companies, people buy and sell stocks, and people are emotional. My whole point of the chapter preceding this one was to convince you of this fact, and even very smart people and institutions can be affected in similar ways. Markets will sometimes respond irrationally because people respond irrationally. As Warren Buffett states it, "because emotions are stronger than reason, fear and greed move stock prices above and below a company's intrinsic value."[93] In the long run, earnings account for most of a stock's performance; in the short run, the "madness of crowds" takes investment prices in all sorts of directions.

As I said, these two observations are somewhat contradictory; but I reconcile the two by saying that most often the market is highly efficient, reflecting all available information, especially closely watched large and midsized company stocks. However, emotion such as excitement, undeserved pessimism, surprise, etc., can cause a stock or the overall market to vary greatly in the short run or be, as Warren Buffett calls it, somewhat manic depressive. This should cause us to be skeptical of any stock tip we hear from our buddy at work and at the same time have a healthy skepticism of the general consensus, because both can be wrong.

Let me expound briefly on this idea of the consensus. As I have already discussed the frailty of being an emotional decision maker in the previous chapter, I want to make sure you get the application of those lessons in how they work in relation to the market. As I have laid out, it is difficult to not pay attention to what others are saying. I know because I hear volumes more than the average person when it comes to the markets. When I am feeling the pull of the crowd, I often remind myself of two quotes by the world's greatest investor (Buffett): "You pay a very high price in the stock market for a cheery consensus" and "Be fearful when others are greedy and be greedy when others are fearful."[94] This sort of contrarian attitude is kind of neat to adopt on the surface, you feel like some sort of rebel, but to really take this sort of attitude and put it into practice is almost unnerving. Built into both of these quotes is the concept that the market is emotional and can move in extremes and that by understanding this you can manage your risks, possibly profit from them, and be more willing to stay the course amidst the daily swings.

There is rarely a week that goes by that someone doesn't ask me my opinion as to what they should expect from the market in the short run. To be honest, it is very difficult to tell. As I have laid out, so many factors affect the movements of the market; and we haven't even discussed foreign forces such as imports/exports, currency, war, etc. The market is normally a leading indicator to the health of the domestic economy, meaning, if the market takes off, that is normally in response to some information that expects the economic prospects to improve. Some say it this way: the market is a barometer, not a thermometer. It is helpful in predicting economic movements in the future, not so much an indicator of what is happening today or tomorrow. I also like to remind people that economic forecasting is like trying to drive a car blindfolded while following directions given by a person looking out the back window. The past is instructive, especially for seeing large trends, but what is going to happen next month or this year is very difficult to tell. As Buffett says, "the future is never clear."

You may be saying to yourself by now, "Well, what do you expect me to do?" Don't get worked up just yet; help is on the way. Before I get into how to navigate the precarious landscape of investing, there are a few more investments that you need to know about. These investments are ways in which you can take advantage of stocks, bonds, and real estate and can assist in the strategies I will mention later on in this chapter.

Some deem the mutual fund the greatest thing to ever happen to the individual investor. While most think of the mutual fund being a fairly new invention, the modern mutual fund actually took shape in the mid-1920s and exploded on the scene in the 1980s and '90s. A mutual fund, also known by its formal name, an open-end investment company, is essentially this: it is a company whose job is to manage and invest money for its shareholders. When you invest in a mutual fund, you are investing money with this investment company which turns around and invests your money along with other investors' money into stocks or bonds or both. Their goal is to manage your and other people's money in accordance with a predetermined investment philosophy or policy. You can tell many of these mutual funds investment criteria and philosophy by their name but this isn't always the case so you should be careful. Example: XYZ Large Cap Value fund is probably going to be investing in large companies utilizing a value-based philosophy.

There are two main *styles* that you will often hear about when it comes to stock investing that I will just briefly mention. Both of these "styles" and others, are active strategies in which mutual fund companies employ analysts and managers who research and pick investments, according to a predetermined set of criteria, that fit within their particular strategy. *Value investing* is based on the idea of trying to buy companies whose stock is currently trading below what it is worth – a good value. Said another way, it's trying to buy a dollar's worth of stock for fifty cents. This style is usually characterized by stocks with low PEs (price to earnings ratios). The other main style of investing is *growth* investing which concentrates on looking for companies who are exhibiting growth and that are going to grow their earnings *more than expected* and are generally characterized by owning high PE stocks. I will point out that many analysts and managers who run these managed investments dislike categorizing their particular style into one of these two camps because it would not only be difficult to do, but it may diminish the true philosophy they are employing. For instance, many "growth" managers *do* care about buying stocks that are a good value today as well as seen as a good value in the further future. Likewise, many value managers aren't scared off by high-PE stocks because they still may exemplify a good value today. The point is that you shouldn't necessarily pigeonhole a manager based on the title of their mutual fund, and a closer look is merited. A close examination will help you to understand exactly the methodology being employed and the risks involved.

While the differences in management styles are sometimes difficult to distinguish, there are differences; and often these style differences perform differently at different times. Many studies have shown that when "value" is doing well, "growth" is not, and vice versa. If you choose to invest employing active management, you should pay close attention to the fund's "style" or philosophy.

Mutual funds are also often categorized by market capitalization and geographic diversification. Market capitalization deals with the size of the companies the fund will invest in. Generally, there are different risk/return characteristics for companies of different sizes with obviously small companies showing more volatility and large companies being more stable. Small companies are generally "one trick ponies" and offer a limited product line or array of services which makes their earnings very dependent on that limited source. Large companies, however, have broad streams of revenues which often make earnings more stable in changing economic environments.

All funds also outline their objective and parameters concerning where they invest geographically. Domestic funds invest all or most of their dollars inside the United States, global funds invest internationally but can be invested domestically as well, and international funds are invested almost solely abroad. There are funds which invest in developing countries and are referred to as emerging market funds. In the past, international investing was considered not only risky, but also inferior because their historical returns were less than the U.S. markets. Today, however, most professionals would suggest that there are great diversification and risk-reduction benefits from investing abroad. I firmly believe, with an increasingly global economy, many great investment opportunities exist outside our borders.

There is another type of mutual fund which uses a passive approach, referred to as indexing, which is an alternative to the active management we have discussed. Created in 1971 by William Fouse and John McQuown of Wells Fargo Bank, but made famous by John Bogle of the Vanguard Group, the index fund has changed the way a lot of people invest their money. Similar to an actively managed mutual fund, this allows investors to instantly diversify their dollars by pooling them with other investors, which is then invested in stocks or bonds or real estate that mimic an index, such as the S&P 500, MSCI World Index, NAREIT, Lehman Aggregate Bond Index, etc. The main difference between an index fund and an actively managed fund is that there should be very little trading activity in what the fund is investing in except when there is a change in the makeup of an index. An example of a trade an index fund would have made would have been when WorldCom went bankrupt and dropped off of the S&P 500 list; index funds mimicking the S&P would have likewise sold it from the portfolio. There are on average about twenty changes per year to the S&P 500. An index fund's goal is to track, as closely as possible, the index it is following. If the S&P 500 ends up heavily weighted in technology because those companies that are comprised in the index have done well (as in the late 1990's), then your S&P 500 index fund will also be heavily weighted in that manner.

Some advantages of index funds are their low cost (since they aren't paying managers and analysts) and tax efficiency – since there is very little trading activity during the year. There are numerous indexes and ways that index funds are constructed which are beyond the scope of this chapter, so it should be noted that all index funds are not created equally. Research shows that this passive approach, in a large majority of cases, outperforms active management over time when you consider fees, transaction costs, and taxes. That is not to say that indexing is right and active management wrong, but it should get your attention and make you carefully scrutinize and evaluate managers if you do use an active approach.

The mutual fund is an incredible invention and has allowed many people to invest their money prudently who would have not been able to do otherwise. They are especially unique for three main reasons. First, they are instant diversifiers. If you buy $100 worth of a stock, you own $100 worth of one stock. In contrast, if you buy $100 worth of shares of a mutual fund, you own a proportionate share of the *whole* investment portfolio. Let's say the mutual fund contains one hundred stocks – theoretically, a $100 investment could allow you to own $1 of each stock (if they were equally weighted). We will discuss the benefits of this later, but mutual funds assist in diversification wonderfully. Second, the mutual fund gives you access to professional management. As I have already clearly laid out, investing is a difficult business. Knowing which stock or bonds to buy, when to buy and sell them, and how much to buy or sell, can be an arduous process. For a small percentage, a management fee that is internally charged, you can have a team of professionals manage your money every day in an actively managed mutual fund. Finally, the mutual fund format allows for small incremental investments. The minimums vary, but some will take as little as $25 a month. If you only had $50 a month to invest and the stock you wanted to buy was Google at $438 a share, you would need to save for nine months to get enough money to buy one share and then you would have $12 left over (not counting any transaction fees). A mutual fund, on the other hand, allows you to buy fractional shares; so if a mutual fund's "price" is $12 a share, your $50 would buy 4.167 shares of that fund, which is then invested in numerous stocks and bonds – much more investor friendly from that standpoint.

Once again, there is a plethora of information that could fill volumes of books in regards to mutual funds to which I need not bore you. However, it should be noted that not all mutual funds are created equal; and unlike children born in Lake Wobegon, not all are above average. Careful scrutiny is required when choosing which mutual funds to use in your portfolio. There are a number of criteria and processes that go into choosing investments, and mutual funds in particular, which are beyond the scope of this book; but just let me say – last quarter's performance is barely considered. This may seem odd to most individuals who pick what are being touted as today's "hottest funds," but I have already discussed the performance that most individuals *actually* experience using these techniques.

Another investment that I feel the need to introduce you to is the ETF, or exchanged-traded fund. Most ETFs, said simply, are index funds that trade like stocks. There are numerous ETFs available today that follow different indexes, and these are becoming more and more popular in the investment management business because of their tax efficiency, low cost, and ease of trading. I will add, while most ETFs track widely used indexes, there are a growing number of ETFs which track sectors of the market, obscure indexes, or "baskets" of stocks – these should probably be avoided as these are speculative in nature and will probably cause more grief than good. While this new breed of investment has broad application, it is not right for every situation, especially for people who are regularly investing small amounts at a time. If you haven't seen or used an ETF yet, it probably won't be too long before you hear and see more about them.

There are numerous other types of investments and ways to invest such as unit investment trusts (UITs), closed-end funds, hedge funds, options, commodities, separate accounts, and the list goes on and on. All of these have merit, but are beyond the scope of what I am trying to accomplish in this introductory section. Chances are, if you are dealing with any of these, you are probably a more sophisticated investor and have been dealing with a professional advisor who *hopefully* has educated you about their proper use. I do, however, want to mention just one more investment vehicle before we move on to other subjects. That investment is an annuity.

There is a lot of discussion and intense scrutiny (some well deserved) regarding annuities. Since this last bear market, annuities have become a topic of increasing popularity; and I feel certain that at some point everyone should at least understand their basics. An annuity is an insurance contract that has an investment component built in. Before I go further, let me quickly clear up the misconception that annuities are these terrible investments that when you die, the insurance company keeps your money. What people are referring to is a feature (annuitization) that *can be* accessed on all annuities but rarely is – don't jump to any conclusions just yet.

Generally, it's good to separate annuities into two main categories: deferred annuities and immediate annuities. Deferred annuities are accumulation vehicles; they can either pay a fixed rate of interest or be "variable" and driven by market performance. A variable annuity can actually get a very similar look and feel of a brokerage account that is holding mutual funds, with the difference being that the annuity is inside an insurance contract. Let's discuss that for a minute. First of all, the primary advantages of deferred annuities are that you get tax deferral of investment gains and you have the ability to "annuitize" and take a lifetime income. The word "annuitize" means a series of payments or cash flows. All annuities, even deferred annuities, have the option to annuitize which can mean a wide array of income options, with some being based on your lifetime. While there are some serious consequences associated with annuitization, this still can be a good solution for some people who need income from their investments.

The other type of annuity I mentioned is an immediate annuity. This investment is simply designed to accept an amount of money and turn it into an immediate stream of income. As with the other types of annuities, there are many options; and the decision to annuitize is one that should only be made after careful consideration.

While some investment purists or financial planners would probably balk at my mentioning annuities in this chapter, I think annuities' application for the average investor is one that is rapidly growing. Many investors, in the wake of the recent bear market, have sought guarantees that only annuities can offer. Also, with the baby boomers at the doorstep of retirement, many investors' main objective is about to switch from accumulation of assets to a need for income; and like it or not, annuities can play a major role in accomplishing just that.

There are a multitude of annuity providers who manufacture annuities of all types and flavors. To be honest, many of them have so many different types of complicated benefits and features; it is very difficult to judge the value that each one may provide. It is because of this that I would caution you concerning annuities, especially considering that many of these are aggressively marketed by all types of salespeople who may not know how they work themselves. Despite some of these snake oil salesmen, we should not throw the baby out with the bathwater. As we have discussed in other chapters, the risk of outliving your income is a growing concern for nearly every investor and annuities can be used in conjunction with the rest of your investment portfolio to curb this risk by transferring some of that liability to an insurance company. My crystal ball tells me that we will be seeing more and more advancements in the world of annuities in the next decade.

We finish this chapter by discussing what you can reasonably expect out of these investments and more importantly from your portfolio as a whole. This might seem a little silly, but I must remind you that just a few years ago, every little old lady out there expected a safe 20 percent return from her all-stock portfolio. To be able to properly plan for your goals and stay the course with your investments, reasonable expectations are needed.

I will ask you to recall the risk-reward relationship that we discussed at the beginning of this chapter and keep that in mind as we discuss reasonable expectations of investment returns for the future. I will readily admit that I have little opinion about what types of returns we can expect next month or next year but looking over longer time frames, it is not hard to see some consistency of past returns and I don't think it is unreasonable to expect those to persist, for the most part, in the future. If you ask what a given stock will return in the future, the "guess" would range from – 100 percent to infinite, because so many things could happen to that individual company. However, when we discuss stock returns in general, with much greater confidence we can project a tighter range of expected returns.

If we look at historical rates of return, we see that stocks have returned in the neighborhood of 10-11 percent annually, bonds around 5 percent, and with inflation around 3.5 percent. Certainly if you look at certain time periods such as the late 1990s, these returns have varied greatly. With a little understanding of economics and barring some society-altering event of biblical magnitude, we can probably expect similar, although maybe slightly lower, levels of returns in the future.

As they say, predictions are very hard to make, especially about the future; but I will make a few anyway. Many today suspect that our days of sustained double-digit stock returns are a thing of the past and that we should adjust our expectation to high single-digit returns. While I won't bore you with why they think that, I will say that anyone's retirement plan that is counting on 10-12 percent sustained returns might be setting themselves up for a big problem. Why? First, I think economists might be right and high single digits might be more warranted. Second, unless you are a fearless investor who throws all caution to the wind and only owns stocks, then a portfolio that also includes bonds has a high likelihood of returns less than double digits over a long period of time.

We have now successfully covered the basic building blocks of investing, the markets and the basics of how they work, as well as some other investments that are integral, and finally ending, armed with expectations that are hopefully a little more reasonable. With this information, you should be able to more closely understand what it is your advisor is trying to tell you and hopefully will steer clear of any "hot tip" your brother-in-law has. With this groundwork laid, we can now learn how to apply this knowledge in a more meaningful strategy to assist us in the pursuit of our financial goals and a truly rich life.

CHAPTER 11

Investing Serious Money

As investing giant Benjamin Graham states, "it is no difficult trick to bring a great deal of energy, study, and native ability into Wall Street and to end up with losses instead of profits."[95] He also says, however, that "to invest successfully over a lifetime does not require a stratospheric IQ, unusual business insights, or inside information. What is needed is a sound intellectual framework for making decisions and the ability to keep emotions from corroding that framework."[96]

I would be foolish to teach the basic building blocks of investing without explaining how you can apply that knowledge in a meaningful way to *actually* invest. Let it be known that there are countless ways to make money with investing, and I will not say that there is only one way to go about it. I will say that the spectrum of what I would call prudent for the average situation is fairly narrow and would not include investing your retirement savings based on the advice of a chair-throwing maniac on TV or letting your broker talk you into options trading dot-coms. As I have mentioned, while you can do those things with your "play" money if you want, I will be discussing how to handle your "serious" money which will be needed for the things of life.

I do not think that the book of knowledge regarding investing is closed; and as the markets continually evolve in response to an ever-increasing global economy, as the ways in which markets operate change, and as the birth of new investment vehicles grows, there will undoubtedly be some adaptations. However, the fundamental principles I am about to share with you have stood the test of time so far; and until something radically changes in the investment world, they will continue to be the primary means by which smart investors manage their money.

To begin this investing process, we first must consider what we are trying to accomplish. This sounds simple, but most people invest the same regardless of the objective or purpose of the money – a big mistake. Are you investing for financial independence (remember, we don't like that "retirement" word anymore), or are you investing for a new car five years from now? Are you in need of income from your portfolio? Each of these goals has different investment objectives and different time horizons, both critically important in determining the appropriate investment allocation. Everybody loves Warren Buffett, but you must realize that his favorite holding period is forever. He is worth *$42 billion* and is not *exactly* in the same situation as you are. This is just one small example, but it should be taken to heart; the "Warren Buffett way" may not be in tune with your investment objectives despite how "good" of an investor he is.

Once you have objectives that you wish to accomplish with approximate time horizons, then it is critically important to have an understanding of your risk tolerance. While it is obvious that no one wants to lose all of their money, you must try and quantify with more precision an appropriate level of risk you are comfortable taking. Just because you skydive on the weekends doesn't mean that you can handle investment risk; and likewise, I have met day-trading grannies who like playing the slots in their free time. A qualified financial planner or investment advisor should have questionnaires to assist in this pursuit. Most have questions like, "If your portfolio went down 10 percent in a quarter, would you (a) panic and sell (b) be concerned but hold tight for another three months (c) not be worried because you are a long-term investor (d) double down and invest more in this "low point." While these tests are not foolproof psychological profiles, they should steer you in the right direction and prevent you from being in a portfolio that is not even close to matching your risk preference/tolerance.

With a clear objective in mind and an understanding of an acceptable amount of risk, you are now ready to move to the next steps in the process. Before I jump right into how the portfolio is constructed, I recommend setting some ground rules and understanding some principles which lay the foundation for why I suggest investing the way I do.

Once you have an investment objective and a risk tolerance, there is one more thing before it is time to actually discuss how to properly allocate or implement a given strategy: an investment policy statement. An investment policy statement is essentially a self instituted set of ground rules. This may seem like an unneeded step in the process – giving yourself rules; but this document outlines your investment goals, the level of returns you need to achieve those goals, the type of investments you will or won't invest in, the general allocation of investments, your time frame for these investments, anticipated tax and inflation rates, liquidity needed in the portfolio, and potential tax consequences. In effect, this policy statement solidifies your strategy, ensures that you and your advisor are on the same page, and holds you and your advisor accountable and insulates you from making poor emotional choices. Any change made to your portfolio should be in line with the investment policy statement; and the statement should only be amended if there is a significant change in your needs and objectives, not just a change in your feelings at the moment. With a detailed investment policy statement in hand, the strategy, implementation, and on-going management of your investments become much easier and the probability of success is greatly increased.

Now let's talk a little strategy. I am sure almost everyone at some point in their life has heard the saying "Don't keep all of your eggs in one basket." While it would be a lot sexier to discuss some other strategy, few can provide as much benefit as simply diversifying. Despite conventional wisdom, probably the single most damaging and prevalent mistake I see investors make is a lack of diversification.

In my experience of reviewing numerous investment accounts, it is very common to see a large percentage of the portfolio in a single security or the aftermath of what used to be a large amount of money in one or a few investments. Many wealthy individuals amassed their fortunes through a single holding and are reluctant to diversify from an investment that has "been so good to them." Likewise, it's common to see entrepreneurs whose company went public or executives who have amassed a majority of their wealth in company stock or stock options and can't bring themselves to sell. This tendency to hold concentrated stock positions is not limited to the wealthy. In a large majority of cases, when reviewing investments of lifelong emplo   f major corporations or recipients of an inheritance of a stock, it is very common to see them hold onto their stock with white knuckles and blinders on as well.

This reluctance to part with the beloved investment is often due to that feeling of safety or sometimes just a sense of loyalty to the company that got them to where they are today. As I mentioned in a previous chapter, these are classic examples of being an emotional investor, confusing familiarity with safety or having a sense of loyalty to an impersonal object. I can assure you that the stock's feelings won't be hurt in the least if you do the prudent thing. Whatever the circumstance, it is extremely important to remember one of the main premises found in modern portfolio theory: you generally are not compensated for risk that you could have reduced through diversification. Said another way, you generally will not get the return to justify the risk that you are taking. The implication of this is you could get the same amount of return while taking a lot less risk if you diversified.

Now that is not blanket advice to sell all of a large position; there may be extenuating factors such as tax consequences and others. Analysis can be run with the tax situation in mind as well as the individual stock's characteristics to determine what potentially is the best strategy to employ to deal with a high concentration of a security. The point to remember is it is always dangerous to play a game of toss with only one egg, especially if you need that egg for cooking. This is one of those situations where emotion can be extremely strong, but you must rely on the "rules" which we know to be in our best interest.

Diversification is simply a risk-reduction strategy used to eliminate company-specific risks and lessen overall risk. The limits of the ways to diversify are extremely vast. It is often wise to diversify among industries. Owning eight telecommunications companies is not being adequately diversified. Diversifying across geography is also important. This can mean not being concentrated in companies in one region or country. In real estate especially, geographic diversification is important. Sizes of companies also differ in how they respond to economic events, so diversification across company size also can provide risk-reduction benefits. The lesson should be clear: when possible, recognize opportunities to spread risk. This diversification strategy begs the question: how do we best allocate across these different factors? This question leads to the next strategy of asset allocation.

Studies show that many, especially 401(k) participants, or as many used to refer to themselves after the tech wreck, "201(k)" participants, allocate or diversify their money in a very "sophisticated" way. They simply put an equal amount in every investment option they have regardless of what that investment might be. One study separated a large group of people into two groups and gave them hypothetical 401(k) investment allocation worksheets in order to study how they invested their money. One group had two investment options: one all-stock mutual fund and one balanced fund (50 percent stocks/50 percent bonds). The other group also had two options: one all-bond mutual fund and one balanced fund. Not to the researchers' surprise, nearly all of the subjects allocated 50 percent of their money in one fund and 50 percent in the other, which resulted in two totally different types of allocations, one much more risky than the other. In reading this study, I could also easily predict the outcome because through the years, I am constantly seeing people who may have five or six funds in their 401(k) accounts allocated to all of the funds, but most if not all are invested in very similar investments.

There is a method or "science" behind how to best allocate among different classes of investments. This "science" of modern portfolio theory created by Nobel Prize winner Harry Markowitz in 1952 describes a methodology of how to construct a portfolio for the maximum amount of return for a given level of risk. Brinson, Hood, and Bebower in their landmark study "Determinants of Portfolio Performance" (1986/1991) asserted that the investment policy, the allocation among the different asset classes, accounted for 94 percent of the variation of returns in a portfolio, with the actual selection and timing of those decisions only accounting for 6 percent. These two breakthroughs have sprung forth a litany of optimizing software packages that help in the complex calculations to devise the "best" allocations of your assets.

I will recognize that these two studies have plenty of detractors, and I am sure that new research can refine the ways in which money is optimally allocated. There have already been huge advances in the ways that software generates portfolios, now being able to include more forward-looking assumptions instead of relying so heavily on historical figures. All of that being said, there is software available that institutions spend big bucks developing and refining which can aid in the pursuit to optimally allocate and diversify. The result is an allocation which gives you the most return for the risk you are willing to take. The end result is a recommendation of exactly how much you should have invested in large company stocks; midsized and small company stocks; short, mid, and long-term bonds; emerging markets; TIPS; real estate; etc. A good financial planner or investment manager should use some similar type of process and technology to construct portfolios as opposed to the "here is my best guess" type of approach.

Now with your strategy and allocation in hand comes the fun part – actually picking investments! In your excitement to find the next greatest thing out there, you must remember your investment policy statement and the allocation that is right for you. The actual investments to fill those slots are so varied that it would take me many more books to address them. I will say that if you or your advisor chooses to use an actively managed mutual fund or separate account, there should be significant due diligence to ensure that you have a high probability of getting the value you are paying for. The firm I am a part of has stringent criteria for selecting investment managers (which I will keep a secret for now), but I do strongly suggest that you not pick based solely on performance – especially not recent performance. I often say that asset allocation is the science of investing, but the implementation is the art. Since I will not go any further on this specific topic, I will say that there are advisors who can assist you with this precarious process.

It only makes sense that if you buy into and believe in the philosophy of proper asset allocation and diversification and have taken the time to actually invest your money accordingly, you would want your portfolio to have a similar allocation at all times (barring a change in objective). So the question arises, what happens when my small company stocks grow substantially, my large company stocks grow a little as well, and my bonds lose money? When looking at your allocation among those funds now, you will notice that your allocation is not like it should be, right? The solution is called rebalancing, simply selling some assets and buying others to get the mix of assets back to its optimal allocation. This sounds easy, but often is emotionally hard to do; after all, sometimes it means selling what is doing well and buying what is doing poorly. This rebalancing process can be done a number of ways, ranging from doing it every quarter, semiannually, or annually, to doing it based on trigger points which are set based on the assets' riskiness. There are a number of studies which confirm that rebalancing reduces volatility of returns, and intuitively it only makes sense. Just think about it, suppose you have an optimal allocation which is well diversified. One year later, due to an extreme run-up of one asset class, say emerging market stocks, your allocation is now extremely heavy in that area. Doesn't it make sense to "take a profit" and buy back those other asset classes because the chances of that kind of run continuing might be unlikely? I'm sure you get my point. As a sidebar, I will add that everyone should know what is called reversion to the mean – simply that returns will generally come back in line with their long run averages, so periods of outperformance are generally followed by a pullback. Now, back to rebalancing. The actual way in which you choose to rebalance depends on a number of factors which include tax consequences. While it may be impractical for your advisor to tweak your portfolio every time it gets slightly skewed, it is important to keep an eye on this type of thing, as over a long period of time without rebalancing, your portfolio may look very little like you initially intended.

While I am on the subject of rebalancing, it only makes sense to bring up another strategy or issue that can enhance your returns over time. Taxes are often an overlooked area of investment planning. Many advisors or brokers take the attitude that "if they have taxes, then I must be making them money." This is not always the case. I would advise you to be as tax sensitive as it makes sense, without materially changing the investment allocation or decisions. What I mean is don't let the tax tail wag the dog. Just because stocks which pay no dividends are more tax conscience than corporate bonds doesn't mean that you should substitute them inappropriately. Often, being tax sensitive means taking in consideration the location of your assets: placing your bonds in your qualified retirement accounts which get tax deferral and placing your dividend-paying stock in a nonqualified account. (This is meant as an example, not a recommendation)

Being tax sensitive also means using mutual funds or other actively managed investments whose managers don't trade feverishly and generate capital gains or employing passively managed index funds or ETFs. A study done by Tom Roseen and Lucas Garland of Lipper showed that mutual fund investors, on average, give up between 1.3 to 2.5 percentage points annually to taxes, which translates to as much as 23 percent of the return (in dollars) getting wiped out by taxes *every year* from internal trading activity.[97] This is a loss you don't see, but trust me, it's there.

If you have money invested outside retirement plans and in "nonqualified" accounts, it also makes sense to take advantage of "harvesting" losses (selling the losers) during the year if you have an investment that loses money. You can use these tax losses to offset future gains and even take some of the losses off of your ordinary income taxes. The specifics of this strategy are beyond the scope of this chapter, but doing such things can lead to real differences over time. Most investors, and even a large percentage of advisors, pay little to no attention to such an important issue. The larger the account, the bigger the difference in real dollars; so I definitely recommend reducing this tax "drag" when it is practical to do so.

The last strategy that I will mention is dollar cost averaging. I hope I have convinced you of the benefits of asset allocation; if you recall the study I mentioned by Brinson, Hood, and Bebower, they found that selection and timing only accounted for 6 percent of the investment returns. Despite this research, the average investor is constantly trying to "time" the market, investing when things are doing well and avoiding when things are doing poorly. Unfortunately, not only is this near impossible to do, it normally leads to sitting on the sidelines and missing opportunities. I can personally attest that I have been in my office watching CNBC or Bloomberg and seen the market falling and thought, "Wow, this doesn't look good." Within a couple of days, the commentators have switched their outlook and the market is soaring. My point is that it is impossible to predict good markets, bad markets, and especially market turns with any high degree of confidence. We also know that over time, our allocation is more important.

The strategy of dollar cost averaging is simple and one that you probably already use. It is simply investing a fixed amount of money regularly regardless of what the market is doing. If the market is going up, you are buying at increasing prices. If the market is going down, you are buying more and more shares because of the decreasing prices. Over time, this strategy accomplishes two things: it keeps you *actually* investing (instead of sitting on the sidelines) and it reduces volatility (price fluctuation).

If you have a large lump sum of money that is in cash, like an inheritance or a pension rollover, and you are uncertain about when you should invest that money – dollar cost averaging it over a period of time helps in making this decision and is effective at reducing the risk of making a poor choice. Of course, this strategy does not prevent against a loss or maximize gains; after all, if the market is going up, you would have been better off just investing it all to begin with. On the other hand, if the market declines, your decision to be invested is actually several decisions whose consequences have a decreasingly negative effect, lessening the overall loss than if you would have invested it all up front. One of the main lessons learned and being applied in the strategy of dollar cost averaging and which has wide application in these other strategies as well, is that it is near impossible to predict markets. If you could predict them, then chances are everybody else could do it as well, which would probably lead to some sort of full-scale worldwide economic meltdown. I think you get my point. Academically, a strong case can be made against timing; but more importantly, practically speaking, timing isn't a viable option.

I will point out a weird phenomenon that I run across which sometimes brings up this discussion of dollar cost averaging. Many times a person about to retire has a 401(k) or something of the sort to roll over into an IRA. While the person may be fully invested in the 401(k), there is often a strange sense of uneasiness when it comes to fully investing the rollover dollars right away. It seems elementary to point out, but I will do so because hopefully you are presently unaffected by the emotions of such a decision – if you are fully invested today, then there should be no fundamental difference to "cash in" your investments in your employer's plan and invest them fully in a rollover IRA. In fact, to want to dollar cost average or to hold cash for a period of time *is* a timing issue which is probably best to avoid – let's move on.

Being invested, properly diversified, allocated, and being aware of such things as taxes are great starting points to building a robust portfolio which can assist in the accomplishment of your financial goals. A detailed investment policy statement is also a great tool to keep you on the right track. This approach is not only a sensible way in which to invest but also a much more freeing way to invest. There is no recommendation from me that you watch the market for a number of hours a day, do research on ten stocks a day, make charts, shake magic eight balls, or read tea leaves. I am not saying that there aren't other ways to make money; but unless that is your calling in life, I would point you to the more practical, risk-sensitive approach that I have laid out. I will also say that this is very similar to the way most large institutions (pension funds, endowments, foundations, etc.) invest their money. May your investments be profitable, but most importantly may your life be truly rich.

CHAPTER 12

The President's Cabinet

"Plans fail for lack of counsel; but with many advisors they succeed."
(Prov. 15:22)

Today, people have more information available to them than was ever thought possible. We are truly in the information age. Whether or not you want to know how to bake a dish or perform a surgery, a few minutes on the computer can probably get you to a site that can provide a lot of information about your topic of interest. A quick trip to the bookstore or library will likewise overwhelm you to the point of almost believing that everything worth knowing has already been written about or studied. I think we would all agree that information is abundant. The paradox, however, is with information overflowing, it remains difficult to make right decisions and take correct actions. I believe this in part because expertise, empathy, experience, and accountability in the form of a person or persons, is difficult to find and rarely sought.

Throughout my life, but especially since the start of my career as a financial planner, I have grown to learn that no one person has a corner on all of the good ideas. I have also learned that in each specific professional discipline, whether it is accounting, law, or the disciplines in financial planning, the depth and breadth of knowledge needed to provide sound advice about every conceivable situation is rarely found in one person. I have also found it to be true that in the more general issues of life, such as parenting, marriage, career, etc., learning from others, as opposed to the school of hard knocks, is an invaluable asset. In this chapter, I hope to convince you that no man is an island; and in this world obese with information and present with all sorts of snares, a team of advisors can add a tremendous amount of assistance in your pursuit to live a truly rich life. Throughout this chapter, I will outline the advantages of having a team of advisors, whom you should have on your team, and what roles they could play.

As a professional advisor myself, of course it would seem as though I am bias in offering my opinion on this subject. While it is true that it is somewhat self-serving of me to argue that everyone needs professional advice, I hope that you will consider my thoughts and see that my advice is not about me and my profession, but rather, it is about you and your success. I have personally met an untold number of people who have utilized a team approach and experienced success as well as been in contact with those who valiantly or, better said, have proudly gone it alone – most often with far less stellar results. You could chalk my experience up to too small of a sample size or some other excuse, so let's continue. Think about any business that has experienced success at some level. Do you think Bill Gates knew how to take a company public or draft legal documents or manufacture anything? Probably not. What about our government? Some may view this as a bad example, but we all know that our government doesn't rely on the intellect or effort of any single individual. Regardless of who is elected president of the United States, no single individual could successfully run any function of that office without tons of help from other experts. The president's cabinet of top advisors play a critical role in the success of the office and country. If you dislike the bureaucracy of the government and that doesn't make a good case for you, let's look to the world of sports.

Every professional sports team has coaches who lead the top athletes in that particular sport – people who know how to play the game well. Almost without question, I would guess that most people would contend that coaching in sports still matters. Even if we look to individual sports like golf, professional guidance and coaching are still an integral part of these athletes' "individual" success. Take Tiger Woods for instance. Tiger is probably the most talented golfer of all time, yet he still has a coach that works with him to help him play at an optimal level. Why is it that the best athlete in a given sport needs a coach? More practically, why would a perfectly intellectually capable individual need assistance with financial planning? Why would a Christian with an average degree of self-discipline, who reads and studies the Bible, need to attend church and/or be discipled by others?

The reasons to involve others in your endeavors to live a truly rich life are very simple. There is tremendous benefit in involving others who possess talents and gifts that are different than yours, or maybe that compliment yours, which could result in real value to many different areas of your life. In many instances, this means surrounding yourself with people who have core competencies that might be your weaknesses; but that doesn't have to be the case in order to provide value, as the Tiger Woods example would prove. Involving others also takes advantage of that hard-to-quantify value of objectivity that only an outside perspective can bring.

This outside perspective helps in providing a clearer picture, unskewed or tainted by the emotions of your particular situation, and often can draw insight from the experiences of others. Yet another element that a team, advisor, coach, or mentor brings is accountability. People hire personal trainers not just to show them the right way to exercise but to make them exercise even when they don't feel like it or to push them harder than they would otherwise. As a financial planner, I can't tell you how many clients that would probably not have the discipline on their own to regularly invest or keep up with tax information or regularly set goals if it wasn't for the encouragement and accountability that comes through a professional relationship. Unfortunately, we can also site numerous examples of Christian leaders who have lost their ministry and tarnished their witness as a result of not having accountability in the more personal and spiritual areas of life. Accountability matters.

There is no wonder that you often hear successful people thank those who have helped them to get them where they are. How often have you heard an Academy Award winner, Super Bowl champ, or Grammy winner give that all-so-familiar "I want to thank God, my family, my team, etc." While these are public examples of recognizing this truth, there are many more private examples of those who have enriched their lives and the lives of those around them by reaching out to others for help.

The question now becomes, who should you have on your "team" of advisors? I will give several suggestions and will start by dividing them into two main categories: nonprofessional and professional advisors. I can assure you that I thought long and hard about some better name for nonprofessional advisors, but I think you will get the point and application despite the bland name. I can also already guess that some level of tension is growing, and you may be thinking, "I don't want to compose a *team*." I can understand that this might seem somewhat awkward, and I am not suggesting that you have to tell these people that they are part of some formalized team or as some would call it, a "personal board of directors." I am suggesting that you have, formal or informal, a network of people you know and trust who can provide experience, expertise, objectivity, and accountability.

The Bible speaks a great deal of discipleship and relationships for good reason. The Christian life is not one that is intuitive; in fact, it is contrary to how we naturally are. Because of that fact, we must pray for the Holy Spirit's direction, read, and study the Bible; but on top of that, the impact that other Christians can have on us is one that is almost indescribable. The only catch to this wonderful situation is that in this busy world, it normally takes initiative on your part to seek out these relationships that can add that teaching and accountability element. As a Christian, there is a world full of things that would pull us from our God-given purposes; without other Christians to encourage, support, teach, and disciple, the probability of discouragement and failures greatly increases. It is sometimes tough to stick to God's promises or your commitments when you don't have physical reminders, actual people, who are there encouraging you, praying with and for you, and helping to carry the load with you. We all know we need it, so we should be about seeking and maintaining these pivotal relationships.

I will add that when looking for someone or several people to develop this kind of relationship with, while it is great to have someone who is your same age and is going through the same things, it should be noted that there is also great benefit to learning from someone older who has the asset of reflection. This elder individual may have already successfully, or maybe even unsuccessfully (but learned from the experience), dealt with the issues of life to which you are going through. Case in point, learning about parenting is best learned from someone who has raised their children fully, as opposed to your buddy who is struggling with the same issues. It should be obvious; but when seeking out spiritual, or just life mentors, look for those people who are truly rich – not just the successful businessman who's been divorced three times or the person who is a walking Bible trivia guru but has no fruit in their life.

I do think it is of some benefit to have other nonprofessional advisors on your team. These might be people who *are* just successful in the business world. While you may not seek their advice or opinion about many areas of life, they may have a great deal of insight and expertise about other areas that can be beneficial, such as your professional life. It is hard to put your finger on it, but there is often a unique quality that some successful people in the business or financial world have – a knack, for lack of a better word, for making money. These people can act as a sounding board for ideas and can add another viewpoint that you might not otherwise have. I hope to make it clear that I do not suggest that your advice from some people go beyond their particular area of expertise, as I would never want to violate Psalms 1, "Blessed is the man who walks not in the counsel of the wicked." However, if I was thinking about opening a particular business and there was a successful businessman who has run similar businesses, it is only common sense that he could add insight into that particular venture that even your most well-intentioned Christian mentor could not.

Next, I will suggest some *professional* advisors that you may include on your team. I fully realize that not all people need a robust professional bench but many people could benefit from these advisors and don't seek them out because of misperceptions and just plain excuses. I can't tell you how often I hear people say, "I don't have enough money to need a financial planner." In reality, anyone who needs to plan financially probably could benefit from professional help. I understand the reality that most advisors don't work for free, but that is a whole other issue altogether and one in which we will deal with shortly.

It is my contention that the three main professional advisors that should be a part of your team are a financial planner, an accountant, and a lawyer. I will briefly discuss my reasoning behind these picks and recognize that other people such as your insurance agent and your banker also can provide advice and services that are meaningful and needed and may even be more important to you depending on your particular situation. When looking for and evaluating any professional advisor, there are three main criteria that should be evaluated and used as your guidelines for hiring: expertise, experience, and ethics.

First and foremost, an advisor should have expertise in their particular area of practice. If they don't, you have a potentially dangerous combination – the blind leading the blind. In most cases, it would be obvious that they have some level of expertise, whether as the result of a formal education in their field or some other evidence of training which has equipped them to handle your issues. I will talk about specific qualifications that each professional should have shortly. The whole point of using an "expert" or professional is to ensure that things are done right, which can save you time, energy, heartache, and money down the road – not so you can just say at dinner parties, "That is my attorney."

Second, but of no less importance, is experience. I must be careful in stating what I mean here. Many people say that experience is the result of making bad decisions, a definition which makes me a little nervous when discussing getting advice about money or, especially, legal or tax issues. I would hope that most competent advisors have learned their lessons through some formal education and by learning from the mistakes of others, rather than having to make them on their own. I prefer to think of experience as having "been there and done that" – hopefully, many times before. I frequently compare the experience you should seek to the difference in a travel agent versus a tour guide. A travel agent may know about a particular place and can point you in the right direction, but a tour guide knows the details and has a firsthand familiarity with the area and can essentially go along with you; it is this familiarity and experience that you should seek.

Experience in dealing with a situation can give both sides confidence in the outcome, because this isn't the first time the advisor has done this sort of thing. When a doctor says, "I've never done this type of surgery; I can't wait to see what happens," you should be concerned; however, when they tell you they have performed this same surgery ten times already this week, you can have much greater confidence in a positive result. An example of a situation where experience is greatly needed would be when someone is about to retire and collect that final paycheck. Often, "retirement" means decisions regarding taking pension options, rolling over 401(k) money, maybe selling a business, or just that the new event of actually starting to draw money from their investment portfolio. An inexperienced investment person may know the "theory" of how to construct a portfolio and what a pension is, but until they have been through this process many times, hopefully under the supervision of an experienced advisor, the outcome could be problematic to say the least. Another example would be setting up an estate distribution plan. If you let Joe Attorney, who does not have expertise or experience in devising such plans, draft your documents – who knows what will really happen once you are gone? I can assure you Joe isn't so sure himself. Dealing with an experienced advisor can provide a peace of mind that things are handled properly.

Unfortunately, the "experience" that many tout could be just poor advice practiced over and over again. Without the proper education, I would heavily discount any "experience" someone may have. Years in the business does not necessarily translate into the type of "experience" you should be looking for, so make sure the expertise criterion is met first.

While I firmly believe in experience as a criterion, I also grudgingly bring it up for the simple fact that I am comparatively young (at the writing of this book) and have less "years" under my belt than some others in my field. Nevertheless, I think you see what I mean, and I think that it goes without saying that there are a number of wonderful advisors, though young, that have the expertise and experience to provide a great deal of value. I will selfishly add that often it is the young professional who is still very energetic about learning and may be more current with information and strategies or may be more proactive than a more established older professional; don't write young advisors off without exploring their qualifications first.

Finally and without a doubt the most important factor in choosing any advisor is ethics. I think it almost goes without saying these days, in the wake of corporate scandal after corporate scandal, that ethics do matter. I think in most of those cases, the individuals involved were both educated and experienced; but the chink in their moral armor led to their downfall as well as those around them. The fact that I am talking about building a team of advisors who will help you with making financial and other decisions should immediately throw up a red flag if you question the advisor's integrity. As the Bible says, "the love of money is the root of *all kinds* of evil," which should make you always stop to consider who you're dealing with and any potential biases that may be present. Although there is no foolproof method for rooting out the "evil advisor," the good news is that for the most part, they are scarce. I would suggest, however, that you be sensitive to this issue and spend a little time researching and asking around about the advisor before you let them guide you in your financial decisions. I believe, and am thankful, that most people are very trusting and not suspicious types, a fact I hope remains, but would ask you to simply guard yourself from being the next sucker. It is unfortunate, but there are people who make a pretty "good living" by practicing bad advice and taking advantage of clients and you certainly don't want to be their next prey. Many of these types of people would fit closely with Groucho Marx's quote, "The secret of life is honesty and fair dealing. If you can fake that, you got it made." So with that in mind, take the advice of Warren Buffett; to paraphrase: be wary of promotional people . . . not all promotional people are crooks, but all crooks are promotional people. So just because you see someone on TV, or have seen their billboard, or – God forbid – read their book (ouch!), you should still dig a little deeper.

How do you find that right person with expertise, experience, and ethics? The easiest way is to get a referral from someone who works with them. A referral represents a few things: experience (they probably helped the person who referred you), competence (the referrer liked the outcome of working with them), and the ethical issue becomes less of a concern as hopefully the person who referred you has gotten a chance to know the advisor and can vouch for their integrity. Most top advisors don't have their face on billboards or have TV commercials. They don't have to, and most wouldn't want the people who respond to that type of advertising. Do you think Bill Gates's advisors are soliciting John Q. Public? Probably not. Think about it – how do you go about choosing your doctor? Of course you wouldn't just choose the one with the best yellow pages ad; you would ask a friend who they use. This same method is great for finding the right professional advisor. Ask around and get a strong referral, not just an "I think I know this guy that does something like that" or "My guy is *okay.*" Find someone who has worked with them and is happy with the relationship. Often, if you find one of the main three advisors, they will know and work with advisors in these other fields that can assist you and be a great referrer.

Now let's briefly touch on why I believe in these three key players and what they bring to the table: the financial planner, attorney, and accountant. As I said, these are the "key" players; others will be involved and may be more important depending on your particular situation. I am sure that I have just offended some people who would suggest that their "profession" should be included on this short list of key players. They are entitled to their opinion and can write their own book if they feel so inclined; however, I will give my reasoning for these three.

I will start by suggesting that the quarterback of the team would be the financial planner. A financial planner is a professional that takes a cross-disciplinary approach to looking at your entire financial situation and uses this big-picture approach in helping you to achieve your life's goals. This individual or firm will spend a good deal of time wanting to know what it is you want out of life, what you want to accomplish, and helping you to prioritize those goals. Then with that end in mind, they make recommendations and specific plans to help you get from where you are today to where you want to be. As I mentioned, this is a holistic or multidisciplinary approach that will involve everything from investing to legal planning to tax planning to insurance planning. It is because of these numerous areas that a financial planner deals with that I suggest this being one of the first advisors to put on your team. They will often act as a "quarterback" in making sure that the "ball" is handed off to another professional, such as an attorney, and makes sure that steps in the process are getting accomplished and working toward your goals. Good financial planners have numerous contacts within the financial, legal, insurance, banking, and accounting communities and could be a great source to refer you to your next team member.

With that being said about financial planners, it is *very* important for you to look for the three *E*s when looking for one. I say this because there is currently no legal restriction on the term "financial planner," and it seems en vogue today to throw around that title regardless of what you actually do. The Certified Financial Planner Board of Standards Inc. suggests that you ask the following ten questions when interviewing a financial planner; their answers should give you a pretty good idea of where they stand.

1. What experience do you have? (Already discussed this one)
2. What are your qualifications? Education? Professional designations (CFP®, ChFC, CLU, PFS, CFA®)?
3. What services do you offer? Is it comprehensive or just investment advice?
4. What is your approach to financial planning? Conservative or leading edge? Holistic or more specific to one area?
5. Will you be the only person working with me? Team approach, other staff, or a one-man shop?
6. How will I pay for your services? Flat fee, percentage of assets, hourly fee, commission on products, combination of these?

7. How much do you typically charge? What does it depend on?
8. Could anyone besides me benefit from your recommendations? Are there any referral fees being paid – conflicts of interest I should know about?
9. Have you ever been publicly disciplined for any unlawful or unethical actions in your professional career? (Show me those skeletons!)
10. Can I have it in writing? Make them put the details of services that will be provided in a written agreement that you keep on file.

These questions are a great guide and start to find that right person for you. You can see this list and other resources at their Web site: *www.cfpboard.org*. With respect to qualifications, I would suggest that a "financial planner" be a *Certified Financial Planner*™ practitioner or CFP® practitioner for short. There is a formalized educational program to becoming a CFP® practitioner, and I can see no reason why a competent planner would have a problem with going through it. To become a CFP one must complete a comprehensive course of study, pass a rigorous comprehensive two-day-long test, have at least three years of financial planning experience, agree to abide to a strict code of professional conduct, and complete ongoing education to stay certified. With planners who have proven a certain level of competence by doing these, why would you choose to have a planner who isn't certified? Would you ask medical advice regarding a serious problem from someone who isn't a doctor? Of course not, and I believe just as strongly about this issue.

There are a number of other professional credentials in the financial services industry that are out there that I will briefly address. The American College, a financial services educational institution, supports the Chartered Financial Consultant designation, or ChFC for short, which is also a comprehensive course of study in financial planning and is highly credible – but in my opinion, does not command quite the same level of respect as the CFP®. They also award the Chartered Life Underwriter designation (CLU) whose course of study is concentrated in the area of life insurance and estate planning. The Chartered Financial Analyst Institute awards the Chartered Financial Analyst designation (CFA®) which is considered the gold standard in the investment management world and requires passing three very rigorous examinations which take on average four years to complete. There are litanies of other professional designations out there, some of which are credible, but possibly much narrower in scope which I haven't mentioned.

I must give warning that there are also an increasing number of bogus credentials whose purpose is simply to instill confidence from the public but are backed by very little education. To put it very bluntly, there are some designations that nearly anyone with a few hours and a couple hundred bucks could become "certified," "chartered," and anything else that sounds fancy.

It *is* important to ask what services one offers, which may seem strange because I just said that planners use a holistic approach. Keep in mind that many people, even some who are CFP®s, choose to only offer investment or only insurance advice and don't do *comprehensive* planning. That is not to say that one is necessarily superior to the other in your situation, just that you need to understand what you are getting. I will contend that the wealthier you are, or the more complex your situation, the more comprehensive planning becomes strongly advisable.

The last question that I will comment on with regards to financial planners is the issue of compensation. I think most would agree that if someone provides a meaningful and valuable service, they deserve to get paid. If you agree, then we can move on to the method of payment; if you don't agree, this world we live in probably seems like an extremely unfair place. As I start, let me say that there is not necessarily a "best way" for a planner to get compensated, only that the client needs to fully understand it and feel comfortable with it. Inherently associated with *all* types of compensation in financial services business are conflicts of interest. *What is really important* is whether or not you are getting value for the service provided, there is full disclosure, and that the planner is acting in your best interest.

The three basic categories of planner compensation are fee only, fee-based, and commission only. Fee only is simply charging a fee, either a flat or hourly fee for the planning work they do. In addition, if the advisor manages the investments, this is also done as a fee based on percentage of the assets they manage. While many fee-only advisors proudly tout their way of doing business as the only ethical way to practice since it presents "no conflicts of interests," this is not entirely the truth and should not be the basis of considering one's ethics or skill. You are obviously not on any kind of moral high ground if you charge an exorbitantly high "flat fee" which goes against the clients' goals of accumulating money. That being said, however, many top planners *do* choose this form of compensation for their practice.

Fee-based is yet another way that financial planners arrange compensation and this simply means that some fee is charged, either flat or hourly, and the potential to make commission exists. There are so many ways that this arrangement can be sliced and diced that I will refrain to comment much more about it, other than to say that this is how I currently structure my practice, and I feel it is a good option for all parties involved. Different advisors have different ways they derive their fee, what it covers, and what services commissions may be a part of. Some fee-based advisors only manage investments on a fee basis, similar to fee-only advisors, but may earn a commission on insurance products if that is a part of your plans implementation. Today I feel like this compensation structure suits my practice and clientele, as I feel I am equitably paid for the service I provide: fees for the planning work my team does, and the potential for commissions (on certain areas) on the implementation of that plan. I will say that disclosure is always an important issue when there are commissions involved, and most all planners do or will disclose all fees being generated at the request of the client.

Finally, there is the full-commission advisor who is often thought of as just a glorified salesperson and his only objective is to sell you something. Of course, this is a destructive generalization and speaks nothing of the advisor's morality, expertise, and experience. I have been watching recent TV advertisements which seem to fixate on this negative perception of commissions; and to be honest, it is focusing on the wrong things altogether. I will say that most credible financial planners serving the affluent marketplace do not find this method practical and recognize that it does present higher degrees of conflicts of interest, but I certainly recognize that it is possible to get good advice from a full-commission advisor. If you are of modest means or are in need of "single-needs" type of planning (buy some insurance or open a Roth IRA), then the advisor who will serve you is probably primarily compensated through commissions. I have thought long and hard about how all socioeconomic classes can be served; and at this point, the commission-based advisor is still an indispensable part of that system. I would remind you that, regardless of the compensation method employed, I firmly believe the advisor you choose should closely meet the other criteria.

In being involved in the financial planning community in the Birmingham, Alabama area, I have met a number of good financial planners. Many offer different levels and types of service, and many are paid in various ways. To make a blanket statement about the validity of these would be absurd. In reality, the way planners choose to be compensated is a business decision based on a multitude of factors and most would be more than happy to discuss them with prospective clients – so don't be shy about asking. With that, I will spare you from all of the potential conflicts of interest, as most are somewhat obvious; and if you have followed my advice about expertise, experience, and ethics, these conflicts should be manageable.

Next, let's discuss another valued advisor that most all can greatly benefit from having on their team: an accountant. I will quickly cut to the chase and recommend that your accountant be a CPA, or certified public accountant. While I am sure that there are probably a number of instances where someone is a good accountant who isn't a CPA, it is probably much safer to say to stick with those who are. The qualifications to become a CPA also aids in getting past the expertise criterion I firmly believe in. If you have a simple financial situation, an accountant is probably not going to do much more than do your tax return every year and may offer some ancillary advice about contributing more to your 401(k) or IRAs and a few other tidbits. However, if your situation is more complex, as many people's are, then an accountant can be an invaluable member of your team. Our tax system is ridiculously complex and constantly changing; and with expert knowledge, it is possible to obtain a real tangible benefit. I am all for "paying Caesar what is Caesar's," but I highly recommend that the government not be your biggest charity. A good accountant is not just someone who correctly calculates the tax you owe but is someone who can assist you and your financial planner in proactively planning to avoid unnecessary taxes and correctly implement other strategies. Because so much of financial planning has tax consequences, the more you have going on financially, the more a CPA becomes an irreplaceable team member. For those of you who own businesses or are in business for yourself, a CPA can aid in many ways to ensure that you are not only doing things correctly from a compliance standpoint, but also can aid a great deal in your profitability.

Finally, it is always good to have a relationship with a good attorney, attorneys, or law firm. It should be noted that both financial planning and accounting have a number of specialties of sorts; however, almost nowhere is specialization more prevalent than in the legal field. It would not be odd to meet with a great real estate attorney who knows very little about estate planning or an estate-planning attorney who would be of no value to you as a defense attorney. I sincerely hope that you never need a defense attorney, but all people need to do estate planning at some point in their life (sooner better than later) so an estate planning attorney would be a good person to have on your team. As Christians, we really shouldn't pretend that death isn't real, and so planning for estate distribution and legacy issues is only prudent. I seriously urge you to take care of this area of planning early on and review and revise your plan as your goals, situation, and tax environment change. I strongly suggest that the attorney who aids you in this pursuit is a specialist in estate planning; after all, your plans are only as good as the documents that are drafted. If your real estate attorney draws up your will and something goes wrong, there is little you will be able to do about it from the grave. I will also take this opportunity to stress to those of you who have special-needs children or spouses with disabilities: estate planning with a good attorney can solve a number of the issues you fear; please don't hesitate in seeking the help of a professional. An estate-planning attorney is also very familiar with asset protection concerns and can be a tremendous resource on a number of other issues as well.

While I am not handily dismissing all one-man legal shops out there, I will bring you back to my comment that rarely does one person have all of the knowledge and experience to provide prudent advice. This is true in financial planning, true in accounting, and is especially true in the legal realm. Thankfully, most attorneys who specialize in estate planning are housed within big firms. This can allow for contact with other attorneys who can aid in other legal issues (that they specialize in) that may arise and can be a valuable resource for you. While you might not meet with your estate-planning attorney often, especially for affluent individuals, their importance cannot be emphasized enough.

These three advisors most often work at different firms which can add a new level of accountability and flexibility. By having these professions not being under one roof, so to speak, it creates somewhat of a system of checks and balances in which the main goal is the success of you, the client. By having other advisers involved, a new sense of accountability and often a new synergy to promote good ideas is created as well. In terms of flexibility, having outside advisors can often allow for more specialized expertise. While there may be some firms which house accountants, attorneys, and financial planners all within one "firm" of sorts; I would caution that this same level of checks and balances I have mentioned may not be present and may leave room or create new conflicts of interest. While many wealthy clients crave bulletproof confidentiality, I don't think that having all advisors under one roof is a necessity.

I want to come back to this issue of compensation with regards to all advisors. I have already discussed the basic ways financial planners get compensated, and for the most part, CPAs and attorneys charge by the hour, with a few exceptions. I do want to address compensation for the primary reason that I find that most people don't seek the advice of professionals because they don't want to pay the "high" fees. What "high" means, I don't know. For some it may mean one thing and yet something entirely different to someone else. There is a saying that goes, "We live in an age where people know the price of everything and the value of nothing." The point this saying makes is that there is a big difference between price and value. Does it make sense to pay an attorney who specializes in the area you need $350 an hour if he can produce a result that is exponentially greater (potentially) as opposed to someone with less expertise who may charge a fraction of that but who's outcome is much less positive (potentially)? Who wins in that situation? It reminds me of a story about a new hair salon in town that in an effort to get into business put out a huge sign in front of their store advertising "$2.99 haircuts." In response, the established salon down the road put up a sign which read, "We fix $2.99 haircuts." The point in both of these examples is clear. It is unfair to make a judgment about a service on price alone without looking at a greater measure I would call value.

Value is comprised of the tangibles of price and performance as well as the intangibles of things like peace of mind. I find it extremely frustrating when I lose a potential prospect to another advisor (whom I deem less qualified) over price. Does it make sense to let the advisor with the lowest bid handle your financial future? While price is certainly a component everyone must consider when hiring an advisor to your team, let value be the deciding factor. Mitch Anthony in his book *The New Retire-Mentality* discusses this issue and describes it as "the high cost of low fees."[98] Some people would rather not pay anyone at all and would rather do it alone, but I hope I have convinced you of the benefits of having advisors. To spare you from a complete recap, it is important to remember that the idea is that the advisor *adds* value to your situation. This means they added more value than they cost, and more than you would have done otherwise, and considers all factors including things like peace of mind. It's okay to be cheap when buying clothes or food; but when it comes to your life plans, don't be a miser.

There is another issue I often hear people discussing that I would like to mention. The issue is the importance of your *professional* advisors being Christian. While truly I wish that all people shared the Christian faith, I do not think in this particular situation that it should be sought *at the expense* of these other criteria I have laid out. Unfortunately, I must also warn you to not substitute further research into an advisor's ethics just because one labels themselves as a Christian. There are those who trade on their religion and hope to instill a blind trust in order to take advantage of you, so you must beware. If you want Christian counsel or are able to find an advisor with a similar belief system who meets these other qualifications – great. However, a true professional is able to take your goals and translate that into aligning actions whether or not they completely agree with them. This is one reason I strongly encourage you to have spiritual accountability from nonprofessional advisors. Looking for spiritual accountability within the framework of a professional relationship creates a difficult dynamic that can be precarious to navigate. Take the example of a situation where a Christian advisor thinks you have a standard of living that is too high, despite your generous giving. Is it the advisors' place to speak their opinion? Will they get fired or hurt the relationship by doing so? As I said, spiritual accountability is paramount, but seeking it in a professional setting can be (not always, but can be) difficult. I also hold this opinion because frankly some of the most technically competent advisors within my profession do not share my faith, but I recognize the value they can bring to *anyone's* situation. I often relate it to this example. Let's say you have a dreaded disease and needed surgery. Would you rather have a nice Christian doctor straight out of medical school or a non-Christian doctor who specializes in that particular surgery? The point being is that in important matters which require a technical skill, expertise outweighs their religious affiliation. I am obviously not making this argument for my benefit, as I am sure you know by now that I am a Christian; but I would encourage you not to overweigh faith as a requirement at the expense of expertise and experience. If your situation is very simple or if you are seeking Christian counsel because you don't have nonprofessional advisors, then I would urge you to seek advisors who are Christian; but if your situation is complex or you have the nonprofessional group of advisors I have recommended, then I don't think it is an extremely relevant criterion. The bottom line is that you deserve good advice, and you should feel comfortable sharing your plans with the advisor.

One last thing in regards to criteria for advisors that should be obvious but I must mention. When I have laid out the criteria for professional advisors, I am making the assumption that they are "professional," meaning it should go without saying that they return your phone calls and are diligent in the work they do for you. You can have the smartest, most experienced, and most ethical advisor in the world; but if he never calls you or does what he says he is going to do, then you have a problem. A referral should lessen the probability that this would be a problem.

Now I am going to assume that you will take my advice and seek out this group of people if you haven't already. Assuming you seek these types of relationships, I want to remind you that these are relationships. If you want to get the most out of any relationship, even your professional ones, it only makes sense that you have to work at it a little. With this, I mean that your professional advisors are people too, not just heads full of knowledge; and they have emotions and feelings just like anybody else. I am just being honest when I tell you that those clients who are easiest and best to work with get the best service and the most out of the relationship. If you, the client, don't return phone calls or are constantly rescheduling meetings, any (I speak for all advisors in saying this) advisor is going to take issue with that. We also like to be thanked from time to time when we have added value, because remember, most advisors don't practice for the sole purpose of making money – we like helping people.

I say all of this not so that I will get thank-you cards but because I think that it affects (whether it should or not) the level of service you get and the relationship you have with the advisor. I have some clients who are far from ultra wealthy, and probably not very profitable for my firm, but they are extremely appreciative and responsive and I would do nearly anything for them. On the other hand, every professional has that ultrawealthy client that treats them like dirt and is constantly evaluating if it is really worth it to keep them as a client. Treat your professional relationships with the same courtesy you would any other, and I can promise you the result will be much better for everyone involved.

I hope I have convinced you of the importance of building a team or network of advisors who can aid you in your pursuit of a truly rich life. This network should provide guidance, support, and accountability in really every area of your life. The benefits of having others with different strengths collectively assisting you not only makes intellectual sense, but also creates a wonderful emotional feeling as well. It is great to know that other people want you to be successful and, in some cases, have a stake in your success. I would also encourage you to make these relationships, if you don't already have them, before you need them. If you wait until you are in a time crunch to make an important decision or if you're struggling with some issue, it is very difficult to pull this sort of thing together in a way that produces the best result. I believe in this concept so much that I have made it my life's work, and I firmly believe that it is an integral part of a truly rich life.

CHAPTER 13

More Pearls to Ponder

Throughout this book I have been laying out for you what I believe it means to be truly rich. I have shown evidence that clearly shows that material abundance and financial assets are not the sole ingredients for true happiness. I have laid out what I believe the central messages of the Bible are concerning money and hopefully have dispelled myths and misconceptions that many hold. While money does not make a life, we do live in a time where it takes money to live; how we handle that money will determine, to a great degree, the options that we have in life. It is for this reason that I have spent considerable effort to point out some suggestions regarding how to best manage the money and resources that you have been given. Finally, while the topic of this book could probably fill volumes, I do feel the need to leave you with a few other items that I believe are important in this pursuit of living a truly rich life. As I will repeat near the end, some of these suggestions are obviously my personal opinion, where others I believe stand on their own as fact. My hope is that since this list is not exhaustive, you will begin to think of other things that you would add and this will motivate you in ways to better your life and others. I in no way believe that there is one cookie-cutter guide to happiness and fulfillment. White picket fences, two kids, and grandparents living in the same town may be wonderful for some, but not for others; however, there are some aspects which are universal. Here are some of those along with some of my opinions:

Have a personal relationship with Jesus Christ as your Lord and Savior. While I have mentioned it numerous times indirectly while discussing stewardship and other topics, which all lead toward a truly rich life, I need to make no mistake in putting it at the forefront of everything we have discussed. All these and even greater issues of life are answered in Christ and I pray that you will seek out the good news of Christ and if you already know of Him or maybe already trust in Him for your salvation, that you would affirm that with a life that would be pleasing to Him. For doing God's will is what it means to be truly rich.

Have children; they teach you what love is really about. God in His wisdom created the family to give us a glimpse at what His love is really like. It is one thing to talk about unconditional love, and it is another thing to experience it. Parents inherently love their children, and children, at least at a young age, likewise love their parents; there is nothing this side of heaven like it. I recognize that all couples can't have kids, which presents another unique blessing: adoption. While anyone can adopt, it is also a gracious provision to couples who can't have children. (It is also an amazing fertility enhancer. I can't explain it, but we all know people who have adopted and who end up having a biological child). Children are also a way we can leave a bigger mark on this world and fulfill God's command to be fruitful and multiply.

Flee from sin. This is not my plea for legalism, where I suggest you do this and not do that. God's plan for our lives is one free from the penalty and bondage of sin (if you are saved by faith in Christ). While many may not recognize the chains of sin, I can guarantee that any short-term enjoyment of sin is followed by a long list of negative consequences. *All sin* has consequences, and it is only God's grace that keeps them from being full-blown. A truly rich life is one free from the guilt and bondage of sin and full of the freedom that is enjoyed with Christ as your Savior.

Have a pet. This may seem a little out of place, especially considering other topics I have just mentioned, but it's my opinion that there is something wonderfully positive about pets. I prefer dogs simply because they are affectionate and love attention. Like children, they too have a wonderful quality of unconditional love (I'm not comparing children to dogs – settle down.). My dog is always ready to greet me when I walk in the door and is a constant companion. God created many animals apparently for no other reason than our enjoyment and I truly believe they add a wonderful element to life. My own experience with pet owners suggests to me that most wouldn't trade their pet for any amount of money. There is some research which supports uplifted attitudes around animals which is why there are organizations which take animals to hospitals to visit patients. I will give fair warning to choose carefully your animal companion, as some, by nature, can be a pain in the neck. Also, recognize that if you don't train them early, you will be dealing with the consequences for their life. For whatever its worth, I am a proponent of pet ownership.

Read books. If you have read this book, I hope it has rewarded you in some way. I really didn't develop a love for reading until I was out of school and didn't *have to* read. It was then that I found the incredible wisdom that is available through books. If you look at those people throughout history who have made an incredible impact in this world, it is not uncommon to find that they were avid readers. It is a shame that much of the wisdom of those before us is being lost, because many today are unwilling to invest in themselves by reading. Of course, when I say reading, I certainly promote casual and fun fictional reading; but mainly I am referring to those books which will have the capacity to add something to your life, not just subtracted time. If we want to know God's plan for our lives, know about who He is and what He has done, as well as His immeasurable wisdom, then the Bible should be our guide. I truly believe every Christian should not only regularly read the Bible, but learn to study it.

Remember that your money can be spent and lost, and later you can make more. Time, on the other hand, can never be regained. I am reminded of a story I heard about an elderly man at my church that at his birthday filled a jar with marbles, each representing days that he hopefully had left to live. Every morning he would get up, say his prayers, and take a marble out. This was a visual reminder to him to not waste any of his time here on earth. If you would like to do this somewhat eerie exercise yourself, the Web has a site call *www.deathclock.com* where you can see how many seconds you have left to live based on actuarial calculations. Even though I firmly know that God has numbered my days, it still kind of gives you a sense of urgency to "get to livin.'" Every day is precious; if you don't believe me, as they say, try missing one. Citibank has a commercial on TV right now that says something to the effect of "overtime pays more because of what you are missing;" not only a great commercial, but a great lesson in life. Capture each moment and use your time wisely – it is truly precious.

Develop and be intentional in your relationships. Surround yourself with people who have qualities you admire. On the flip side, remember, bad company corrupts good moral character. However, if you have an opportunity to befriend someone who doesn't know Christ, be intentional in your friendship and model the love of Christ to them and teach them of the good news. At some point in all of our lives, our relationship with the Lord, family, and friends are all that will matter to us. Ask anyone who has been stricken with a serious illness if they care about what year model their car is or if they are a member of the "right" country club. I can assure you that these seemingly "important" things are inconsequential. Striving to be intentional in relationship building is not only "good for you" but also enriches the lives of others and can be what God uses to build His kingdom. Despite increases in communication technology, the fast pace of life is causing people to become more and more isolated; we should resist this trend and seek meaningful friendships, not just having tons of acquaintances. Friends can be there to share our joys, carry our burdens, ask the tough questions, and give godly encouragement. A man with many true friends is rich indeed.

Invest in your health. There is a strong connection between the physical and the spiritual and between the physical and the mental. In fact, I can't think of many things that your physical well-being doesn't affect. It only makes sense that a truly rich life involves one that is healthy as possible. Of course, God is in control of our health and He is always the first cause, but there does exist the phenomenon of second causes. That being said, eating junk food all day and smoking cigarettes will probably affect your health at some time, which affects all aspects of your life. Our bodies are the temple of the Holy Spirit; keep it in good shape. Go to the doctor. This sounds so simple and it is, but many people, especially as we start to age, fear going to the doctor as if going is what will make them sick. Trust me, if you have a health issue, you want to know about it early and seek treatment. I heard a doctor on the radio recently who said that one of his patients told him that he would have taken better care of himself had he known he was going to live that long. Make the most out of what you have been given. It is not about adding years to your life, but life to your years.

Do hands-on work to help those less fortunate. Whether it's an out-of-the-country mission trip or delivering Christmas gifts to those who can't afford them, it gives you a reality check as to how materially blessed you are. For me, it is a check on my pride and makes me so thankful for all that I have been given. It is impossible to be thankful and greedy at the same time; so if you need an antidote for the "gotta-haves," go and do for the less fortunate. Most importantly, you are acting out part of the mission of Christ's church which is to "love your neighbor as yourself." People who are often hostile or uninterested in the Gospel message have had a negative experience with Christians in the past or are hopeless and don't know where to turn. An outward showing of love and mercy is paving inroads for the Gospel to be delivered unencumbered. Doing works of compassion are not done to make you feel good, but there is an undeniable benefit which God bestows on those who are about His work.

Learn something new. Learn a new skill, a new language, a craft, or a sport. There is something exciting about learning. Many people who work with the elderly know firsthand that learning something new keeps the mind active and sharp and spirits lifted. Children are a great example of the joy of learning. When my son learns something new, he giggles and repeats what he learned incessantly. This isn't a coincidence. Learning is fun. If you need something new to learn, think about some of the things mentioned earlier and how you might combine these. For instance, you could learn how to build things by getting involved with Habitat for Humanity or a short-term mission project. This would help you to build relationships with others, help the less fortunate, do something physical, and help build something lasting. Forget the so-called linear life plan: youth (learning), middle age (working), and old age (leisure); develop a mantra of lifelong learning. There should never be a time in one's life when they have "arrived"; this attitude can lead to a stranglehold of the past, no excitement about the future, and is not an attitude that reflects a truly rich life.

Invest in your marriage. If you have been blessed with a spouse, then this is the person God has chosen for you to travel the road of life with. Try to stay out of the rut of the mundane everyday hustle and bustle. Take the time to enjoy your spouse and love them the way you are commanded to. Although I don't remember much of what was said at my wedding, I do remember the pastor commending me to "date your wife all your life," meaning to try and treat them with the esteem and special courtesy that they once were given. One who has a strong marriage is truly rich. Be your spouse's biggest fan, not their biggest critic, their biggest ally instead of their opposition. I am sure most everyone who is married can remember a time early on in your relationship when you felt like as long as you had this person in your life, nothing else mattered. I can remember living in a little apartment when I was first married, working days and going to graduate school at night, and somehow I didn't care much because I was so "in love." Unfortunately this feeling of infatuation nearly always fades; and instead of a mature love that is even much greater, we often replace it with the cares of this world and selfish desires. I encourage everyone to work on their marriage as if it was one of the greatest missions in life, because it is. The institution of marriage is under attack today; and if you have been blessed with a spouse, you should work to make your marriage a testament to the bond and blessing that God has given which is found nowhere else. It is without question that a good marriage can be your greatest asset, or a bad one, your greatest liability. Having a healthy and happy marriage is an invaluable part to a truly rich life.

To those of you who are unmarried, choose carefully your spouse and look not to the world for advice. While beauty, money, and power are all attractive qualities that the world champions; they are contrary to what the Bible prescribes. Men, remember Proverbs 12:4 and 31:30, "An excellent wife is the crown of her husband, but she who brings shame is like rottenness to his bones" and "Charm is deceitful, and beauty is vain, but a woman who fears the Lord is to be praised." Likewise, women, seek men who are godly and who cannot only provide financially, but spiritually as well. Oprah and Dr. Phil should not be your guide, and bars are probably not the best place to find your future spouse. Seek godly counsel and pray for the spouse God would have for you. Marriage is a wonderful blessing, but treated flippantly will produce unwanted consequences.

Invest in your children. In terms of leaving an inheritance or a lasting legacy, there is no better way than raising God-fearing children. Of course at some time, children become adults and have to make decisions for themselves as to the lives they will lead; it is for this reason that you should pour as much into their lives as you can, when you can. People who dread their kids turning teenagers probably should. You can't expect respectful kids who love the Lord if you haven't modeled that to them from the beginning. In this area, I am not speaking from personal experience, but from what I have seen from people I respect and what I desire for my children. Studies show people develop their moral foundation and their sensitivity to spiritual things at a very early age; so especially for parents with young children, the need to seize those precious opportunities is paramount. After all, we would all wish for our child's life to be God honoring from the start and not rely on some Damascus-road experience later in life. Another quick comment that I recently heard my pastor say and I thought was profound: "In today's society, it is all too common that we teach our children to depend on us and to need us." We *should* be raising our children to leave us, to "leave and cleave" to their spouse, and to be their own person. Dependent children may be endearing, but dependent adults are a strain emotionally and financially. As they say, kids learn more by what is caught than by what is taught. If you model the behavior you desire for them, pray for them diligently; God will do the rest. Of course, I should add here that grandparents can participate in this process as well.

Life is really a series of investing decisions. Stewardship is the allocation of your time, talents, and resources to the accomplishments of God-given goals; and as they say, you will reap what you sow. It is always important to start with the end in mind. Being truly rich requires a lot of investing – money being just a small part of the bigger picture.

Invest in prayer for others and yourself. Christ has uniquely provided the open door to communication with God; we have His ear, and He cares for us as His children. Prayer enables us to participate in what God is doing and can serve as His way of molding us more and more in His image. Life apart from prayer is like hearing the score of a game after it is over. Prayer allows us to be involved, maybe just as an active observer, but in some way in what God is doing; it is exciting to see Him answer. Ask others if you can pray for them; it may be the door to building that connection God will use to draw them to Himself.

Exercise. Certainly all physicians and people in the medical community suggest it in order to keep you healthy. The human body is truly unique in that when we work muscles, they grow stronger, when we use energy, we have more energy. I can't really explain it, but I do know that it doesn't take very long without exercising for you to quickly lose needed energy, as well as the cascade of implications from dormancy, such as weight gain, muscles and ligaments tightening, etc. Everyone knows that exercise is good for you, but I think it can be a lot of fun as well. It can come in the form of sports, classes with others, or even just the enjoyment of working out on your own. By the way, age is really not an excuse. Here is my disclaimer: consult your doctor before engaging in any exercise program, yada, yada, yada.

Travel from time to time. All are certainly not able for one reason or another; but getting out of your own little world is refreshing, exciting, relaxing, and mind expanding. A few days in a foreign country will make you quickly recognize that life isn't all about what is going on in your own little world; heck, these people don't even know you exist! Whether or not you like to fly, all would have to agree, looking back at the ground from thousands of feet in the air, that God is pretty awesome to have made it all. I always land with my jaded perspective wiped away and a renewed since of awe. Travel forcibly breaks the rut of everyday life that we often find ourselves in. It is not uncommon for bickering spouses to get past their pettiness or children to enjoy their parents just by getting away from it all. Some of my most vivid memories as a child were on vacations or short trips with my family.

Have accountability. There is something about people as they become adults that shun any idea of accountability; we don't want to have to answer to anyone. In reality, this attitude is what leads many to a fall in numerous areas of their life. Have people that can hold you spiritually accountable and can serve as encouragement during difficult times. Have someone, maybe it's a financial planner, who can hold you financially accountable. Try and develop mutual relationships with people who love you enough to ask the tough questions and can provide godly advice, as we are all prone to wander in various parts of our life. While this can be painful or uncomfortable in the short term, in the long run it is a key to a truly rich life.

Pursue your passion. God has uniquely planted most people with a passion for something. If it is a healthy passion (this is my disclaimer), embrace it and use it for God's glory. If you are able to have your passion as your occupation – great. Most people spend more time at work than in any other single activity, including sleep – might as well do something that you like. People whom I have observed that live a truly rich life often have something that they are very passionate about; maybe it's their occupation or mission work or maybe even a sport.

I have learned in my own life as well as observing others that what you feed grows. If you feed cynicism, you will become cynical. If you feed laziness, it will dominate your life. However, this principle can also be powerfully positive; if you feed your mind with positive thoughts, you will be a positive person. If you love on others, your love for others will increase; and many times they will love you back. If you seek after God, you will be satisfied in Him. Feed what you want to grow and starve the rest.

I find that many people like to put areas of their life in neat little boxes, separated from one another: this is my spiritual life, this is my social life, here is my financial life, my family life, my work life, etc. Life doesn't fit into neat little boxes, and trying to keep these areas separated is an impossible task apart from having a clone. Our life purpose should be to glorify God and to enjoy Him. All of these areas *can* fit within that framework. How it fits for you may be different than how it fits for me, but that is all Christians' purpose in life. To live a truly rich life depends on our ability, with God's help of course, to make all areas of our life line up with this purpose. We should strive to have all of these areas work together in harmony instead of conflict. If your work life puts undue pressures at home or your social life and spiritual life are diametrically opposed, something has to give. Chances are the result of such an example will be stress and grief. Being truly rich is being of one purpose.

As I have mentioned in several places in this book, the Christian life is not one that is easily, or should be, lived in isolation. I would encourage every believer to find a good church home. This church should be one that presents opportunities to grow you spiritually through effective preaching and teaching. Of course, a church is also a great deal about community, so I encourage you to be proactive in finding activities to be involved in as this is the way that you build relationships that are invaluable in your Christian walk. Everyone is busy these days, so as I mention these recommendations, I fully realize that if you don't make it a priority and a commitment, then it probably won't become a reality. The purpose of being plugged into the body of Christ through His church is to not check the box off of some kind of religious checklist, but to keep you plugged into His people and His purposes.

Finally, while the focus of this book appears to be "how to make my life 'rich,'" I hope I have made the point that it is not all about me or all about you. With that I would be doing a real injustice to this book, to myself, to you, and to the cause of Christ if I didn't specifically say that part of being truly rich is being involved in ministry. In previous chapters, I have mentioned giving money specifically and touched on the greater concept of stewardship. I have also mentioned being intentional with our relationships, also a wonderful way of making yourself available to evangelistic opportunities. Whatever the avenue, I believe we are all called to play a part in the building of God's kingdom; it is an exciting opportunity that everyone has. We all have unique giftings and audiences which can make a difference. In the end, it is really our only lasting legacy, so we should take hold of the opportunity and privilege of being a part of something bigger than all of us.

As I am sure you have noticed reading my recommendations for a truly rich life, some are obviously my opinions (pet ownership, traveling, etc.); others I would contend are simply truth revealed through Scripture. I do want to call your attention to the fact that none of these require substantial material wealth, if any at all. Whether you are white collar or no collar, make minimum wage or are a decamillionaire, I still believe these principles hold true and are parts of a truly rich life. Although our world believes that the only absolute is relativism, I believe firmly in the following absolutes. Without a doubt, money will not buy you happiness. Also, how you view and handle your money shapes everything around you. Stewardship is an all-encompassing term not relegated to just money but to your entire life. And finally, one's fulfillment and purpose will only be found in God and specifically in a relationship with Jesus Christ.

Now my challenge to you as well as to myself is to try to apply these principles and live in view of these absolutes. My frustration in life is rarely with external forces, but in my inability or lack of putting these things I know to be true in practice. However, I do know that through prayer and God's all-sufficient grace, He can help us to live a life which is truly rich and glorifying to Him. If you are a Christian, you have this same opportunity. I pray that you will see progress in your life and be encouraged by what God is doing. We only get one life to live; my prayer is that yours is *truly rich*.

God bless!

CHAPTER 14

Homework

I find that it is easy to read some books, even some good ones; and either because of the setting I read them in, what else was going on in my life, or some other reason, I didn't fully absorb or internalize what the author was getting at. The most effective way I know to invoke a deeper thought process is to ask some insightful questions. I have listed a few questions which deal with the big issues of life and finances, and I am confident that these will get your wheels spinning and hopefully will assist you in focusing on the things that matter in life. While breezing through them may be enjoyable, I encourage you to take the time and write down your answer, as this will force you to think about them much deeper. I would not be the least bit surprised that one or more of these may even result in an epiphany of sorts.

Once you have had the opportunity to go through this list, give it to your spouse and friends to complete, even discuss your answers if you feel so inclined. If I have aided in changing or strengthening your view with regards to even one of these questions, then I will have considered this book a success. While I won't be grading your answers, my guess is that if you can firmly answer these questions, then you are probably on a path to a truly rich life. These questions are also wonderfully insightful in pulling out what you truly value or what changes you should make. While it may be neat to just think about these questions, it would be a terrible waste to not make changes or live in view of these values. It also may be a fun exercise, just as in the planning process, to review these questions over time to see how your answers may change, which I hope they do. God grows everyone at different speeds, but He does promise to grow us. With that, we hopefully will have new insights and strengthened commitments as we grow.

Why were you created? What is your purpose or purposes for being put on this earth?

Where are you going, when all is said and done and your time is up?

With these in mind, what is your overarching goal in life?

If you had so much money that you could never reasonably spend it all (Bill Gates as an example with $50 billion), what would you do? How would you use the money?

If you were told today with a medical certainty that you had a month to live, what would you do with your time left?

What would you do with your possessions and money?

If you were told with a medical certainty that you were going to live a healthy life and die on your one hundredth birthday, what would you do differently?

If you could snap your fingers and have a different career, what would it be?

What is the most satisfying way you have ever spent money?

How much would you pay to do one year of your life over again? What would you do differently?

What are the most valuable things you treasure?

If you had an extra two hours every day, how would you spend them?

What are you passionate about?

What is the smartest financial decision you ever made? What made you make that decision?

If you had a clear undeniable opportunity to tell someone something that has been on your heart, who would it be and what would you tell them?

If you could have more close friends or 25 percent more income, which would you choose? Fifty percent more income? One hundred percent more income?

Who is the most impressive, most admired person you know? Why?

What do you hope people say about you when you are not around?

What do you want people to say about you at your funeral?

What is the most important lesson you learned from your parents?

What is the most important thing you hope to teach your children?

What is the biggest mistake you have ever made? How did you end up making that decision, and what did you learn?

If you could take ultimate control of your life away from God, would you do it; and if so, what would you do differently?

If you could pick a spouse for your child, what would they be like? What qualities would they have? Do you think they value these same qualities? Do you have these qualities?

If you could go back to college, or go to college, what would you study?

What is your favorite book of the Bible, and why?

If you could request to God that one more book of the Bible be written, what would you want to know about most?

Is it true that it "is better to have loved and lost than to have never loved?"

What could you do today to make your marriage richer?

If your profession/job no longer existed (wiped from the face of the earth), what would you do?

When was the last time you did a random, secret act of kindness for someone else? How do you feel about that?

What are the things you wouldn't trade for money?

If you had to rank yourself from 1-100, 1 being poor and 100 being abundantly rich, in a material sense, how would you rank yourself? In a truly rich sense?

I hope you enjoyed those questions, and my prayer is that you are glad you took the time to think about them. I wish you and your family and friends the best, and may you take hold of life, which is truly life, and live it richly!

NOTES

Chapter 1: Porsches and Prozac

1. De Graaf, John, David Wann, and Thomas H. Naylor. *Affluenza: The All-Consuming Epidemic*. San Francisco: Berrett-Koehler Publishers, 2002. 14.
2. Ibid, p.85.
3. Ibid, p.83.
4. Ibid, p.32.
5. Getlen, Larry. *Good Debt and Bad Debt*. 1 Nov. 2005. Bankrate. 1 Nov.2005. *<http://www.bankrate.com>*.
6. De Graaf, John, David Wann, and Thomas H. Naylor. *Affluenza: The All-Consuming Epidemic*. San Francisco: Berrett-Koehler Publishers, 2002. 42.
7. Ibid, p.57.
8. Nelson, Jennifer. "Cutting Down Debt." Bloomberg Wealth Manager April 2004:43.
9. "All-Consuming Passion." Pamphlet Produced by New Road Map Foundation and Northwest Environment Watch, 1998. 11.
10. Nelson, Jennifer. "Cutting Down Debt." Bloomberg Wealth Manager April 2004:43.
11. Myers, David. *The American Paradox*. New Haven, Conn.:Yale, 2000. 6-7.
12. De Graaf, John, David Wann, and Thomas H. Naylor. *Affluenza: The All-Consuming Epidemic*. San Francisco: Berrett-Koehler Publishers, 2002. 2.
13. Easterbrook, Gregg. *The Progress Paradox: How Life Gets Better While People Feel Worse*. New York: Random House, 2003. XVI.
14. Moeller, Steve. "Money and Happiness." Investment Advisor March 2006.
15. Ibid.
16. Ibid.
17. Ibid.

Chapter 2: Adam, Eve, and the Mega-mall

18. Moeller, Steve. "Money and Happiness." Investment Advisor March 2006.
19. Miller, Will., Dr. Speech. 15 March 2004.
20. De Graaf, John, David Wann, and Thomas H. Naylor. *Affluenza: The All-Consuming Epidemic.* San Francisco: Berrett-Koehler Publishers, 2002. 84
21. "All – Consuming Passion." Pamphlet Produced by New Road Map Foundation and Northwest Environment Watch, 1998. 6.
22. Bernstein, William J. *The Birth of Plenty: How the Prosperity of the Modern World Was Created.* New York, NY:2004.328-331.
23. "Tips to Reduce TV Watching in Children and Adults." state.sd.us. Sept. 2003. South Dakota Department of Health. 12 Oct. 2004 <*http://www.state.sd.us/doh/Nutrition/TV.pdf*>.
24. Ibid.
25. Nelson, Jennifer. "Cutting Down Debt." Bloomberg Wealth Manager April 2004:43.

Chapter 3: Designer Theology

26. Westminster Confession of Faith.
27. Edwards, Jonathan, Dr. "Christian Charity or the Duty of Charity to the Poor, Explained and Enforced." The *Works of Jonathan Edwards.* Vol. 4. Yale University Press, 1972.
28. "Giving to Churches Rose Substantially in 2003." 14 April 2004. The Barna Group. 10 May 2005. <*http://www.barna.org*>.
29. Schultze, Quentin. *Televangelism and American Culture.* Grand Rapids, MI: Baker Book House, 1991. 132-133.
30. Magliato, Joe. *The Wall Street Gospel.* Eugene, OR: Harvest House Publishers, 1981. 20.
31. Ibid, p.32.

Chapter 4: Mammon, Man, and Our Maker

32. MacArthur, John F., Jr. "Investing in Eternity: Part 1." Sermon. 1990.
33. Ryken, Leland. "That Which God Hath Lent Thee: The Puritans and Money." A Puritan's Mind. 10 June 2005. <*http://www.apuritansmind.com*>.
34. Calvin, John. *The Best of John Calvin.* Choteau, MT: Old Paths Gospel Press. 326.
35. "Short Quotes on Wealth from Church History." A Puritan's Mind. 18 April 2005 <*http://www.apuritansmind.com*>.
36. Blue, Ron. *Generous Living: Finding Contentment Through Giving.* Grand Rapids, MI: Zondervan Publishing House, 1997. 67.

37. Spurgeon, Charles H. "Charles Spurgeon's Thoughts on Money." From a number of Works. 10 Dec. 2004 <*http://www.apuritansmind.com/stewardship*>.

38. Manton, Thomas. *The Complete Works of Thomas Manton.* Vol.01. Lafayette, IN: Sovereign Grace Publishers, 2002. 524.

39. Edwards, Jonathan, Dr. "Christian Charity or the Duty of Charity to the Poor, Explained and Enforced." The *Works of Jonathan Edwards.* Vol. 4. Yale University Press, 1972.

40. Calvin, John. *The Best of John Calvin.* Choteau, MT: Old Paths Gospel Press.234.

41. Spurgeon, Charles H. "Wealth and Riches." From his *Works.* 17 Dec. 2004 <*http://www.apuritansmind.com/stewardship*>.

42. Spurgeon, Charles H. *Faith's Checkbook.*

43. Piper, John. *God's Passion for His Glory: Living the Vision of Jonathan Edwards.* Wheaton, IL: Crossway Books, 1998.

44. Magliato, Joe. *The Wall Street Gospel.* Eugene, OR: Harvest House Publishers, 1981. 42.

45. Burkett, Larry, and Ron Blue. *Wealth to Last: Money Essentials for the Second Half Of Life.* Nashville, TN: Broadman & Holman Publishers, 2003. 204.

46. De Graaf, John, David Wann, and Thomas H. Naylor. *Affluenza: The All-Consuming Epidemic.* San Francisco: Berrett-Koehler Publishers, 2002. 75.

47. Spurgeon, Charles H. "Peter's Shortest Prayer." Sermon. 2 Oct. 1873.

48. Manton, Thomas. *Works.*

Chapter 5: Planning For the Trip Called Life

49. Carlson, Richard. *Don't Worry Make Money: Spiritual and Practical Ways to Create Abundance and More Fun in Life.* New York, NY: Hyperion Books, 1997. 208.

50. Burkett, Larry, and Ron Blue. *Wealth to Last: Money Essentials for the Second Half Of Life.* Nashville, TN: Broadman & Holman Publishers, 2003.34.

Chapter 6: The Imaginary Finish Line

51. "Social Security: A Brief History." *Ssa.gov.* Social Security Administration. 24 Oct. 2005. <http://www.ssa.gov/history/pdf/2005pamphlet.pdf>

52. Dychtwald, Ken, Ph.D. *Age Power: How the 21st Century Will Be Ruled By the Old.* New York, NY: Jeremy P.Tarcher/Putnam, 1999. 11.

53. Ibid, p.57.

54. Dychtwald, Ken, Ph.D. Speech. 15 March 2004.

55. "Social Security: A Brief History." *Ssa.gov.* Social Security Administration. 24 Oct. 2005. <http://www.ssa.gov/history/pdf/2005pamphlet.pdf>

56. Henderson, Nell. "Greenspan Urges Pension Benefit Cuts." Washington Post 27 August 2004.

57. Stein, Michael K. *The Prosperous Retirement: Guide to the New Reality.* Boulder, Co: EMSTCO, 1998.
58. *TV Dimensions.* New York, NY: Media Dynamics, 2004.
59. Anthony, Mitch. The New Retire-mentality:Planning Your Life and Living Your Dreams . . . At Any Age You Want. Chicago, IL: Dearborn, 2001. 7.

Chapter 7: Blocking and Tackling

60. "The Lottery as a Wealth-building Strategy." *Journal of Financial Planning* March 2006:15.
61. Stanley, Thomas J. *The Millionaire Next Door: The Surprising Secrets of America's Wealthy.* New York, NY: Pocket Books, 1996.
62. "The Richest People in the World." *Forbes* March 2006: 148.
63. Pond, Jonathan. *Your Money Matters: 21 Tips for Achieving Financial Security in The 21ˢᵗ Century.* New York, NY: G.P. Putnam's Sons, 1999. 7.
64. Dychtwald, Ken, Ph.D. *Age Power: How the 21ˢᵗ Century Will Be Ruled By the Old* New York, NY: Jeremy P.Tarcher/Putnam, 1999. 80.
65. Ibid
66. Carlson, Richard. *Don't Worry Make Money: Spiritual and Practical Ways to Create Abundance and More Fun in Life.* New York, NY: Hyperion Books, 1997. 208.
67. Spurgeon, Charles H. *The Salt Cellars: A Collection of Proverbs and Quaint Sayings.* Vol. 2. M.

Chapter 8: The Flight Attendant Hand Jive

68. "History of Insurance." *Wikipedia.* 10 Jan. 2006 <*http://en.wikipedia.org/wiki/ Insurance#History_of_insurance*>
69. "Healthy Aging Project" 1999. Health Care Financing Administration. 14 Sept. 2005 <*http://www.hcfa.gov/quality/3b.htm*>.
70. Dychtwald, Ken, Ph.D. *Age Power: How the 21ˢᵗ Century Will Be Ruled By the Old* New York, NY: Jeremy P.Tarcher /Putnam, 1999. 144.
71. Hing, E., and B. Bloom. "Long-term Care for the Functionally Dependant Elderly." *American Journal of Public Health* Feb 1991. Series 13. no. 104.
72. "Providing Care for Another Adult: A Second Job for Many." *Aarp.org.* 6 April 2004. National Alliance for Caregiving. 10 June 2004 <*http://www.aarp.org*>.
73. "Key Concepts and Facts." Asset Protection Corporation. 22 Nov. 2005 <*http:// www.assetprotectioncorp.com/keyfacts.htm*>.
74. Ibid.

Chapter 9: The Psychologically Impaired Investor

75. Belsky, Gary, and Thomas Gilovich. *Why Smart People Make Big Money Mistakes And How to Correct Them*. New York, NY: Fireside, 2000. 154.
76. Ibid, p.151.
77. Kahneman, Daniel, and Amos Tversky. "Prospect Theory: An Analysis of Decision Under Risk." *Econometrica* 47.2 (1979).
78. "Exploiting the Effects of Emotions on the Capital Markets: Part 2 Exploiting Biases." 8 Oct. 2003. Bernstein. 24 Nov. 2004. <*http://www.bernstein.com*>.
79. Lynch, Peter. *One Up On Wall Street*. New York, NY: Fireside, 1989. 24.
80. Parisse, Alan. Speech. 15 March 2004.
81. Lynch, Peter. *One Up On Wall Street*. New York, NY: Fireside, 1989. 20.
82. Ibid, p.48, 66.
83. Horwitz, Michael. "Mob Mentality." *Financial Planning* May 2005:81.
84. Maranjian, Selena. *The Motley Fool Money Guide*. Alexandria, VA: Motley Fool, 2001. 380.
85. Hagstrom, Robert G. *The Warren Buffett Way*. New York, NY: John Wiley & Sons, 1995. 31.
86. Eisenberger, and Leiberman. "Why Rejection Hurts: A Common Neural Alarm System for Physical and Social Pain." *Trend in Cognitive Sciences* Vol 8 no. 7 (2004).
87. "Quantitative Analysis of Investor Behavior, 1984-2003." *Wall Street* Nov. 2004:60.
88. Buffett, Warren. "Bershire Letter to Shareholders" 1977-1983. 53.

Chapter 10: The Raw Materials in the Construction of Wealth

89. Hagstrom, Robert G. *The Warren Buffett Way*. New York, NY: John Wiley & Sons, 1995. 29.
90. Lynch, Peter. *One Up On Wall Street*. New York, NY: Fireside, 1989. 13.
91. Hagstrom, Robert G. *The Warren Buffett Way*. New York, NY: John Wiley & Sons, 1995. 45.
92. Pond, Jonathan. *Your Money Matters: 21 Tips for Achieving Financial Security in The 21st Century*. New York, NY: G.P. Putnam's Sons, 1999. 102.
93. Hagstrom, Robert G. *The Warren Buffett Way*. New York, NY: John Wiley & Sons, 1995. 49.
94. Ibid, p. 52.

Chapter 11: Investing Serious Money

95. Graham, Benjamin. The Intelligent Investor. New York, NY: HarperCollins Books, 1973. 11.
96. Ibid, p. 1.
97. Goodman, Beverly. "You Can Spare Your Returns the Tax Ax." 26 August 2002. The Street. 24 Oct. 2004. <*http://www.thestreet.com*>.

Chapter 12: The President's Cabinet

98. Anthony, Mitch. The New Retire-mentality: Planning Your Life and Living Your Dreams . . . At Any Age You Want. Chicago, IL: Dearborn, 2001. 204.

Chapter 13: More Pearls to Ponder

Chapter 14: Homework